Power Tools for Woodcarving

David Tippey

Guild of Master Craftsman Publications Ltd

First published 1999 by
Guild of Master Craftsman Publications Ltd,
166 High Street, Lewes, East Sussex, BN7 1XU

Reprinted 1999

Photographs by David Tippey except where otherwise stated

ISBN 1 86108 104 9

Designed by Fineline Studios

Set in Utopia

Colour origination by Viscan Graphics (Singapore)

Printed in Hong Kong by H & Y Printing Ltd

Power Tools for Woodcarving

Dedicated to Angela
for her unstinting support

Warning

All the tools described in this book are potentially dangerous. Always follow the manufacturer's recommendations in terms of safe working practices, and ensure that appropriate protective clothing is worn at all times. Do not remove safety guards from power tools when toothed or abrasive cutters are being used. Do not use tools or tooling which are damaged or excessively worn, and do not work when your concentration is impaired by drugs, alcohol, or fatigue. The safety advice in this book is intended for your guidance, but cannot cover every eventuality: the safe use of power tools is the responsibility of the user. If you are unhappy with a particular technique or procedure, do not use it – there is always another way.

Contents

Notice

Whilst every effort has been made to ensure that the information in this book is accurate at the time of writing, it is inevitable that prices, specifications, and availability of tools will change from time to time. Readers are therefore urged to contact manufacturers or suppliers for up-to-date information before ordering tools. A list of suppliers will be found on pages 115–23.

Measurements

Depending on their country of origin, some tools are supplied in metric sizes, some in Imperial, and some are available in a choice of metric or Imperial. Equivalents have been given in the text where possible, but readers should be aware that measurements cited in brackets (parentheses) may have been rounded up or down to the nearest convenient equivalent; they are intended only as a guide for readers unfamiliar with the system of measurement used by the manufacturer. If in doubt, contact the manufacturer or supplier for further information.

Acknowledgements

I would like to thank all the suppliers mentioned in the text for their kind co-operation in the preparation of this book.

CHAPTER ONE

Introduction

UNTIL the last quarter of the twentieth century, woodcarving tools had changed very little from the ones used by medieval craftsmen to create the masterpieces which adorn the palaces and cathedrals of Europe. The last few years have seen a variety of new woodcarving tools and techniques becoming available to carvers. Power carving tools have become very much a part of the carving process for many woodcarvers, and as we move into the twenty-first century, the range of tools which can be used to speed up or enhance the craft continues to expand rapidly (Fig 1.1).

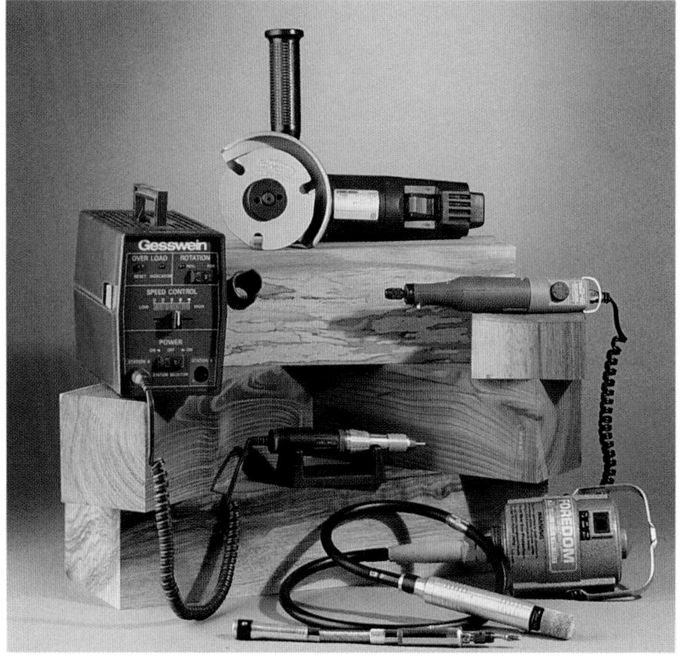

Fig 1.1 *Power carving tools come in many forms.*

There are those who decry the use of power tools, and cite poor finish and design as a product of their use, but I am convinced that the master carvers of the past would have welcomed them with open arms and their work would not have been diminished. It is the craftsman who creates the carving, using his vision and skill; tools are merely that, a means to the creation of the carving. Poor finish on carvings is not a product of power carving techniques, but an indication of the level of craftsmanship employed.

The use of power tools for carving opens up the craft to many who could not or would not have taken it up in the past, reducing the need for in-depth knowledge of timbers, and the manipulation and sharpening of edge tools. If flexi-shafts, angle-grinder carving discs, copy-carving machines, etc. had been available to the master carvers of the past, I am sure they would have used them, if only to cut down on the number of journeymen and apprentices they had to find, and pay!

With the exception of copying machines, power tools are still basically hand tools, requiring selection and guidance by the carver. They are merely a means to an end: the saving of time, money, and effort. The wide range of equipment and tooling now available is capable of fast stock removal on the one hand, and on the other, the most delicate detailing work. Power tools can also open up the world of carving to those whose disabilities prevent them using conventional tools and those who do not

Fig 1.2 The use of a machine and these burr-type cutters allows many people to carve who for various reasons cannot cope with sharpening and using edge tools.

have the time, skill, or inclination to sharpen edge tools (Fig 1.2).

Power carving tools are not a panacea, but they are a very useful addition to the woodcarver's arsenal: new tools to be used where appropriate, to speed up work or achieve effects not available by other, more traditional means.

The ease of use and the increased working speed afforded by power tools leave the craftsman with more time to concentrate on the form and finish of the work and less on the mechanics of carving and tool manipulation. However, Luddite tendencies still exist in some quarters of the woodcarving fraternity, eschewing all forms of mechanization and thinking wood should still only be worked and finished in the 'traditional' manner. Whilst I have a certain sympathy with this view, and enjoy the peaceful, contemplative use of timber, mallet, and gouge occasionally too, we have now reached the end of the twentieth century. Power carving tools have been invented and, however hard some may wish, they won't go away, so they might as well be accepted for the advantages they bring. I enjoy the use of both traditional hand tools and modern power carving tools in my own workshop, and see them as being complementary; I wouldn't like to give up the use of either.

Power carving tools are here to stay, and this volume is a guide to the wide range of powered tools – and their appropriate tooling – which woodcarvers may employ in their work. It introduces the machines which can be used in woodcarving (although some are of only slight use, as they are not carving-specific), and discusses what they may be suitable for, what tooling is available for them, and some of the safety implications of their use.

Choosing suitable machines

When you have decided that power carving is for you, there is the question of what type of machine to buy, which make to choose, and also what tooling and safety equipment is needed in addition to the basic machine. You will hope to buy a machine that will last you some considerable time and will be productive, so take some time over its purchase, considering as many factors as possible.

Very few workshops have access to compressed air, so I have not included details of the sanders, grinders, polishers, etc. which use compressed air as a power source. In the list of suppliers at the back of the book I have included some manufacturers of compressed-air-powered tools, because if you already have an air supply they can be an economical option.

First you need to decide what type of machine you require. This will depend upon many things including the scale of the carving, what you want the tool to do, what tooling is available, and of course, how much you have to spend.

The first machine I bought to aid my carving was a two-wheel bandsaw, which was rapidly followed by the very versatile flexible-shaft carving machine. Both machines have already done a decade of hard, regular work without problems. They have proved to be good purchases, but that wasn't just luck; I did my homework first. If you are about to buy any new machine or tooling for your workshop, you should think hard about what you require and look at everything that is available; don't just go to the first tool dealer you come across.

Although price will always be a major factor, particularly for the non-professional carver, it is wise to look at more than just the price and the paper specification when deciding on your purchase. You must decide at the outset what you want the machine to do, and then collect and study the literature and the specifications of suitable machines.

Unfortunately, motors are often confusingly marked, as both the electrical input and the mechanical output power can be measured in the same unit, the watt (W). Some motor plates show the input power in watts, while some quote the output power, also in watts; these are entirely different figures, and the difference between them depends on the efficiency of the motor. Sadly, when advertising products, many manufacturers quote the larger, more impressive number. When used to indicate *output* power, a 750W motor equates to about one horsepower (1hp). However, when electrical *input* is quoted 1,000W (1kW), depending on the motor efficiency, will only give you an output power of between 450 and 750W (0.6-1hp), and not the 1.33hp you might expect. This is a point which should be borne in mind whenever you are comparing any motor-driven equipment: make sure that you are comparing the true *output power* specifications, and not confusing them with power *requirements*.

Two areas which are not usually covered in the manufacturers' literature are reliability of the goods, and backup or after-sales service. It is not in a marketing department's interest to point out that their machine may break down like any others, so few will tell you about the cost and availability of spares and service, unless you ask. Dealers may be perfectly honest about the different products they stock, but often they will have little practical knowledge of the various machines they sell. Ask amongst your friends and acquaintances for their experiences of different makes, and of course consult this book. You may feel that you want to ask the dealers a few pertinent questions, such as:

- How long has the supplier dealt with that manufacturer? Are they good on backup and spares?
- How long has that model been made and sold? Has it shown any consistent faults, or have there been high return rates?
- Would they describe it as a light, medium, or heavy-duty machine; DIY, trade, or industrial?
- Is it suitable for continuous use eight hours a day, or only intermittently for short periods?
- Is it suitable for the use you have in mind?
- Have they had any problems with previously sold machines failing, and if so, why?

- Have they had difficulty with the manufacturer's backup, spares, or service?
- Do they keep stocks of spares? What are the prices of typical renewable items?
- Do they perform in-house servicing and repairs? What are their charges?
- Do they stock a full range of accessories?
- What is the guarantee period, and what does it cover?
- What is actually included in the price, and (if you are like me) is there a discount for cash?

This is quite a lot of questions really, but if you can't get satisfactory answers to the questions you consider important, maybe you should ask yourself if you are thinking of buying the right piece of equipment, or if you have gone to the right shop.

Having perused the literature, and being armed with the answers to all your questions, you should then have enough confidence to make your decision and spend your hard-earned cash. Hopefully, having gone through that process, the machine of your choice will be the right one for your application and will give many years' reliable service.

Tooling

Expenditure doesn't end with the purchase of the tool. Many come with little tooling or none at all, and some even arrive without the basic spanners and Allen keys needed for regular tool changing or adjustments. Always budget for a small basic kit of good-quality tooling before you buy the machine. Good tools and cutters are expensive, and a full range of tooling may easily cost more than the machine it is used with. Poor-quality tooling is a bad bargain and can lead to much disappointment with the machine's performance; it may even cause damage to the machine itself. It is much better to buy one or two top-quality accessories at the

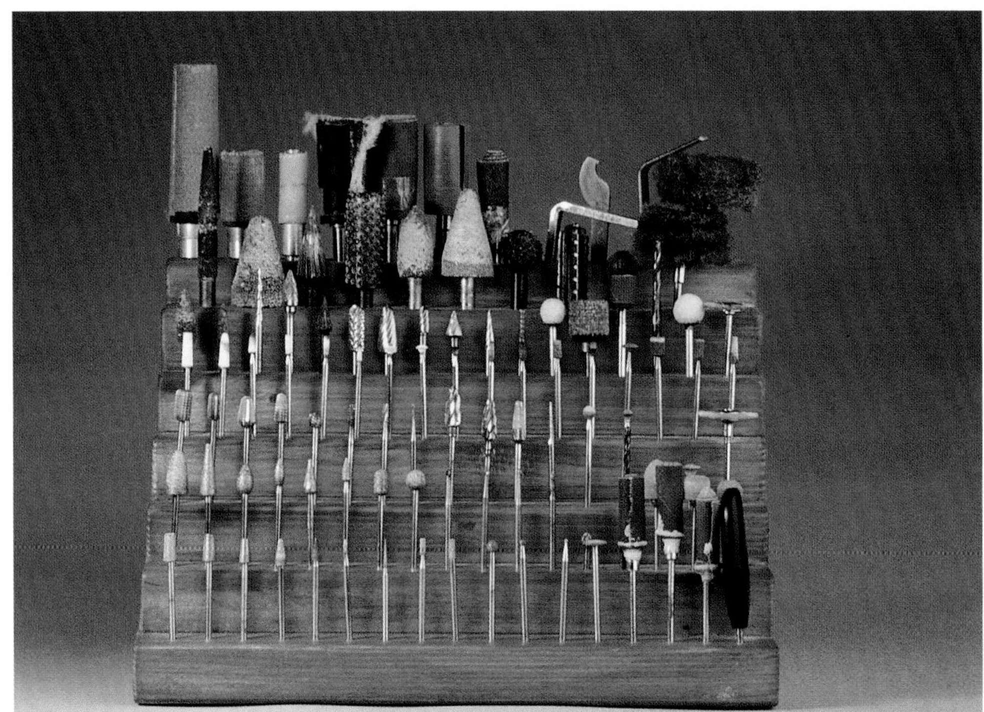

Fig 1.3 *Just as you might build up a collection of hand tools, you also amass burrs, cutters, and sanding devices, rather like fishermen with floats and flies!*

outset , and add to them as you find it necessary. Don't buy tooling just for the sake of it; I have dozens of tools for my flexi-shaft machines, but the ones that I pick up and use regularly probably amount to about six or eight small burrs and four large ones. Some of my large collection were bought for specific jobs, some just to try, and many will never be used again. Fishermen collect flies and floats; power carvers collect burrs and cutters (Fig 1.3). As the saying goes, 'Don't do as I do, do as I say': so save your money and don't buy that extra tool until you really need it.

Safety

The last thing many people think about when buying new equipment is safety gear – it can't be used to make anything, and so can seem almost an extravagance. But your health and safety are important to you, and to your family and friends, so look at the money spent as a necessary investment in your future good health. Make sure you budget for any additional safety equipment you may require, whenever you are purchasing new power tools. Obviously you may own some items already, but any additional equipment you are likely to need should be obtained at the outset, not somewhere down the line. Professionals and hobbyists alike need safety equipment – the consequences of not owning and using it are so severe that it shouldn't even be contemplated.

What safety equipment you need, and how much it will cost, varies depending on the tool. A basic set of head-to-toe equipment for a chainsaw costs about £200 (at 1999 prices), while at the other end of the scale a would-be flexible-shaft carver could probably purchase a leather apron, goggles, and a disposable respirator for £25.

Whatever safety equipment your power tool needs, buy it at the outset. Don't think of it as a later addition: something else may keep cropping up – until it is too late!

What tools do you need?

Just which power tools you want to buy will depend on a number of factors, including the scale and type of work you envisage carrying out. The work which can be accomplished with any particular tool can vary enormously in both scale and approach. Large sculpture would require the use of heavy-duty equipment such as the chainsaw, and perhaps an angle grinder fitted with an appropriate carving disc. However, the angle grinder is also suitable for roughing out medium-sized sculpture too, where a flexible-drive rotary carving machine or a die grinder might be a useful addition. The flexible-drive machine is one of the most versatile power carving tools, and is equally at home on small work, alongside miniature high-speed die grinders and air-turbine carvers.

To sum up the applications for various types of machines and tooling in an easily assimilated visual form, I have prepared a series of bar-graph charts. These attempt to show the usefulness of the equipment for different operations, such as roughing out, detail carving, and sanding, on work of various scales. The taller the bars in the chart, the more useful the tool is for the specified task performed on work of the specified scale. The more columns are coloured in, the more versatile the tool is; items with entries in only a couple of columns are useful in comparatively few situations. The charts are intended to be self-explanatory and a useful résumé of each power carving tool's abilities.

CHAPTER TWO

Health and Safety

SAFETY should always be paramount when you are working with machines; you only have one life, and I would wish it a long and healthy one. Buying and using safety equipment should not be something that is left until 'later', even though its purchase may seem an expensive and unproductive use of your funds. Your health and safety are important to you and your family, so don't leave it until it's too late. But remember that no amount of safety clothing and equipment will provide total protection against an accident; you won't be invincible, so safe working practices are very important too.

The hazards posed by power carving equipment vary to some extent from one type of machine to another, but some basic, sensible safety measures are common to all.

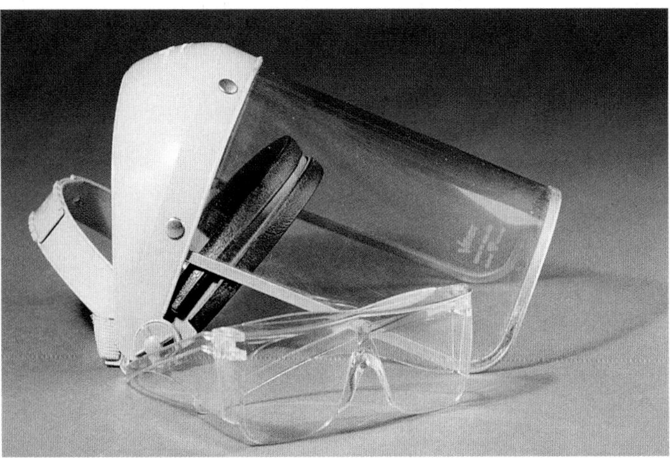

Fig 2.1 Face shields and safety glasses (which can be worn over prescription spectacles) are useful alternatives to goggles.

There are many possible hazards or accidents which can have very immediate and dramatic results, from debris being thrown into your eye, to attacking your leg with an angle grinder or chainsaw. However, more insidious hazards exist, such as long-term hearing loss or lung damage, and these need to be taken into account too. Their effect on your quality of life can be just as devastating, if not more so, than the more traumatic and immediate results of accidents.

Properly approved safety equipment should be looked upon as the first, most essential accessory to any power carving equipment, and should be bought at the same time as the machine and other associated tooling. Visiting a specialist industrial safety equipment shop or using a mail-order supplier is the best way to find a good range of safety products. Ordinary tool shops tend to offer little or no choice. Most large towns and cities will have local safety equipment suppliers, or you could use an industrial mail-order company like Arco (see Suppliers on pages 115–23).

Eye protection

Protection for your eyesight should always be a priority when using portable tools which create dust and wood chips. When using any rotary equipment, always wear suitable approved eye protection (Fig 2.1). Tool bits can chip or break and abrasive stones disintegrate, tools work out of their collets, and wood chips and dust fly everywhere. Your eyes are particularly vulnerable when working on small, detailed work, because of the proximity of the work to your face. Goggles offer the best all-round protection, because they fit close to your face, but the cheaper ones often suffer from steaming up. My latest ones, made by Bolle, are effectively double-glazed and work very well, and you can find others that don't tend to fog for very little extra money, so try and seek them out. Goggles can be worn over glasses, or you can get prescription safety glasses with impact-resistant lenses and side shields. These tend to be rather expensive unless you get them supplied for your employment, and another alternative is a face shield or visor. Ordinary visors, however, especially large ones, may not give adequate eye protection when working close to your body, as they can allow debris to come up behind the visor, and may even make matters worse by trapping flying objects. If you use one, do not get one that is too large, and don't wear one where your face will be sited immediately above the work.

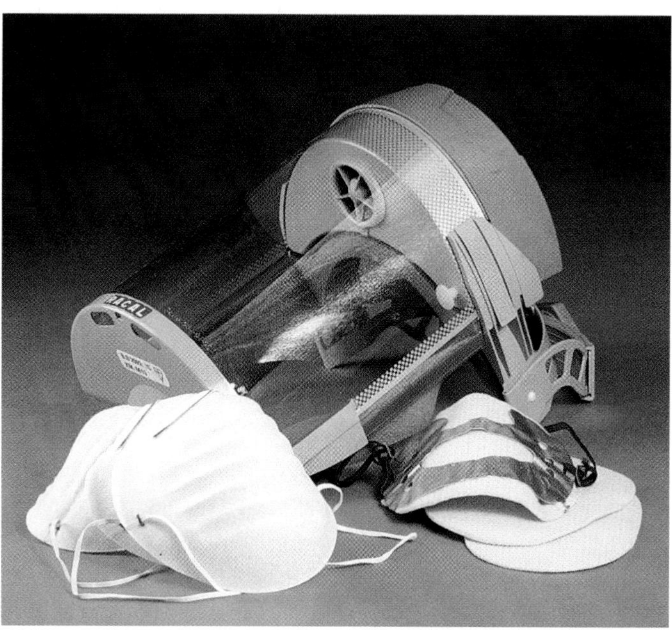

Fig 2.2 *Disposable masks and powered respirators are the most pleasant solutions for respiratory protection.*

● **Use special cleaners for your eye-safety wear to help repel dust and reduce misting; remember to keep all your safety equipment clean and hygienic.**

Respiratory protection

Operations which create fine wood dust are potentially hazardous to your health even if you apparently show no reaction to them. Some timbers are known to be particularly bad, but the long-term effects of any fine wood dust should be considered dangerous and a suitable mask worn at all times. Over time, sensitization can occur, so that allergic reactions can be triggered by any wood dust, not just the notorious ones like rosewood. It is quite possible to work for years with a certain type of timber and have no problems, then suddenly to become sensitized to it. I am sensitive to at least one type of timber, and a careless few minutes of sanding without a mask can leave me with a running nose, sore throat, and catarrh for a couple of days. I now rarely use that variety for any work, as I have no wish for the symptoms to become any worse, as they may with further exposure. Your breathing and general health can be permanently affected, and some conditions are life-threatening.

Masks

For most people a disposable dust mask is a reasonable solution (Fig 2.2, foreground). These are available in a wide variety of styles and types suitable for dealing with toxic and non-toxic dusts, and are made by many well-known manufacturers such as 3M and Racal. I prefer the idea of disposables because no maintenance is involved: you just take a fresh mask out of the packet and throw the old one away. However, I have a beard and, short of shaving it off, I cannot use a disposable mask because it is prevented from sealing to my face.

Powered respirators

The worst problem with masks comes when you wear spectacles. Exhaled air, warm and moisture-laden, is very effectively diffused and passes over your cool glasses, misting them up, like a car windscreen demist in reverse. If you have a beard, then the problem is compounded by the fact that you cannot get an effective seal against your face, rendering the dust mask much less effective. If you have a beard *and* wear glasses you really have problems, and the best solution to your breathing and eye protection is a powered respirator. Although they seem expensive, powered respirators with built-in visors are an excellent investment for the regular woodworker, combining protection for both sight and breathing (Fig 2.2, background). Unlike ordinary face shields, they have sufficient sealing at the bottom of the visor to prevent light objects from being thrown up behind them. Filtered air is blown into a partially sealed visor-type face shield. This overcomes the problem of glasses and goggles steaming up, provides full face and eye-impact protection, and the positive air pressure within the partially sealed visor prevents the ingress of unfiltered air – making it very effective even with beards. This is a solution that many woodworkers are now turning to.

I have been successfully using a Pulsafe unit (now Dalloz Safety; see Fig 2.3) for around eight years; this is similar to the Record Power units which are manufactured by the same company. Once bought, it has proved very economical to own. Besides regular changes of the main and pre-filters, I have replaced the battery pack, as the original would no longer hold much of a charge; the visor is only now ready for replacement.

Cheaper units have appeared since I bought mine; then, only the expensive, heavy-duty industrial units were available. Both Racal (now owned by 3M) and Helmet Integrated Systems produce powered respirators aimed at the

Fig 2.3 *The Dalloz Safety Pulsafe Turbovisor MV; this firm also makes the Record Power Turbo respirators.*

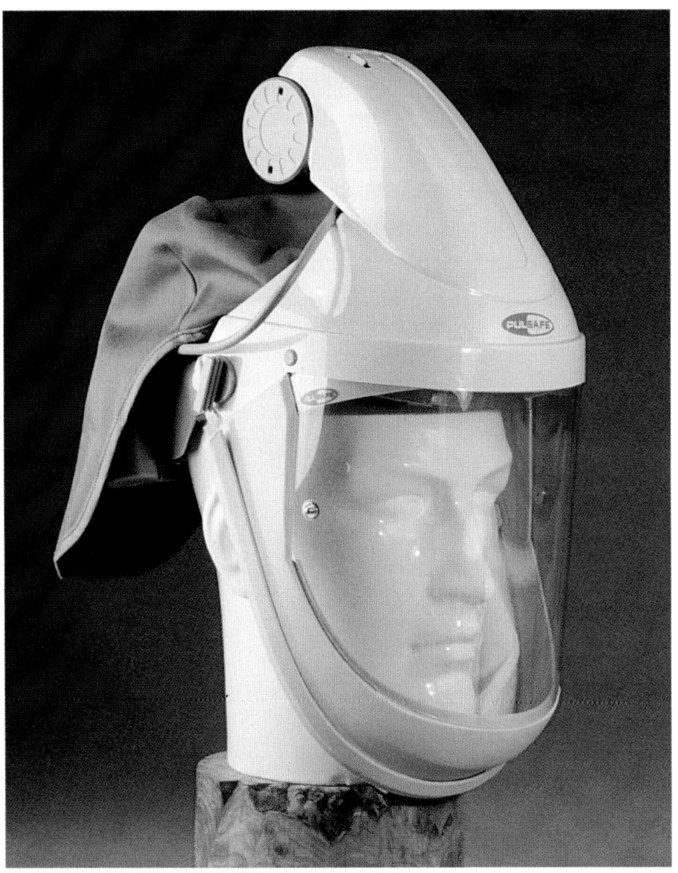

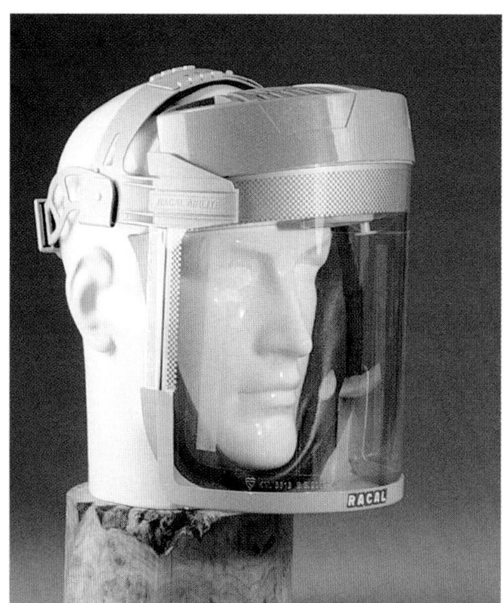

Fig 2.4 (Left) Racal Airlite powered respirator.

Fig 2.5 (Below) Helmet Integrated Systems Purelite respirator.

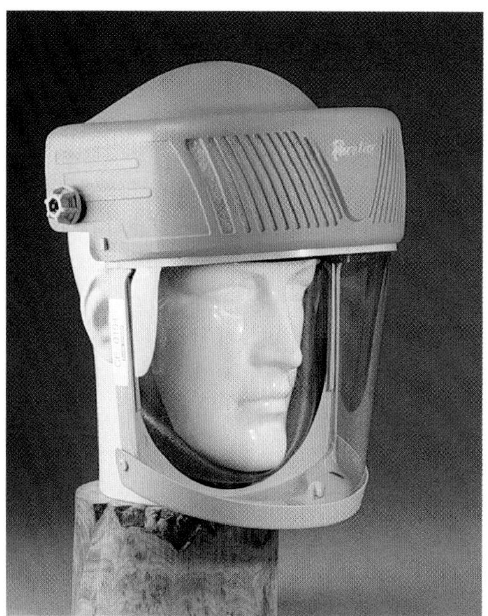

woodworking market, with prices around £130–150 (Figs 2.4 and 2.5); Record Power and Dalloz Safety sell basic units in the £200–250 range. I found the Racal noisier, and less convenient, as it will not flip up on to your head. It also uses the most expensive filter, and doesn't have a pre-filter to increase its life.

All powered respirators effectively combine the eye protection of a face shield, and protection for your lungs from fine dust, in one convenient unit which is not a chore to use. Various battery options are available with the different respirators, giving from 4 to 8 hours' continuous usage on one battery charge. You can check for yourself on the state of the filter and change it as necessary, which gives greater peace of mind (Fig 2.6).

Respirators are much more convenient to use than separate masks and goggles, so you are much more likely to use them, which makes them a very worthwhile investment for the regular woodworker or carver.

Respiratory protection should be worn as much as possible; the British Government's safety guidelines say that not wearing your mask for only 5 minutes in an 8-hour shift reduces its effectiveness by 40%. That is a rather sobering thought for those who do not use their masks for the odd 'little job'.

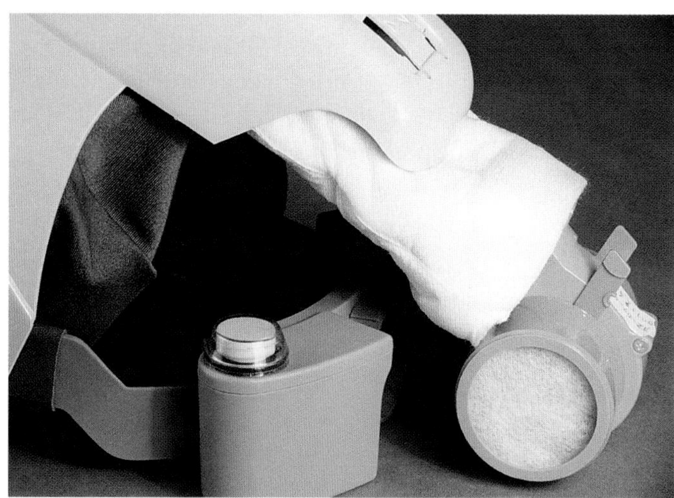

Fig 2.6 Powered respirators provide convenient protection for sight and breathing in one easy-to-use package; it is easy to check on the filter condition.

Hearing protection

The sound level of most carving machines is not excessive, so earplugs or similar hearing protection may not be necessary, especially for occasional use. Take note of the manufacturer's instructions, and bear in mind, for example, that a flexi-shaft motor is generally used at around ear level and quite close to your head. If you work for many hours at a time you should consider hearing protection (Fig 2.7). I know of one carver who wears ear-protection muffs to prevent him getting earache caused by the draught from the motor's cooling fan! However, if in any doubt at all, err on the safe side and wear hearing protection. I'm not keen on bulky earmuffs, and usually wear the soft Bilsom type of earplugs, which are comfortable and cheap to replace.

Fig 2.7 *Three alternative forms of hearing protection – the ear plugs are washable and disposable.*

Skin care

It is not just your breathing which can become sensitized to wood dust; it can also irritate your skin, causing itchiness, rashes, and dermatitis. This can happen particularly on your hands and between your fingers. Washing your hands regularly to remove the dust will help stop any potential problems. If you do develop a reaction, use a non-greasy barrier cream to help prevent it recurring. Suitable creams are available from safety suppliers such as Arco, and large chemists.

Wash all your work clothing, overalls, etc. regularly to remove the fine dust that soon builds up in the fabric; otherwise you will be constantly breathing it in and getting it on your skin. Obviously, you should stop using any particular timbers that cause you problems in case the effects become more severe.

First-aid box

Keep a small first-aid box in the workshop, and make sure that it is properly restocked after use (Fig 2.8). It is no use having one if you don't know how to use it, so make sure that you have at least rudimentary knowledge of first aid. Local further education colleges, and

Fig 2.8 *Keep a well-provisioned first-aid box near at hand.*

voluntary organizations such as the St John Ambulance Brigade, frequently run short courses in first aid, and some of these are particularly aimed at emergency situations like those which may occur in the workshop.

Clothing

Overalls will help prevent wood dust getting where you don't want it, including the lounge carpet, and will help to preserve your clothes, but they will not offer much protection against power carving equipment. Work clothing should be worn to prevent heavy contamination and damage to your ordinary clothes, and to keep dust away from your skin. Close-woven cotton material is both effective and comfortable to wear, and I use woodturners' smocks when I'm power-carving. They slip over your head easily and fasten right up to the neck to help keep out flying chips. Even so, I find dust and wood chips in some strange places!

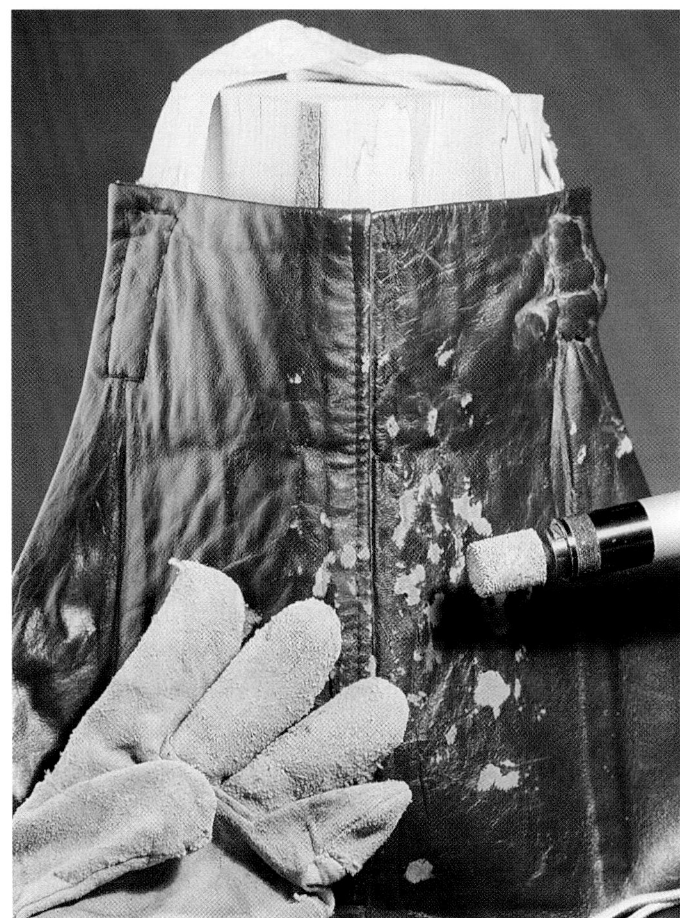

Fig 2.9 *Leather aprons and gloves provide some protection and extra reaction time for many power carving operations.*

A thick leather welder's or blacksmith's apron offers some protection and extra 'reaction time' when using power carving equipment (Fig 2.9). It is especially effective when using flexible-shaft carving tools, where it offers a good level of protection when working with carving burrs. Unlike cloth, the leather scuffs and doesn't allow the cutters and burrs to grab hold; this saves on clothing, flexible shafts, and personal damage.

Chainsaws have their own complete safety clothing system, which you should purchase at the outset and use whenever you pick up the saw, but this is not the case with other tools. Chainsaw clothing offers little protection against any other type of power carving tool, and is not intended to work as body armour. It contains long Kevlar fibres which are intended to jam the chain and sprockets on a chainsaw, an action which will be less than effective against an angle grinder.

General safety

It is all very well to buy and wear safety equipment, but it only reduces risks and doesn't make you invincible. If you do not adopt sensible, safe working practices you are still at risk. Obvious precautions are often overlooked, and can lead to serious incidents, so here is my ten-point plan for general power carving safety:

1 Carry out a full safety check of the equipment and tooling before you start, particularly the electrical safety checks listed in the next section; also check the security and adjustment of cutters in machines.
2 Wear appropriate safety gear whilst you are working, even if the job lasts just a few seconds – that is as long as it takes to have an accident.
3 Have a suitably equipped first-aid kit to hand, and the knowledge to use it. Try and make sure that you can contact someone easily in an emergency.
4 Make sure your working area, both floor and bench, is clear and doesn't present any hazards.
5 Think about how you will tackle the job in hand, and devise and use a safe working system. Particularly look at the secure clamping and holding of workpieces when power-carving.
6 Do not work if you are tired, or too cold to control the tools properly.
7 Do not use power tools when under the effects of alcohol, or of drugs which may make you drowsy or affect your judgement.
8 Keep the working area clear of all distractions – especially pets and children, who can easily put themselves in danger without realizing it.
9 Particularly if you are using a chainsaw or angle grinder, tell someone before you start work and preferably have them remain within calling distance, to be of help in an emergency – but don't have them hanging around causing a distraction.
10 Double-check ALL NINE of the previous points!

Electrical safety

Most of the machines used for carving will be electrically powered, and you should take steps to prevent accidents relating to the potentially lethal (240V in the UK) mains electrical system. Some of these points are covered in my ten-point general safety check, but it doesn't hurt to double-check.

1 Check cables for any damage and replace or repair if necessary.
2 Check plug and cable connections, including the security of the cable clamps and the fuse rating.
3 Don't work in the rain or in damp conditions.
4 Do use a residual current device (RCD) to supply the tool (Fig 2.10). An RCD adapter can be bought for less than £15 at most tool or gardening shops and

***Fig 2.10** Residual Current Devices (RCDs), which used to be known as ELCBs (Earth Leakage Circuit Breakers), are cheaply available as adapters and should be used on all portable power tools.*

could well save your life. (They used to be called ELCBs or earth leakage circuit breakers.)

5 Keep your work area clear and the supply cable away from the work and from the tool's cutting edges. I find it is usually convenient to bring the cable from behind and over my shoulder to keep it clear.

6 Make sure that you can switch off the machine easily. If necessary, fit a secondary foot switch in the supply line (Draper supply a suitable model: Fig 2.11), or use an easily reached NVR (no volt release) switch with emergency stop button (Trend supply one). NVR switches also prevent the tool from restarting by itself after the power has been interrupted.

7 Make sure the tool cannot be accidentally started. If controlled by a foot switch only, it is possible to stand on the switch inadvertently, so use the isolating switch as well, for additional safety. Alternatively, an NVR switch combined with a foot switch makes a much better foolproof combination to prevent accidental and unexpected restarting of tools.

Dust extraction

If you think that dust extraction is unnecessary providing you are wearing a mask or respirator, think again. Fine wood dust created by the abrasive burrs will still be drifting about when you remove your mask, so extraction to take the dust away from your work area and safely contain it is really an essential too. Without extraction, all the dust you create whilst working will descend as a fine layer over your entire workshop. Every time you disturb anything in your workshop you will then release more dust into the atmosphere to be breathed in, so dust extraction is not a luxury. Both respiratory protection and extraction are required when using any processes which create fine dust.

Fig 2.11 *A foot switch is a useful safety addition when you need both hands to operate the tool; this one is by Draper.*

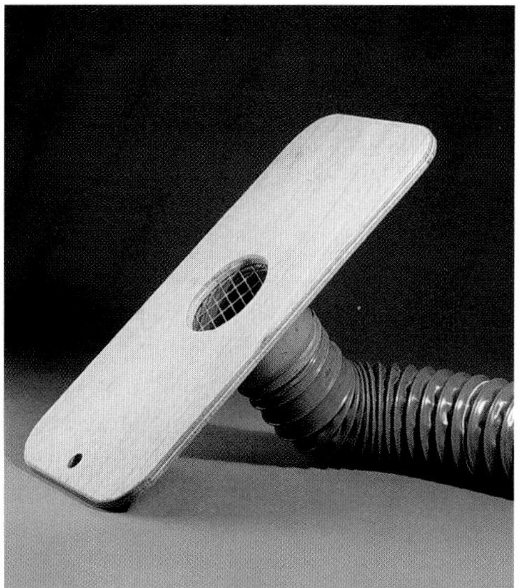

There are lots of dust extractors available (Figs 2.12–2.14), but make sure the one you choose is suitable for fine dust and not just the sort of chips produced by planer-thicknessing machines. Some chip extractors have only thin cotton filter bags, which allow the fine dust to be blown straight back into the atmosphere for you to breathe in. If you are in doubt about the suitability of an extractor unit, consult the manufacturer or supplier.

Some machines are suitable for localized extraction, using the wet-and-dry type of workshop vacuum cleaner

Fig 2.12 (Above and Right) *Dust extraction is really essential, and a trough or lap board is convenient when working on small-to-medium-sized projects.*

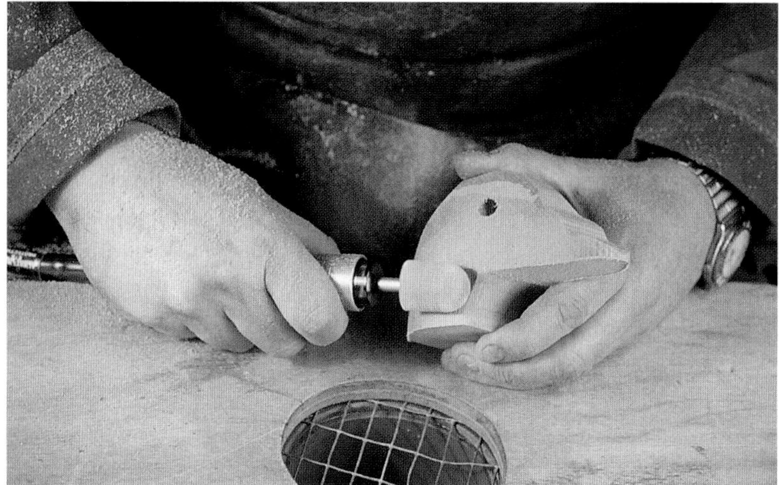

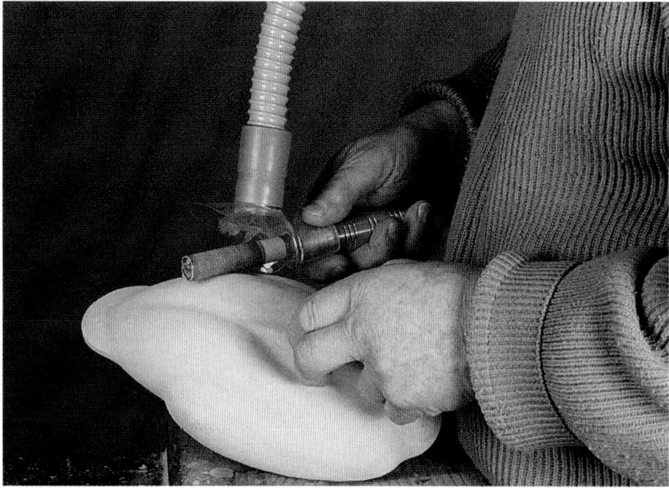

Fig 2.13 *Dust extraction should be as near as possible to the point where dust is being generated. This American Vac-U-Shield extractor clips onto a flexi-shaft tool's handpiece, but it can get in the way at times.*

Fig 2.14 *A home-made extractor fitting, fabricated from empty soft drinks bottles.*

fitted with an appropriate fine dust filter.

If your dust extractor has to share your workshop space, make sure that the noise level is acceptable too. I tried one fine dust extractor which was extremely noisy and had a high-frequency whistle which would have driven me mad, even if it wasn't affecting my hearing. It would be ideal to locate the dust extractor outside the workshop, so that no dust could get back, and you didn't have any noise. The drawback with that idea, though, is that all the warm air will also be extracted along with the dust.

Ambient air filters

Dusty, shaving-filled workshops should not be part of the image of the modern safety-conscious woodcarver – such images belong to the era of Charles Dickens. We now have much greater knowledge of the dangers presented by dust, and it would seem that late twentieth-century homo sapiens are much more prone to allergic reactions than their forebears. A spot of regular cleaning with the workshop vacuum cleaner will leave you with a safer, more pleasant environment to work in. Finally, to get rid of those last floating motes of dust, you can now buy ambient air cleaners to filter fine dust from your workshop air too. These work in much the same way as some of the filters found in pubs to remove dust and cigarette smoke. They run quietly in the background, filtering out the fine dust particles which have escaped your other eradication efforts. Axminster Power Tools sell a couple of imported models, while in the UK, Faron Enterprises are now manufacturing a range of ambient air cleaners too.

Work-holding methods

When carving with power tools, it is essential that both the tool and work can be safely controlled. All work must be securely held, by whatever means is necessary to suit the work and the power tool in use.

When using a flexible-shaft carver or micromotor with abrasive cutters, hand-holding is suitable for small, easily handled items, but the risk is far greater when using cutters with teeth, and alternative work-holding methods are necessary. Hand-holding requires great care, as you will definitely not have both hands behind the tool – which is often given as one of the basic rules for safe working. A thick leather glove on your work-holding hand would offer some degree of protection.

There are now dozens of multi-positional work-holders available for carving, some better than others. These can be happily used with flexi-shaft carvers, powered chisels, angle grinders, etc.; but before buying a carving clamp, make sure you examine the actual item, and try it out if possible, as some are fairly ineffective. The snag with using carving clamps is that they constantly need adjusting, if you are not to end up doing contortions in order to carve, so make sure you choose one which adjusts easily as well as holding securely.

Ordinary vices, both joiners' and engineers' styles, can happily be used with the addition of some suitable fixtures to secure your work. In fact an engineers' vice, mounted on the corner of a heavy bench or pillar, at 45 degrees to the front and side of the bench, and used with fixtures made from heavy, square-section steel pipe with mounting plates of various sizes and shapes welded to their ends, makes a strong, versatile, and cheap work-holding system.

Sandbags, and tie-down straps made of webbing with ratcheted fasteners (of the type used on trucks and trailers), are useful for holding larger work when you are using chainsaws and angle grinders. Whatever method you use, the work must be securely held when you are using power tools.

SUPPLIERS INCLUDE (for addresses see pages 115–23):

Draper
Dalloz Safety
3M/Racal
Helmet Integrated Systems
Craft Supplies (UK)
Arco
Trend
Record Power
Yorkleen
Faron Enterprises
Axminster Power Tools
Fercell
P&J

CHAPTER THREE

Flexible-Shaft Machines

Of all the machinery available to assist the carver, the flexible-shaft machine is probably the most versatile (Fig 3.1). Its use is applicable to carvings of all scales: it is capable of adding details to the largest of carvings, yet the same machine can be used to create the most delicate miniatures too. It is because of its versatility, and the wide range of tooling available, that it is to be found in some guise in the workshops of most professional woodcarvers, including many who show a marked preference for using hand tools.

Using a good machine and well-chosen cutters can be likened to the freedom enjoyed in sketching, enabling you to concentrate on line and form instead of the mechanics of timber removal. Novices are able to achieve good results quickly, because learning to control a flexi-shaft is a much quicker experience than learning to master the use of edge tools, their sharpening, and the vagaries of the timber and grain. The flexi-shaft is probably the most useful machine that a woodcarver can buy after the bandsaw, and, unlike many 'gadgets', I don't know of anyone who has bought a good-quality one and regretted it.

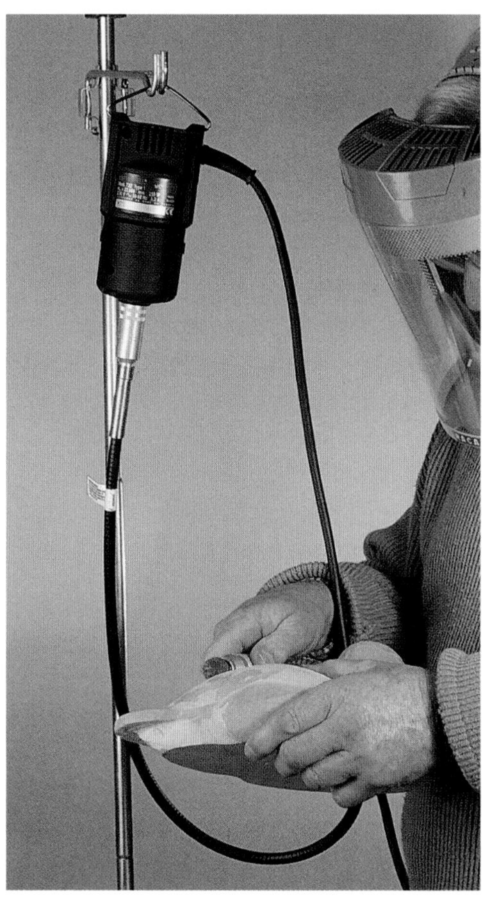

Fig 3.1 *The flexible-shaft carving machine is probably the most versatile power carver for medium-to-small-scale work. This Dremel unit would be a welcome addition to any workshop.*

There is a fairly wide choice of machines from various manufacturers, all offering slightly different products and combinations. If can be very hard to choose from a pile of manufacturers' price lists, so check out all the models, specifications, and prices to see what is currently available before you decide. The larger flexi-shaft machines found in UK carvers' workshops are mostly of American origin, although there are some European and Far Eastern machines about too. I have examples of light-duty, entry-level machines from

Dremel and Foredom, as well as more heavyweight units from Dremel, Foredom, and Pfingst in my workshop. These are simple and generally very reliable machines, as long as they are not abused and receive some routine servicing (see below, page 24).

The machine consists of a high-speed motor, usually having a combined foot switch and speed control, connected by a very flexible shaft to a handpiece with a chuck or collet to hold the tools. Accessory flexible shafts are available for many low-voltage drill/grinders, but these are too underpowered to be of any real use in woodcarving, because too much of the drill/grinder's power is absorbed in friction losses in the shaft. Shafts are also available for use with electric drills, but these are totally unsuitable for general carving: the shafts are too stiff, and electric drills run too slowly (Fig 3.2). Dedicated flexible-shaft machines available at present appear to be manufactured mainly in France and the USA, but don't ask me why that is.

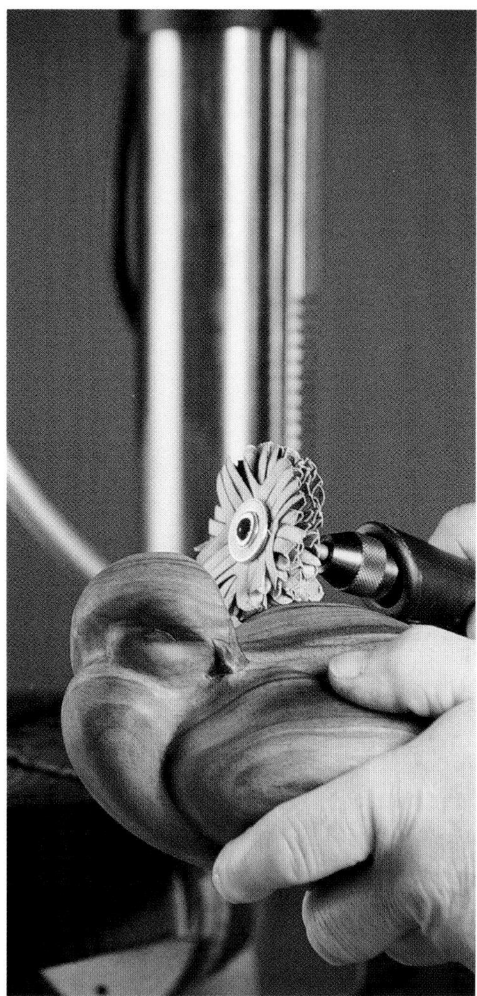

Fig 3.2 *Flexible shafts run from drills are too stiff and slow for tasks other than sanding.*

The motors are most often suspended, although some sit in a cradle on the bench; they usually have top speeds between 14,000 and 30,000rpm. They vary greatly in power from model to model, smaller units being suitable for only very light carving and texturing, while the larger, more powerful models are quite capable of roughing out large carvings when combined with suitable tooling. The range of useful machines for carving available in the UK runs from the light but useful Dremel Multi, with ⅙hp motor, to the heavyweight 1.3hp Moviluty Movix.

With one exception – the Dremel Multi – I have not mentioned any of the small units which offer an accessory flexible shaft, particularly the low-voltage ones. They are generally rather underpowered except for the lightest tasks, and are more suited to less arduous work such as model-making. Adding a flexible shaft to a low-powered motor only absorbs much of the available power as friction in the shaft, rendering such machines of no use in woodcarving.

The 125W Dremel Multi is the only machine mentioned in this section which does not come with a permanent flexible shaft; the shaft is an additional accessory. The Multi is quite powerful, though, and makes a good, budget-priced, entry-level

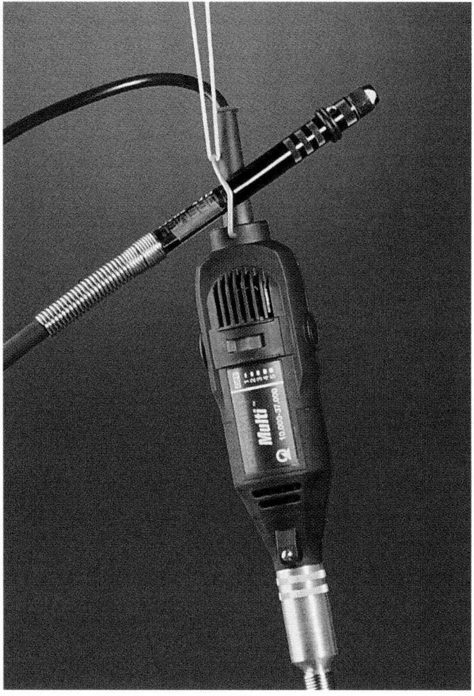

Fig 3.3 *The Dremel Multi with an accessory shaft makes a good entry-level machine for light carving and texturing.*

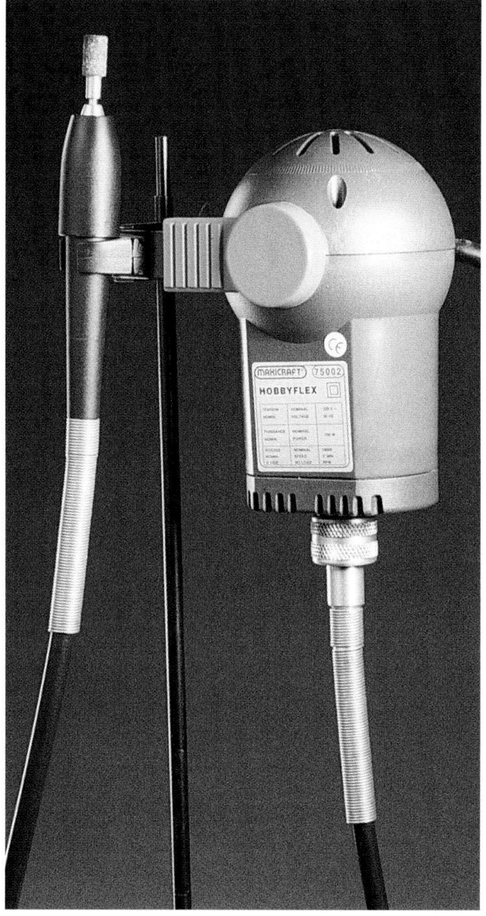

Fig 3.4 *Other entry-level units, like this French-made Maxicraft available in the UK, are suitable for light carving and texturing.*

machine (Fig 3.3). The on/off switch and speed control situated on the motor body is not as convenient as a foot switch, but it could always be plugged into a foot switch such as that supplied by Draper. The 32,000rpm top speed is very useful when working with very small-diameter burrs and cutters which just won't perform properly at low speeds. I have had one around my workshop for a number of years and find it handy to take to demonstrations or to my college classes, because it is light, but still a very useful and capable machine.

Another light, entry-level machine is the Maxicraft, a French machine with a 90W, 1,400rpm motor (Fig 3.4). This has its own combined foot switch and speed control, giving it the convenience of the larger, more expensive machines.

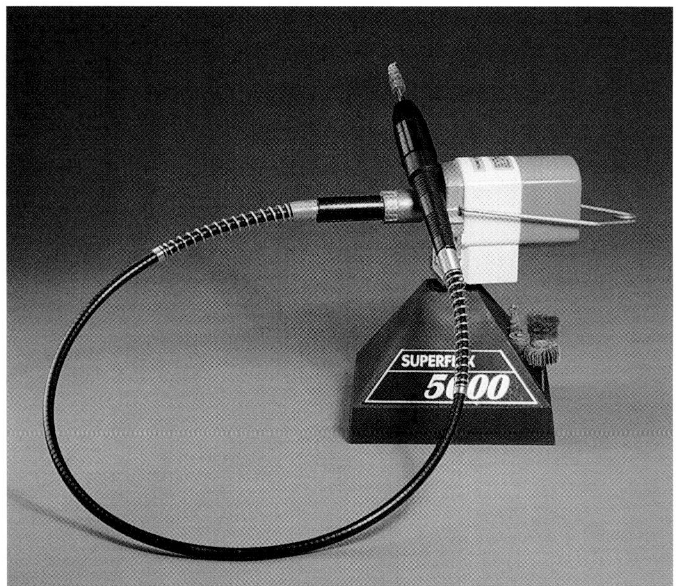

Fig 3.5 *The Inca flexible shaft may be suspended or fitted on a swivelling bench mount, but the top speed is too low for many applications.*

Flexible-shaft machine: entry-level

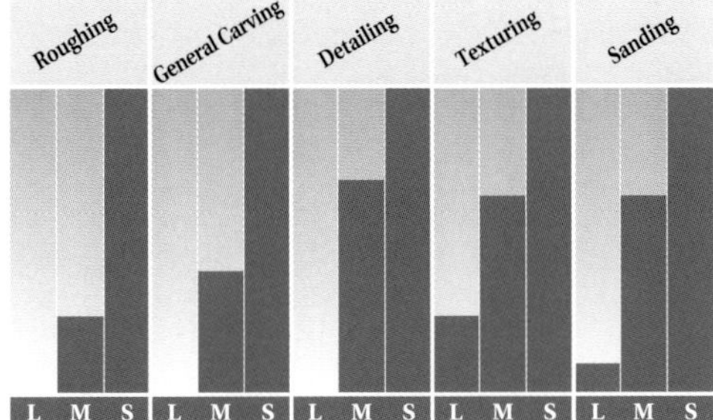

Flexible-shaft machine: heavy-duty

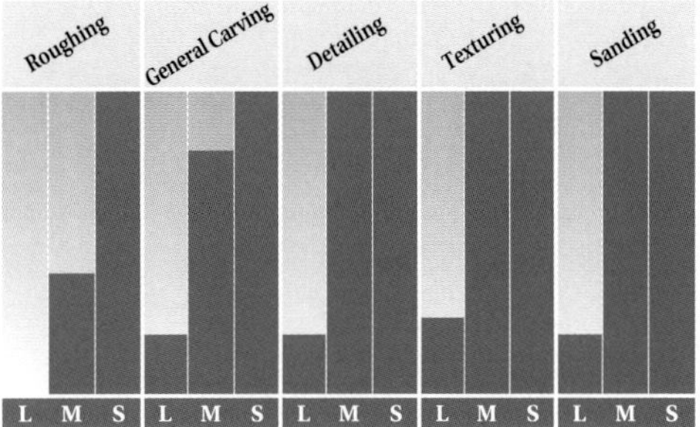

The Inca Superflex 500 can be suspended or put on a swivel stand on the bench (Fig 3.5). It also has a 90W motor, but the top speed is only 6,000rpm; this is rather too slow for most small-diameter tooling, which needs to be running at 10,000+ rpm before it starts to cut properly.

The Moviluty Minyflex is another French machine, with a 150W, 20,000rpm motor. The variable-speed foot control has a preset device so that you can set a maximum motor speed.

Small power tools are useful, providing you correctly match the capacity of the job to the size of the tool. If you are creating netsuke, or are going to perform only light carving and texturing operations on small areas of carving, they may provide all you will ever need. However, once you start using one of these versatile machines, unless you are a miniaturist, you will soon regret buying a small machine, either because it won't perform the tasks you want or because you will quickly wear it out. Unfortunately, the axiom that 'you get what you pay for' is never more true than when applied to tools, and the only people I have met who were disappointed with their flexi-shaft machines were those who had bought cheap or low-powered ones.

To get a useful general-purpose tool, with plenty of ability to grow with you, I would recommend you buy a machine of 100+ watts output. Suppliers report that many cases of failed motors and damaged shafts are associated with very heavy usage, particularly on the harder timbers. These problems are much more likely to occur with small machines, which are asked to perform work they weren't designed for. One of the smaller entry-level machines will probably last for years when used for detailing and texturing, but may fail in weeks if used for heavy roughing-out work. If your budget only runs to one of the smaller machines, look after it by using sharp cutters and letting them cut at their own pace – don't force them. This will give you better results and a longer machine life.

Of the larger, more powerful machines, which are suitable for regular carving, The Dremel Motoflex is probably the best-known. Unlike the Multi, this is a dedicated 250W, 22,000rpm flexible-shaft motor, which is widely distributed. The motor is controlled by a metal-clad combined foot switch and speed control, which stays where you put it on the floor and doesn't walk away when you need it.

New European electrical regulations stopped the UK sale of the popular Pfingst and Foredom flexi-shaft carving machines for a while, but the new Foredom motor has been redesigned to meet the

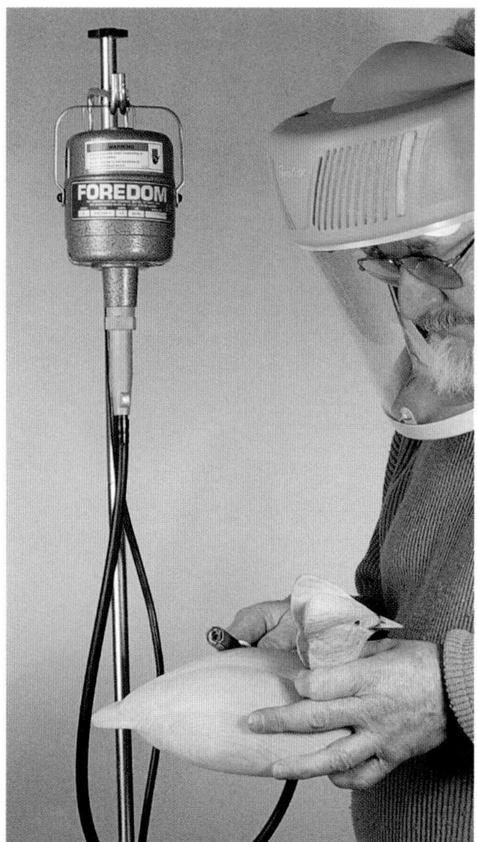

Fig 3.6 *The new CE-approved Foredom machine for the European market appears little different from their other models, and certainly works as well as the old non-approved versions.*

European directives (Fig 3.6). The new Series K CE motor is a well-made 270W output, 18,000rpm machine from this popular American manufacturer. The foot control is plastic, but is mounted on a plate and doesn't wander about the floor as much as the old version did.

The French Moviluty Movix is the real heavyweight of flexible-shaft machines, with its 900W, 25,000rpm motor. It is cradle-mounted and can be either hung or stood on a bench; the foot control has this manufacturer's unique preset feature to adjust the maximum speed.

At least one motor unit is available which allows the direction of rotation to be changed; the unit is made by Foredom in the USA, but is not available in the UK any more (Fig 3.7). When used with suitable sanding and burr-type cutters which do not have conventional teeth, this feature enables you to change the cutter direction to suit the grain direction of the area of carving you are working on. This reduces the tendency to tear out wood fibres, and allows smoother cutting and sanding.

The flexible shafts are of similar construction to that used for bicycle brakes and speedometer cables. They are generally much more flexible than the so-called 'flexible shafts' sold as accessories to ordinary electric drills, which are heavy and unyielding. This allows much greater freedom of tool movement and better control, although the shaft's flexibility

Fig 3.7 *Foredom machines are very popular in the USA, but this reversible-motor unit is no longer available in Europe because of new electrical regulations.*

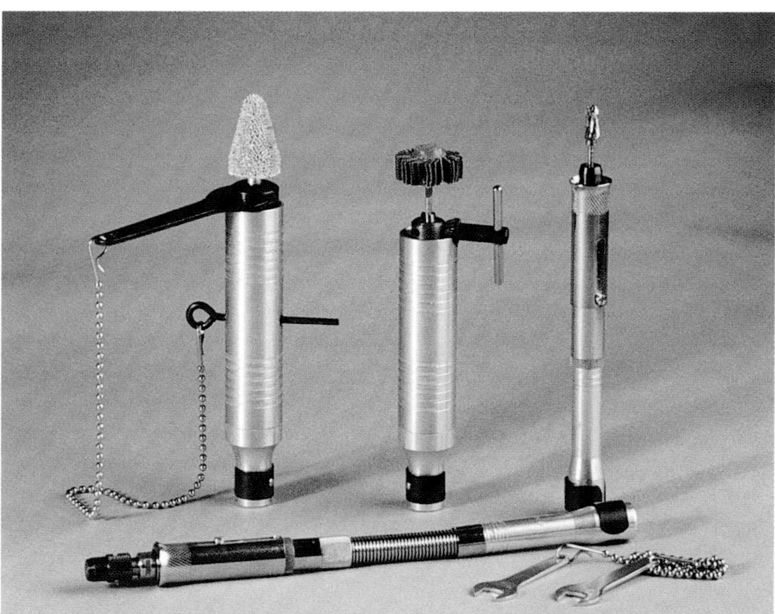

Fig 3.8 (Left) Most of the better machines use interchangeable handpieces.

Fig 3.9 (Below) Collet chucks give a less bulky handpiece than 3-jaw chucks; the Inca (illustrated) and Maxiflex machines provide a chuck cover so that you can hold the handpieces nearer the tool for better control.

does still vary from one make to another. An electric drill and one of the cheap 'inflexi-shafts' is no match for a proper flexible-shaft carving machine, as the speed is too slow for operations other than sanding or drilling, and the shaft too stiff to allow proper tool control.

Handpieces are fixed permanently to the shafts of some, mainly entry-level, machines. The better heavy-duty units have handpieces which are interchangeable between detail and heavy-duty ones (Fig 3.8). These handpieces usually connect to the shaft with a standard American-style snap connector, allowing different sizes and types of handpiece to be selected for different jobs. The handpieces use either collets or small chucks to grip the tool. Those using collets tend to be less bulky, especially when using small burrs, where a conventional chuck can restrict tool access to the work quite badly (Fig 3.9).

The accessory shaft for the Dremel Multi suffers from being rather stiff, and I find it reduces tool control when completing delicate operations. The handpiece uses collets and is pencil-slim, giving very good accessibility on complex carvings. The finger-grip is not too good, though, and you can find your fingers slipping forward onto the rotating collet. I put a couple of O-rings on the handpiece of my machine, and that fixed the problem.

The Maxicraft, another entry-level machine, has a much more flexible shaft than the Dremel Multi, and gives better tool control on fine work, but the handpiece is a little bulky. It uses a 3-jaw chuck, which is less accurate than collets, but has a neat plastic cover that slips on and covers the rotating chuck when you are using the machine, leaving only the tool projecting and allowing you to grip nearer the tool for greater control.

The handpieces for most of the larger machines used regularly by carvers are quick-change, and most are even interchangeable between different makes. I have a collection of handpieces from Dremel, Foredom, and Pfingst in my studio, and they will all interchange between my different machines.

Handpieces are available in both heavy-duty types and pencil-style detailing models, and it is beneficial to have both, with complete sets of collets (Figs 3.10 and 3.11). Each handpiece requires a different collet for each size of tool shank, but tool shafts are standardized and the most common ones you will find are ¼, ⅛, and 3/32in, and 6, 3, and 2.3mm. Most collets are designed to take only one size of tool shank, and should not be strained to clamp a smaller one. Overtightening collets to accommodate a smaller tool shank will lead to the tool shaft being clamped only at the front of the collet, and not being securely held; collet damage can also occur. This is not the case with the collets for the large Dremel 236 heavy-duty handpiece, though. This uses a much more effective double-ended collet which will tighten from both ends, and close securely on any tool shaft within its size range. In practice, you could settle for a ¼in and a 6mm collet for the large

Fig 3.10 (Above) *Large handpieces are better suited to ¼in and 6mm tool shanks, although you can get collets for smaller tools too.*

Fig 3.11 (Right) *The smaller handpieces are ideal for detail work using ⅛in, 3mm, 3/32in, and 2.4mm shank tools. The extra-flexible 'Duplex' section on some handpieces gives you more freedom of movement at the wrist.*

handpiece, plus ⅛ and 3⁄32in for the pencil one. These will usually hold all the common tool-shank sizes, both metric and Imperial. You can buy handpieces from some makers with a small and very flexible section of spring between the handpiece and the snap connector (see Fig 3.11, and Fig 4.1 on page 36). Often called a 'Duplex', this is a very useful addition to the pencil-style detail handpieces, because it flexes at your wrist where you need the flexibility most, and stops you wagging the motor and main shaft about as you work. This greatly increases your control of the tool tip when doing intricate work, but it forms the weak link in the power train and I would only recommend using the smaller tools with 3⁄32in (2.4mm) shanks in a handpiece fitted with a Duplex spring.

It is important for the long life and cool running of the shaft that it is not bent into too tight a radius as you work. It is much easier to achieve this if the motor is suspended so that it can be raised or lowered and also moved laterally to suit the work you are doing. It needs to be easily adjustable as you work, and such an arrangement will also help give you maximum tool control. I replaced my Heath Robinson homemade affair with a neat little foldaway Dremel flexi-shaft gantry, which I find adequate for demonstrations, but for permanent use I have a more flexible arrangement in my workshop (Fig 3.12). My machines are all hung on a very simple adjustable cord loop, based on the tent guy-rope adjuster (you could actually use one of these, although a piece of dowel with two holes works just as well). The top end of the suspension cord is tied to a ring which runs on a length of wardrobe rail fastened to the ceiling, running parallel to the front of my workbench and about 12in (300mm) in front of it. This allows the motor to be positioned correctly when working, and slid clear of my work area when I'm not using it. If you do not always work in the same spot, you may need to use some other arrangement, and the commercial gantry might be your answer. My workshop arrangement makes it quicker and easier to make adjustments, giving optimum tool control and preventing any unnecessary excess bending of the shaft. I think it is better to spend money on tool bits than a fancy 'sky hook' for the machine!

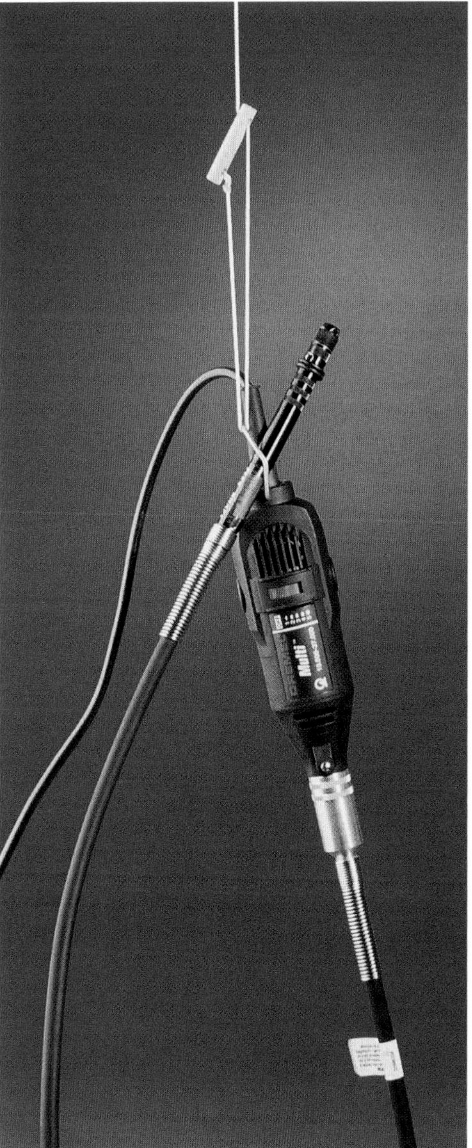

Fig 3.12 *It is important to be able to adjust the height of the motor to suit the work. My guy-rope-style adjuster is a simple solution – a piece of chain or a commercial adjustable stand will work well too.*

I have found that the machines I have used required very little maintenance, five minutes every month or so being all it takes for the routine service of a heavily used machine. Before you start, read your supplier's instructions first to see what they recommend.

Besides the normal safety checks, routine maintenance checks along the following lines would be suitable for most machines, and should increase their life and reliability:

1. Vacuum out the air cooling ports on the motor to remove dust and debris.
2. Lubricate the motor-shaft bearings, but *only* if recommended in the manufacturer's instructions; this applies mainly to motors with bronze bearings and not ball races.
3. Remove the motor brushes and check them for wear, being careful to replace them the correct way round.
4. Remove the outer sheath from the flexible shaft and wipe off the excess grease from the inner shaft.
5. Check that it is securely clamped to the motor shaft and that the drive 'flag' which drives the handpiece is not damaged.
6. Put a smear of fresh grease on the inner shaft and reassemble. Don't overdo the grease: just a smear is needed; filling the shaft will put more load on the motor and may lead to overheating, and the motor's premature death.
7. Some handpieces need lubrication, some are sealed for life (the bearing's, not yours!), so follow the manufacturer's instructions, and don't lubricate unless they say so. Too much grease can cause the handpiece to overheat, and oiling may actually wash the grease out of ball races.
8. Collets should be removed and cleaned, as dust build-up can reduce their grip on the tool. I soak them in acetone or paint stripper to break down wood residues and use a small spiral brush to clean them. I then wipe them with WD40 (or whatever lubricant is recommended by the manufacturer) before refitting them. You can buy collet-care kits from Trend, which will suit the larger collets used.

A full check-up every month or so, or even six-monthly if you don't use your machine much, should keep it trouble-free for years.

Inner shafts break relatively easily if you are careless. Catching your clothing in the burr, starting the motor with the cutter already in contact with the work, and trying to force the cutting action by using excess pressure are the most likely causes of shaft breakages, and all of these are easily avoidable.

Safety

Make sure you work in a comfortable position with tools and switches close to hand and that you check cable and plugs regularly. Foot controls need to be always 'to foot' and not wandering around the floor where you can't find them or might stand on them accidentally. Some foot controls are very light and move all over the floor: the Foredom plastic ones are particularly prone to getting lost. Others, like Dremel's, are heavy enough not to move, but to keep mine always in the right spot I have them all mounted on a heavy, angled board which just sits under the bench.

If your carver has a separate motor switch, get into the habit of flicking it off when you put the handpiece down. Otherwise, accidentally stepping on the foot control can send the shaft and tool whipping dangerously around the workshop. If you do not have a motor switch, make sure the outlet socket is within reach, and turn the power off there.

If your machine has a reversible motor, make sure you get into the habit of switching the direction switch back to the 'off' position (or at least the forward direction) every time you stop using the machine. This will stop the palpitations caused by that large burr shooting alarmingly towards you when you next switch on.

Most carvers hand-hold their work in their lap when using a flexible-shaft carver: the great beauty of their use is that for most situations clamping is unnecessary, and would be a hindrance to the work (Fig 3.13). You are the most quickly adjustable and efficient workholding device invented, but you are also the most vulnerable, so safety should always loom large in your mind.

You will soon work out how to hold the carving and work safely, keeping your hand away from the burr; but, as when using edge tools, you will sometimes make mistakes and will get the odd cuts and scratches. The small abrasive-type burrs, which are the main tools used, do not do too much damage, but large abrasive burrs and toothed cutters, especially the chainsaw-style carvers, demand more caution from the user. A work-holding clamp of some kind is strongly recommended when using these larger tools, and is essential when using a chainsaw-type cutter. 'Prevention is better than cure,' the saying goes, and so as well as the box of plasters (just to be on the safe side), some protective clothing is called for. A stout leather apron, of the type used by blacksmiths and welders, gives good protection to the chest and legs when sitting carving. Leather scuffs away, rather than catching and tearing on carving burrs, which is why it is used for motorcycle clothing. Although it can be cut through, thick leather gives you a lot more reaction time than a pair of trousers or a shirt. My apron has been reinforced by gluing two extra pieces of leather inside it, one in the chest area and one over the legs. This allows it to bend at the waist, but gives extra protection where it is most needed, making it more suitable for whittling too.

Some power carvers wear a stout leather glove on the hand holding the carving in their lap, although I think that

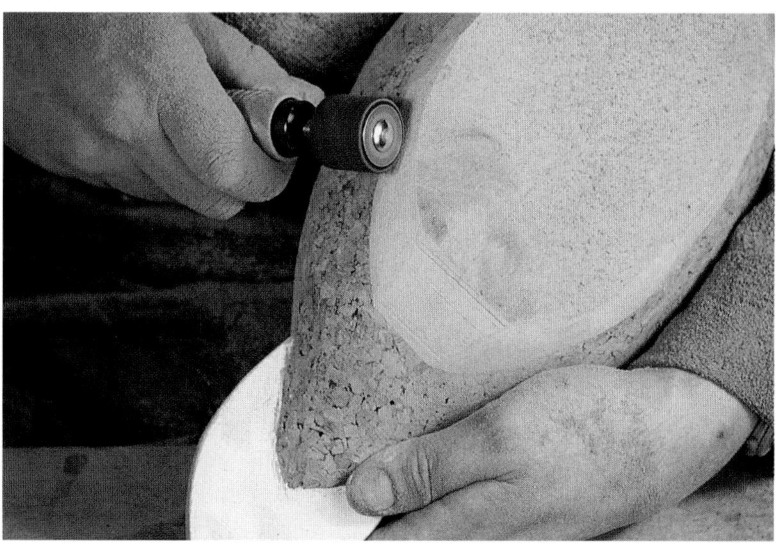

Fig 3.13 *Most carving is done with the work hand-held. Here a rigid-sleeve rubber sanding drum is being used as a carving and shaping tool.*

SUPPLIERS INCLUDE:

Dremel
Bosch (Dremel)
Foredom
Shesto (Foredom)
Axminster Power Tools (Inca)
Macford (Maxicraft)
Moviluty (Hegner)
Pintail (Pfingst)
Pfingst
Protective Specialties (Vac-U-Shield)

this can be more of a hindrance than a help: gloves can actually make firm holding of the carving more difficult.

Before you tackle any operation you should work out how to perform it in the safest manner. Consider both tool control and safe work-holding, and don't carve when you are tired or distracted. About the only time that I would *never* consider hand-holding the work when using a flexi-shaft carver is when using chainsaw-type cutters. Their action is too swift and severe to even contemplate doing it. Other tooling can give you a nasty bite, though, so if you are at all nervous about hand-holding work for some operations, use a work-holder.

The burr-type cutters and sanding drums used so much with flexi-shaft carvers require adequate extraction. Workshop drum-type vacuum cleaners can be adapted to remove dust from the cutting area, and one US company makes a special dust-extraction fitting to clip on the heavy-duty handpieces, called Vac-U-Shield (Fig 3.14). It works reasonably well, although it can get in the way at times. The unit is fairly expensive, especially if you have to import it yourself, and I would think that most carvers could rig up something similar themselves, using their workshop vacuum cleaner, for very little outlay. If you have a large dust extractor, the hose can be connected to a collection hopper or a simple lap board. Don't skimp by using a cheap or unsuitable extractor which allows the very fine, virtually invisible particles back into the workshop air: these are the ones which do your lungs the most damage.

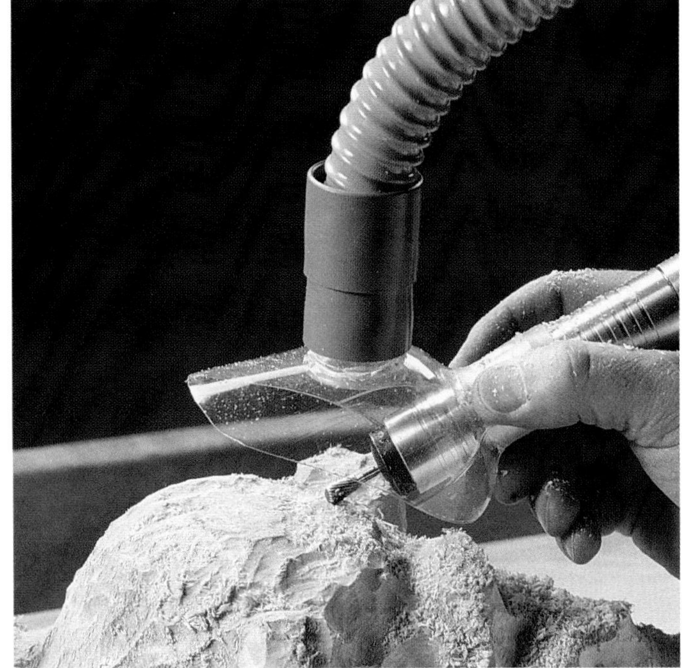

Fig 3.14 *The Vac-U-Shield is an extraction device that clips on to the handpiece; although it is a good idea in principle to keep the extraction point as near the cutter as possible, I find it gets in the way rather a lot. (Photo by courtesy of Protective Specialties)*

Tooling for flexible-shaft machines

Tooling is very important to the proper working of these machines, and good burrs and cutters are not cheap. Poor cutters will diminish the value of the machine: don't expect cheap, blunt, or worn-out carbon cutters to work with your power carver. It will fail to perform, no matter how much force you put on the cutter, and you could even assist its premature demise. Sharp cutters work well without undue force, giving you more control and putting less strain on the machine, so make sure that you budget for a few good-quality cutters to start off with.

The four main functions performed with flexible-shaft machines are:

1 bulk stock removal (roughing out)
2 detail carving and shaping
3 sanding and smoothing
4 texturing.

Consult the bar charts in each section to see which cutters are most suitable for these different applications.

Tooth-form cutters

Suitable cutters for flexible shafts fall into two styles: abrasive burrs, and those with a proper cutting tooth. Abrasive burrs leave a coarse, rasped or sanded finish to the work, whereas toothed cutters can leave the surface rough or beautifully smooth.

Tooth-form cutters vary from the crude, cheap cast-steel type with punched, rasp-like teeth, through chainsaw circlet cutters to the beautifully made solid tungsten-carbide-headed cutters with teeth as sharp as a razor. All toothed cutters suffer from the disadvantage that when used against the wood grain, they are liable to catch and tear out bits of the grain, leaving a poor finish. On end grain, they are liable to compress and break the timber, again leaving a poor finish, especially on soft timbers. This makes them unsuitable for any area of a carving where the cutter cannot be presented in such a way as not to tear the wood. They are more difficult to control, being affected by grain and knots, and even the carbide ones have a relatively limited life before they become too blunt to use.

Carbon steel rasp cutters (Fig 3.15) leave a very poor finish, and only really work on soft timbers, where they are likely to rip pieces out of the grain. They can be used on jelutong or similar timbers as roughing-out cutters, but the punched teeth leave a very rough finish. They blunt quickly and, although cheap, they are best avoided.

HSS (high-speed steel) toothed cutters are much better made and look very similar to their tungsten-carbide-headed counterparts. The teeth are accurately ground into the head of the cutter and they are of a much higher quality than the rasp cutters. Even high-speed steel cutters quickly blunt when working timber, but the cutters are not too expensive and can leave a very good finish.

Fig 3.15 *Carbon steel rasp-toothed cutters are not very effective on most timbers.*

Vanadium steel cutters, sometimes called **'stump'** cutters, are quite popular with carvers. They are in many ways similar to the solid HSS cutters above, but are generally available in smaller sizes. The same comments apply to these as to the HSS cutters.

Carbon steel rasp cutters

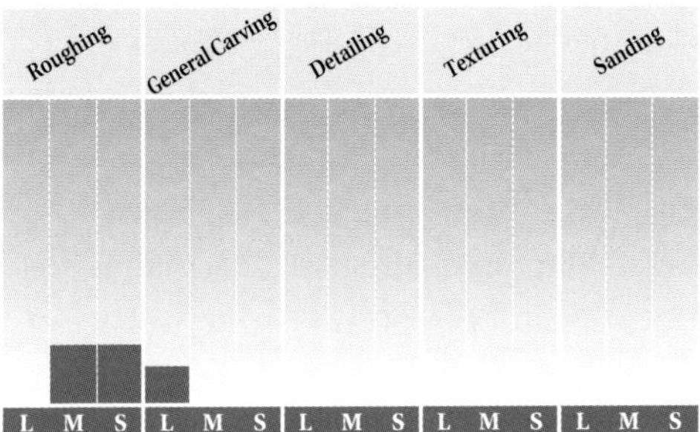

HSS toothed cutters and vanadium steel 'stump' cutters

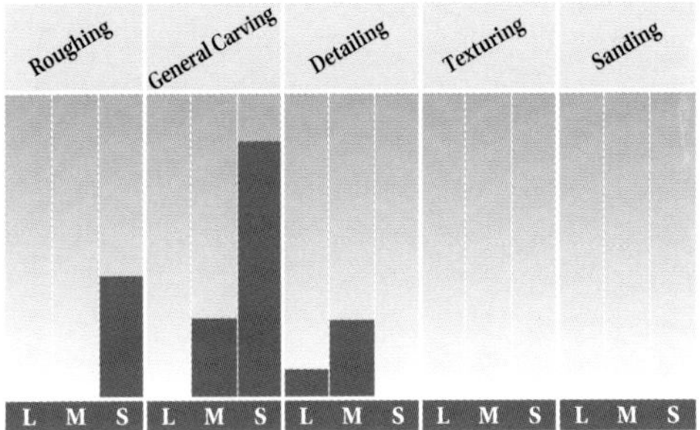

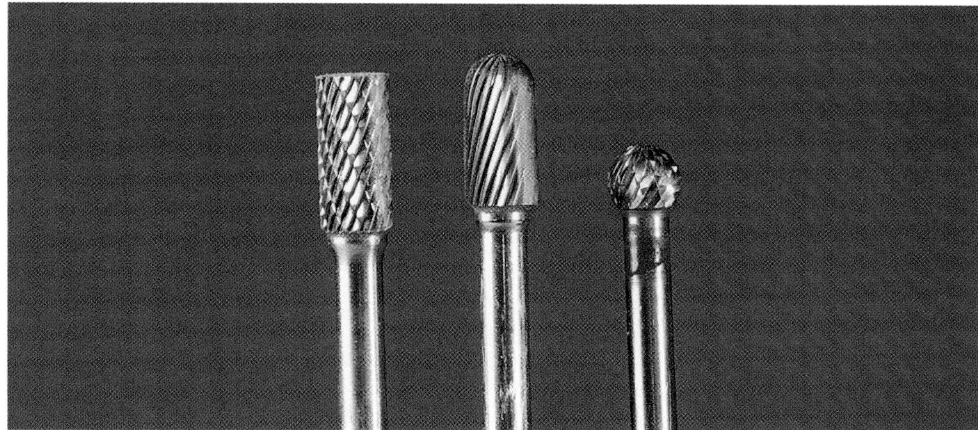

Fig 3.16 Tungsten carbide toothed cutters can leave a clean cut but are affected by grain direction.

Tungsten carbide cutters (Fig 3.16) usually comprise a steel shaft with a carbide head brazed on, although small ones are often machined out of solid tungsten carbide. Few woodworkers would choose to use anything other than tungsten-tipped cutters in a router or saw, and these cutters offer the same advantage, keeping their very sharp cutting edges for much longer than other types; their biggest drawback is the cost.

Carbide cutters with ground teeth cut cleanly and can leave the same sort of polished cut as a well-honed edge tool. In fact, a round-ended cutter can be used to give the impression of a hand-tooled finish to a carving in a fraction of the time. But they are still subject to the vagaries of grain and knots, and prone to ripping out end grain when they start to get worn.

Tungsten carbide toothed cutters

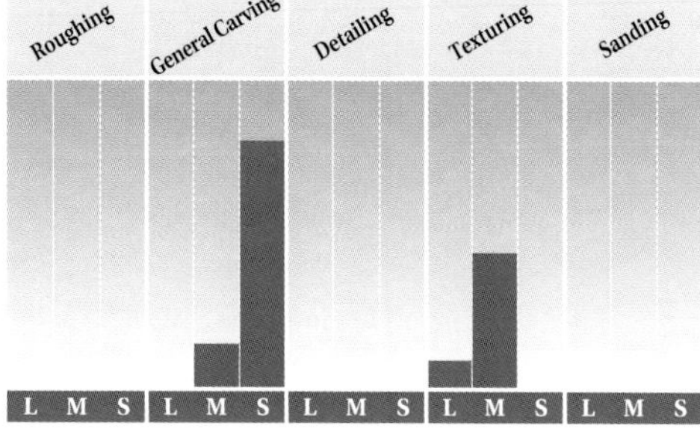

Fig 3.17 Chainsaw cutters like the Tornado are very effective at removing stock rapidly, but they demand respect, with the work firmly clamped and both hands on the handpiece!

The cutting edges chip easily if they are not handled and stored correctly, and although they have a reasonable life span, they cannot be resharpened economically.

Chainsaw circlet cutters are a relatively new development, based on the chainsaw carving discs for angle grinders. One or more small circles of saw chain are clamped between plates and fixed on a spindle to form the cutter (Fig 3.17). They are easily sharpened with a chainsaw file, and remove timber quickly as quite large chips. They are the best roughing-out cutters for medium-to-large carvings that I have used, easily coping with very tough timbers such as elm burr. They require a large amount of respect, though, and careful use.

I have come across two similar makes: the Percival from King Arthur's Tools, which has quite a long reach of 4 or 6in (100–150mm), and the Tornado from Rod Naylor. The Tornado now forms an indispensable part of my power carving kit, and I prefer not to have the cutter projecting too far out of the handpiece. Lessening the length of tool in front of the handpiece bearing restricts access a little, but will greatly increase the life of the front bearing. If I need extra reach, though, I'll call for Percival.

Rod Naylor's latest incarnation of his Tornado chainsaw circlet cutter has a solid steel head with three replaceable tungsten carbide tool tips. It has a smaller diameter than the chainsaw version, but its main advantages are better cutting and longer tool life on tough timbers. The

Fig 3.18 *The smaller 'Ruby carvers' use corundum as the abrasive; diamond burrs tend to be smaller and have finer grit than rubies.*

circular teeth can be rotated to expose fresh cutting edges, before being replaced when completely blunt.

Abrasive burrs

All the previously mentioned cutters have conventional teeth that point and cut in one direction, but there is a whole family of cutters whose cutting action is omnidirectional, and these are probably the most useful style for power carving. There are four types of abrasive cutting burrs: tungsten carbide, synthetic ruby (Fig 3.18), diamond, and vitrified abrasive stones. All of these are used to good effect by woodcarvers, although most of the tools are suitable for working a wide variety of other materials.

Ruby carvers

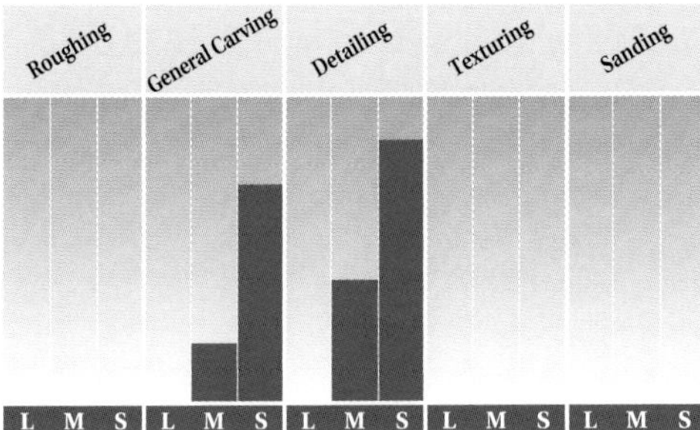

Diamond burrs

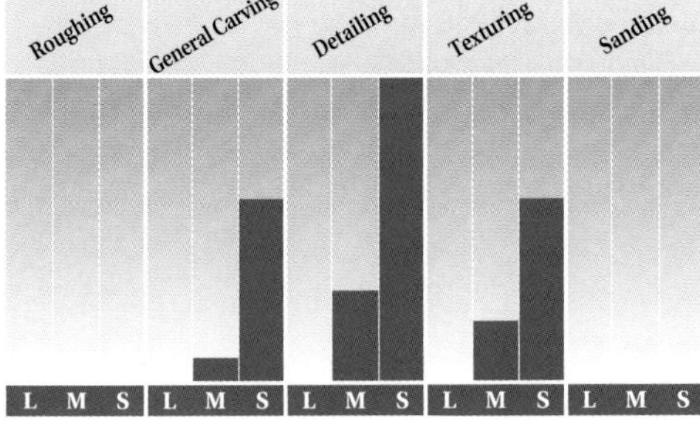

Vitrified abrasive stones

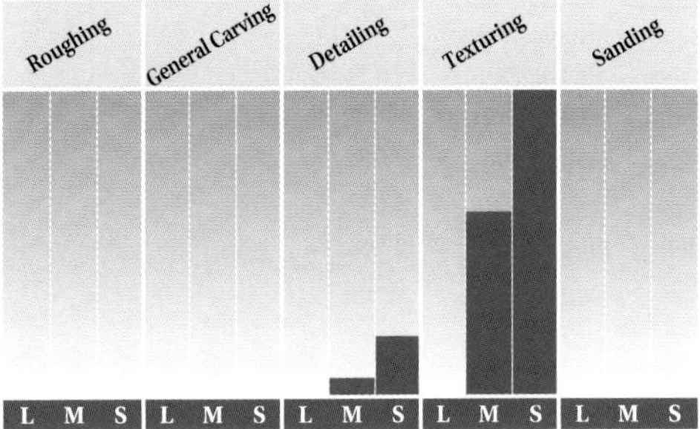

Fig 3.19 *Structured carbide toothed burrs are available in a wide variety of shapes, sizes, and grits.*

Tungsten carbide abrasive burrs (Fig 3.19) come in two basic types: those with random TC particles brazed to the surface, and those where the particles are 'structured', or made into teeth. These structured burrs are further split into two styles: those with randomly positioned teeth, like the Karbide Kutzall, and those with teeth aligned in rows, like the Typhoon. The Karbide Kutzall (Fig 3.20) is the original random-spaced, structured-tooth burr; the teeth give the tool an aggressive abrasive action, rather than a true cutting action.

All these cutters basically consist of a steel shaft, with a machined steel mandrel shape on to which the graded carbide particles are sintered or brazed. The manufacturing process used to create the structured carbide teeth on these burrs is quite interesting, and worth a mention. A machined steel arbor is coated with a temporary adhesive, then with a layer of small steel balls. The size of the ball used determines the size of the finished tooth. The cutter is then magnetized to attract the carbide grains, which build up on each ball to form a conical point, like iron

Fig 3.20 *Oliver's Karbide Kutzalls have been available for many years and are a favourite with many carvers. The carbide grit is 'structured' into teeth which are randomly distributed on the surface of the tool.*

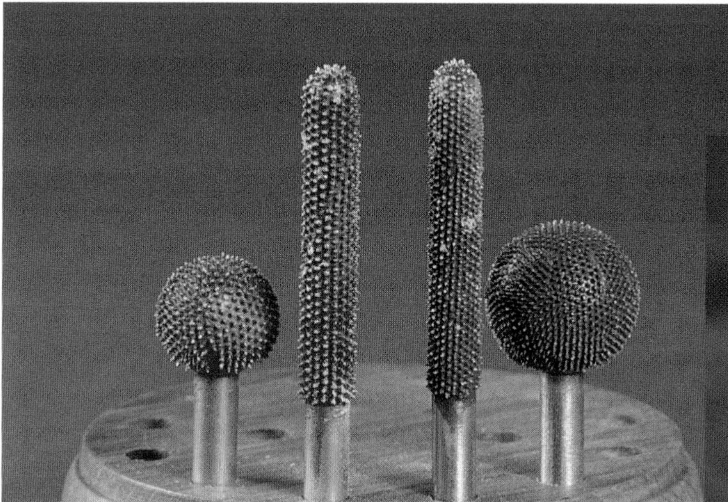

***Fig 3.21.(Left)** The structured teeth on Foredom's Typhoon burrs are aligned over the surface of the tool.*

***Fig 3.22** Abrasive burrs with structured tungsten carbide teeth, like this Foredom Typhoon cutter, are most useful, being largely unaffected by grain direction.*

filings on a magnet. The entire burr is then coated with another layer of temporary adhesive to hold the carbide in place. Finally, they go into a furnace which burns away the adhesive and fuses all the parts together. This unique process produces an aggressive abrasive cutter with a very long life. In fact the life of the carving burrs is quite exceptional – on timber they are just about impossible to wear out, and my oldest KK burr is coming up to its tenth birthday and still working.

Tungsten carbide abrasive-style cutters leave a rougher finish than their toothed counterparts, but are largely unaffected by knots and changes in grain direction. They are especially good for roughing out and the early stages of shaping and detailing. Coarse grades usually leave a similar finish to a fine rasp, or very coarse sandpaper of about 30–40 grit. The finer burrs leave a finer sanded finish similar to that achieved with a 60–80 grit paper.

Carbide cutters cost much more than steel ones, but like the saw blades and router cutters they last far longer. Carbide abrasive cutters are not as vulnerable to damage as the ground-tooth versions, and although the cutting action does dull with use, they have a remarkably long life.

The newest arrivals of this type are Typhoon burrs, which have more even-sized teeth, arranged in rows rather than at random (Fig 3.21). They do not seem to clog as much as random-toothed structured burrs, and do not leave any deep scratching (Fig 3.22).

Good sharp cutters mean that less pressure need be applied, causing less strain on the machine and operator, so cutters with long working lives are a good investment.

Simple brazed or sintered carbide cutters have carbide granules randomly arranged across the whole surface. The tool head is dipped in a copper powder and then into a tungsten grit and adhesive mix. They are then put in a vacuum furnace and the temperature raised until the copper melts and fuses the carbide granules to the steel. They work reasonably well, the coarser ones being fairly fast-cutting, although they tend to

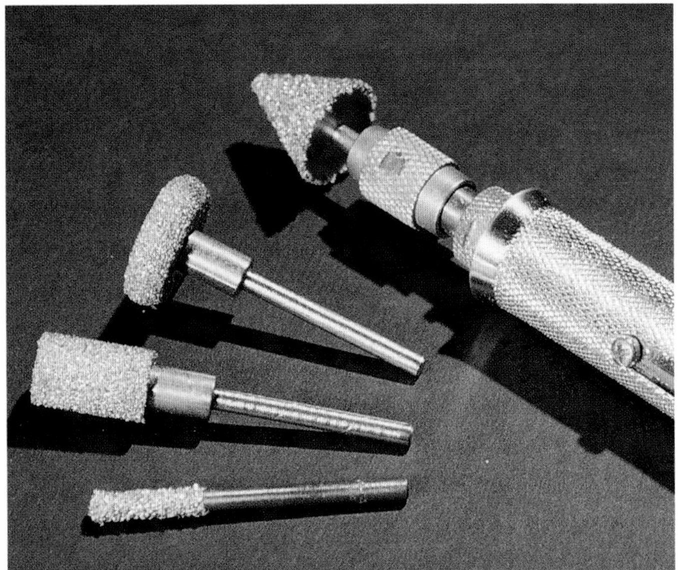

Fig 3.23 (Left and Below) *Perma-Grit manufacture a range of ⅛in-shank burrs with random carbide grit particles bonded to the surface. They include a rotor saw (below) which is useful for forming undercuts, or texturing larger carvings.*

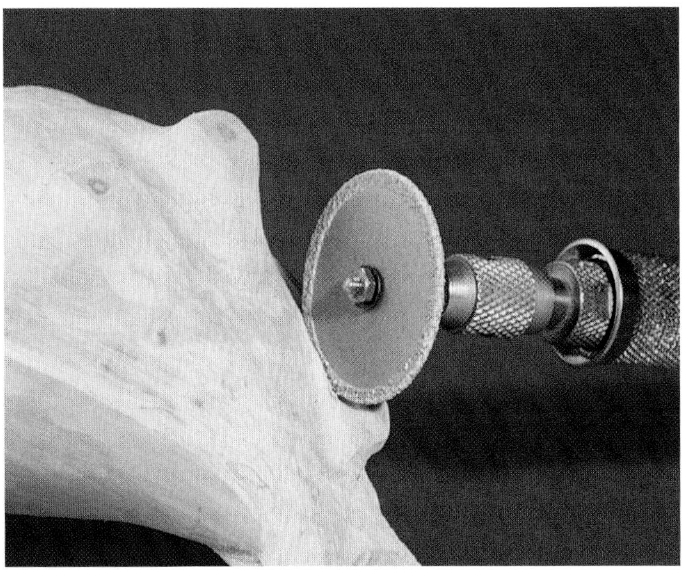

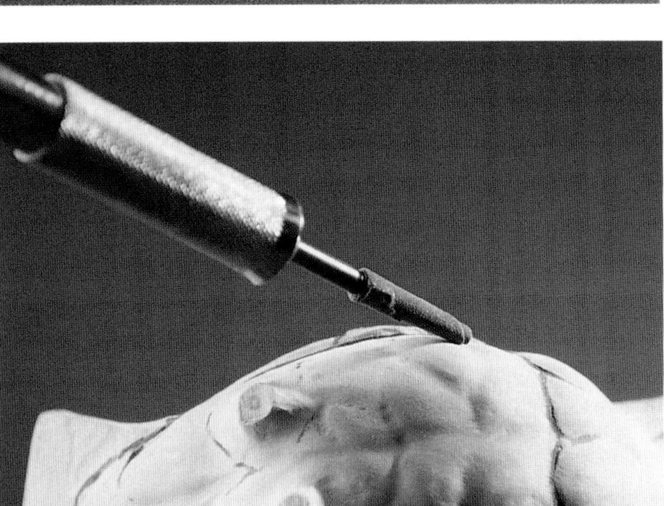

Fig 3.24 *Cartridge sanding rolls screw on to a tapered steel mandrel. They are available in a range of sizes and are good for reaching odd corners.*

clog up with some timbers, particularly resinous ones. They are also the cheapest of the three types to buy, making them a particularly attractive proposition if you regularly use timbers on which they perform well. Perma-Grit Tools make a series of ⅛in-shank tools which I have been using for a few years on smaller projects, finding them quite good on the jelutong and tupelo used for realistic bird carving (Fig 3.23). Rod Naylor sells a series of larger models with ¼in shank.

Cartridge sanding rolls

Cartridge sanding rolls screw onto the nose of a specially made, small tapered arbor, similar to the nose of a polishing machine. They are available in both cylindrical and tapered forms, in a choice of grit sizes (Fig 3.24). The abrasive is solidly wound and when you first use a new roll it tends to bounce on the surface; when it starts to wear a little, the edges soften and it becomes more controllable. The spirally wound rolls can be successfully used to sand very small nooks

Tungsten carbide abrasive cutters

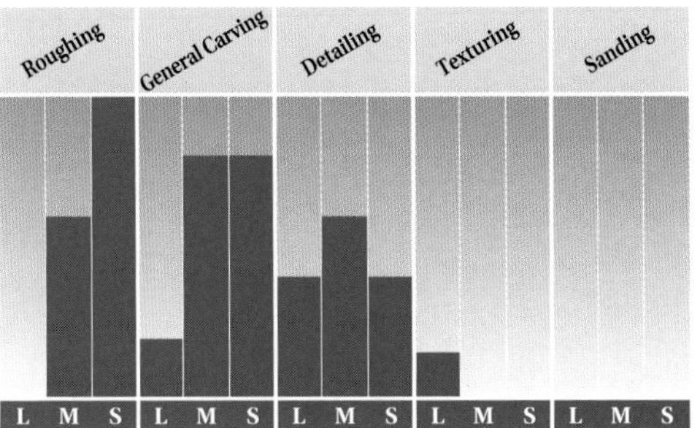

and crannies in a carving, although the end of the metal mandrel can poke through the end of the smaller rolls and mark the work. I have shortened the ends of my tapered arbors to help prevent this.

Sanding drums

Foam-cushioned sanding drums are very useful in the smaller sizes, and I use the range from Carroll Tools (Figs 3.25 and 3.26). They can save you hours of hand-sanding and can tackle quite large areas. Beware of running them at too high a speed, though: check the manufacturer's recommendations.

Pneumatic sanding drums are also suitable in the smaller sizes. I particularly like the compact and well-made Kirjes sanding drums from Sweden (Fig 3.27).

Cartridge sanding rolls

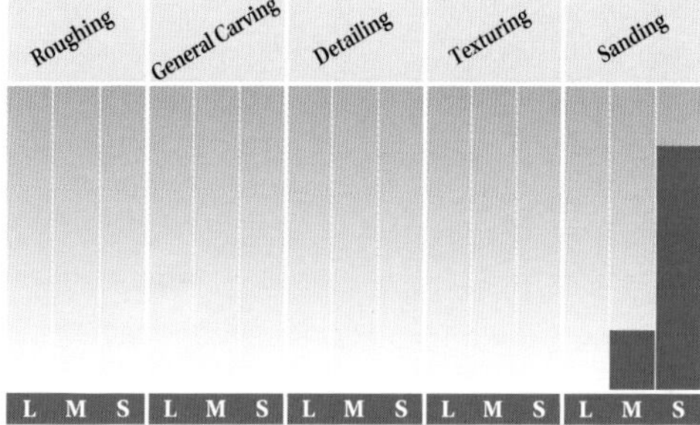

Cushioned and pneumatic sanding drums

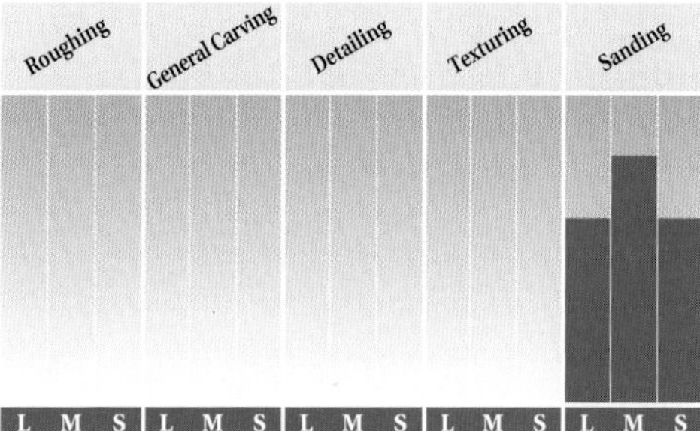

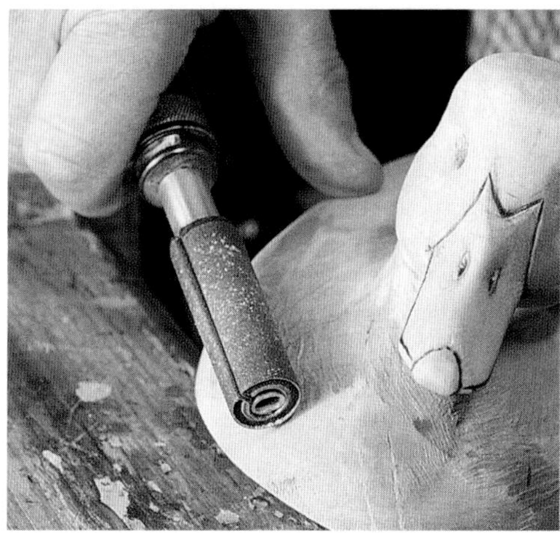

Fig 3.25 (Above) *Foam-covered sanding drums give a better finish than rigid drums.*

Fig 3.26 (Above right) *Carroll Tools have a range of well-engineered foam-cushioned drums which take inexpensive sheet abrasives. The smaller sizes are suitable for use in flexible-shaft machines.*

Fig 3.27 (Right) *Pneumatic drums are the ultimate in cushioned drums, but they require expensive ready-made abrasive sleeves. I particularly like the smaller Kirjes drum shown here.*

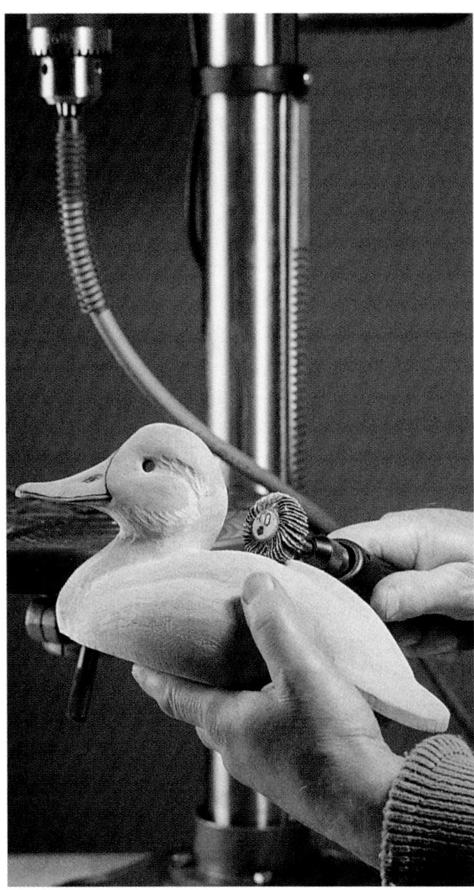

Fig 3.28 (Left) *Flap sanders are relatively stiff and require more care in use; this one is being used on a slower shaft run from a pillar drill.*

Fig 3.29 (Below) *Non-woven abrasive brushes can produce a silky finish, but if run too fast they burn; keep the speed low or use a drill-powered shaft.*

Other sanding aids

Various other sanding aids are available, including cloth-backed abrasive flap wheels, sanding star mops, non-woven nylon abrasive flap wheels, and simple split mandrels on which a piece of abrasive can be wound (Figs 3.28–3.30). Further information is included on pages 84–90. Make sure that you don't overload the shaft and motor by applying too much pressure when using flap wheels, and keep the speeds low, well within the manufacturer's recommended maximum.

TOOLING SUPPLIERS INCLUDE:

Rod Naylor
Pintail Decoy Supplies
Shesto
Bosch (Dremel)
Hegner UK
Perma-Grit Tools
Foredom
Gesswein
UltraSpeed

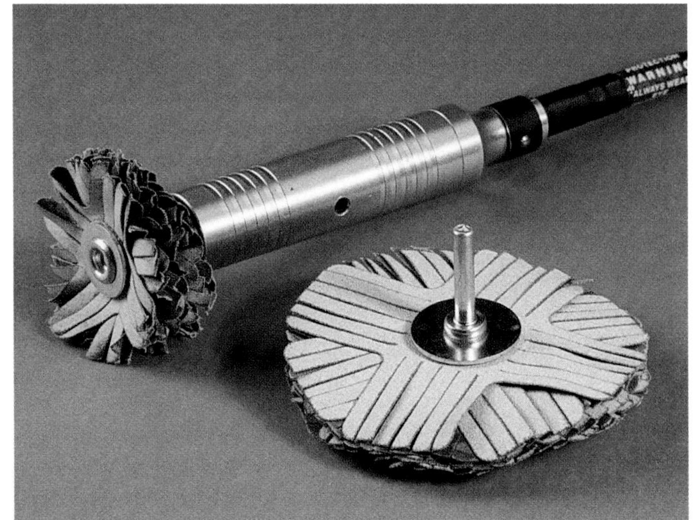

Fig 3.30 *Sanding stars are quite gentle in action and work well on carvings.*

Cleaning Cutters

The most useful cleaning tool is a brass spark-plug or suede-cleaning brush. This can be used to remove wood dust and fibres safely from all cutters and burrs *when they are stationary* (Fig 3.31).

The rubbery cleaning blocks used on belt and disc sanding machines can also be used to clean ruby and diamond burrs and abrasive sanding drums. These are used with the tool rotating, and great care must be taken not to overstrain the motor when cleaning the larger sanding devices.

Burnt-on wood residues can be loosened if necessary by soaking in a solvent such as acetone or paint stripper, before rinsing and brushing the cutters clean. This works with HS and vanadium steel, carbide, ruby, or diamond burrs. The Trendicote PTFE spray supplied by Trend also appears to help prevent residue build-up.

The larger Karbide Kutzall-style burrs can be heated with a small blowtorch flame to char the residues, instead of using solvent. Don't overheat the cutter – just get it hot enough to burn the wood residue. Remove the cutter from the handpiece first, and *don't try this on other types of cutter.*

Abrasive stones are cleaned and shaped by running them against a special coarse abrasive stone, or a small diamond file or old diamond burr. Do not use heat or solvents on these stones.

Diamond particles are bonded to the surface of burrs by a layer of metal plating. As they wear, less diamond sticks through the plating, but you can refresh the cutter by removing some plating to reveal more diamond surface. Use a special soft abrasive stone, soaked in water, and take great care not to remove too much plating, or you will lose the diamond.

Fig 3.31 *Clean tools work better – a brass-wire brush is the first line of defence.*

- **Abrasive cutters are less affected by grain, knots, and the general character of the wood being carved. Toothed cutters are often better where clogging is a problem – on timbers with a high resin content, for instance.**
- **Cutters should be kept clean, and in the case of those with teeth, sharpened or discarded when they become blunt.**
- **Keep collets clean, and insert the tool shank fully in the collet before tightening. Don't use the wrong size collet for the tool shank, or be tempted to insert only a little of the tool shank into the collet to improve the tool's reach.**
- **Don't apply excess pressure to try and make the cutter work faster – find the point at which the minimum pressure on the tool gives the best stock removal without overloading the machine. If you constantly use very large cutters, or tough timbers, and need to remove a lot of wood, consider using a die grinder instead.**
- **Make sure the tooling is suitable for the machine's speed – sanding drums, in particular, usually need to be run at reduced speeds.**
- **Do not exceed the manufacturer's maximum recommended speed for the cutter.**

CHAPTER FOUR

Micromotors and Miniature Turbines

If you are carving small items, or are wanting to put very fine texture and small details on larger carvings, then you may find the shaft and hanging motor of the flexible-shaft carving machine hampers your efforts. A swinging motor and shaft can make the tool tip difficult to control properly. You may also find that the top speed available is a little too slow for the very small stones used for texturing. You can improve the handling by making the motor adjustable in height and by using a detail handpiece with the extra-flexible Duplex spring, which falls at your wrist (Fig 4.1; see also pages 22–3). However, various types of self-contained, motorized units are available which don't have a heavy shaft and are hampered only be a thin cable or tube. These fall into three basic categories: the mini-drill/grinder, the mini industrial die grinder, and the miniature air turbine.

Mini-drill/grinders

These are mainly low-voltage machines aimed at the model-maker and hobbyist, and range in cost from around £20 to

Fig 4.1 Flexible-shaft tools have more available power, and handpieces with Duplex springs give you more flexibility where you need it: at the wrist.

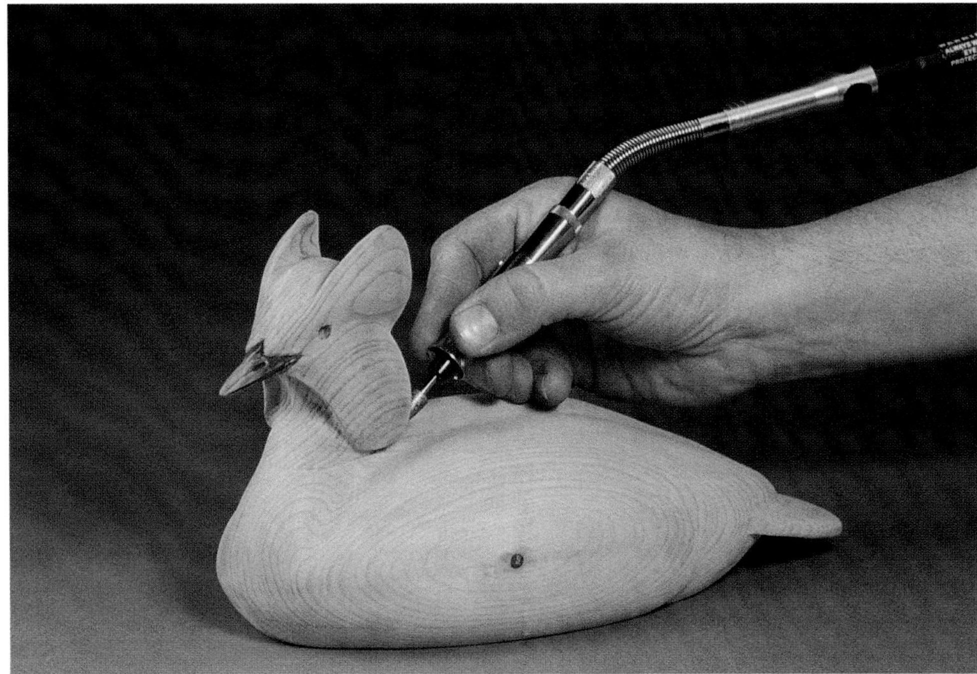

£100 (Fig 4.2). They are generally rather low-powered and not really suitable for heavy or frequent use. I have used several different ones, and the first texturing and detail carving I performed on decoy ducks was using a low-voltage drill bought from Electromail. Proxxon make a nice slim model, which is comfortable to use, and unlike some low-voltage units has roller bearings rather than bronze bushes (Fig 4.3). Bushes wear very quickly, and the tip of the tool starts to run in a small orbit, making it look blurred and preventing you from exercising accurate control over the tool tip. A couple of my students have had considerable use from their Proxxon units, but they are good-quality machines and not the cheapest. They require the special Proxxon low-voltage power supply if the speed control is to work.

I have a Minicraft unit (Fig 4.4) which is several years old now and travels with me

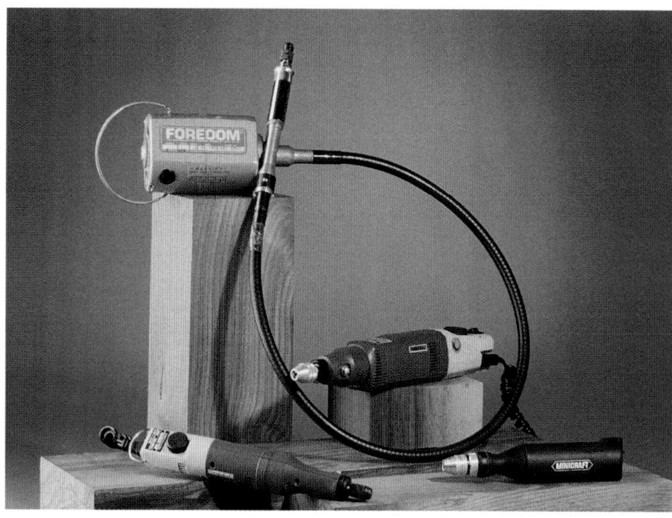

Fig 4.2 *There are various small drill/grinding units on the market; most are low-voltage and fairly low-powered too. Mains-powered units are usually more powerful.*

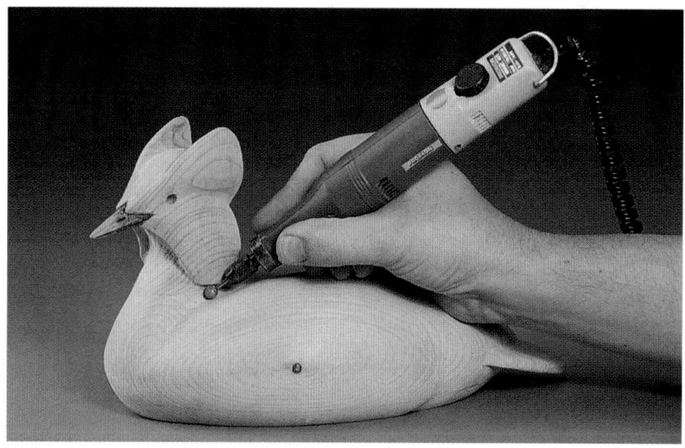

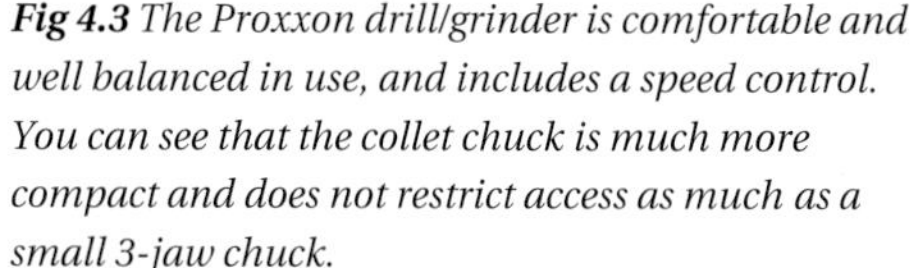

Fig 4.3 *The Proxxon drill/grinder is comfortable and well balanced in use, and includes a speed control. You can see that the collet chuck is much more compact and does not restrict access as much as a small 3-jaw chuck.*

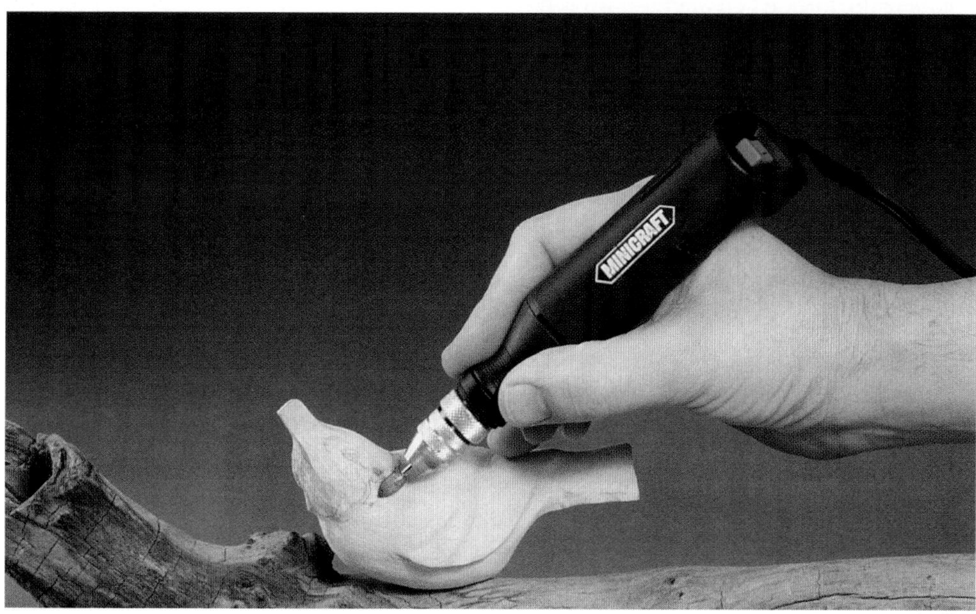

Fig 4.4 *A Minicraft low-voltage drill/grinder. I find the chuck bulky, and you can friction-burn your fingers on it quite easily; I prefer one-size collet chucks.*

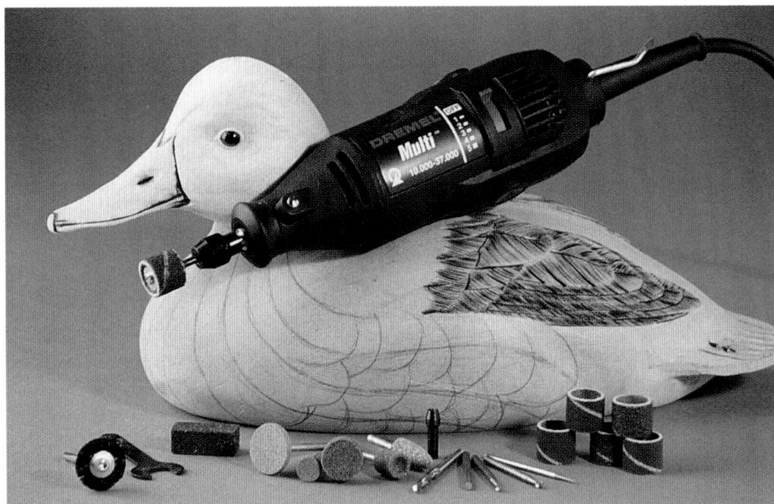

Fig 4.5 *The Dremel Multi is a little bulky to hand-hold for delicate work, but a flexible shaft accessory is available. It is a powerful carving tool for small work and its high top speed makes it good for texturing too.*

to my nightclasses, so that students can add a few odd details, or clean up an awkward spot. It hasn't done a lot of work really, and if you do a lot of carving and texturing with one of these small machines you could easily wear it out in a year. I wore out two in my first nine months of carving and texturing decoys!

The main drawbacks with all the cheaper low-voltage machines are the necessity of an expensive transformer, and (in most cases) their lack of power. The low-voltage motors used in them do not have the torque of a mains-powered model.

The small Dremel Multi (Fig 4.5) requires no transformer and certainly doesn't lack power. This is the latest version of the Moto-Tool, which has been around for many years. This machine is a much more capable tool for the carver, and if you are looking for a relatively cheap, but well-made and reliable machine for detailing and texturing, I would highly recommend it. It will quite likely be cheaper than the combination of a good-quality low-voltage drill and transformer, and will deliver more power and speed. The Multi is a bit larger than the low-voltage units, making it more difficult to hold pencil-fashion, but there is a flexible shaft available for use with it. The shaft is somewhat stiffer than that found on the larger flexible-shaft machines, and has a tendency to wag the motor about, but as the motor is not too heavy, the pendulum action is not too great.

Low-voltage mini-drill/grinder

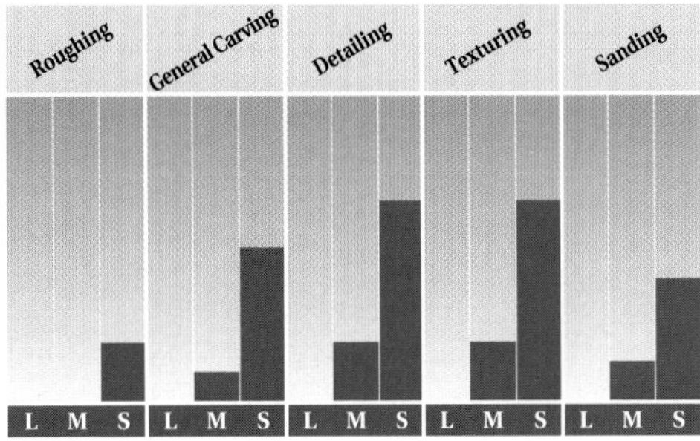

Dremel Multi or mains-operated drill/grinder

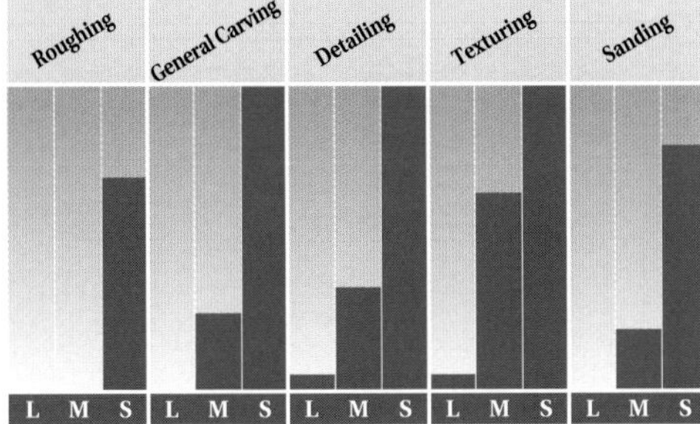

SUPPLIERS INCLUDE:

Bosch (Dremel)
Record Power
Macford (Minicraft)

Safety

The usual general safety precautions should be taken when using mini-drills, but ensure that your eye protection is very close-fitting, as you tend to use such tools much nearer your face.

Miniature industrial die grinders

These machines are industrial in both specification and price, costing from around £600. They are widely used in finishing precision-engineered components, and in dental laboratories. The ones you will find being used by carvers are usually those with high-precision electric handpieces, although air-driven versions are available. The electric models have very precise electronics controlling the speed, direction, torque, and braking of the motors. I use an American unit made by Gesswein, which is supplied in the UK by Pintail (Fig 4.6). They have very high top speeds from 35,000rpm upwards (mine has a top speed of 55,000rpm), which enables them to use very small-diameter burrs and stones to give incredible detail. They are very popular with carvers of realistic birds or animals, as well as makers of netsuke and similar miniature carvings.

Besides the ability to use very small tooling, most of them are reversible too. This enables you to change direction when working on different areas of the carving to reduce any tendency to pull up wood fibres. The high-precision collet handpieces usually have quick-change twist or lever tool changes, making them very convenient to use. Although quite powerful lower-speed motors and geared handpieces can be used with these units, the handpieces are still only connected to the controller by a light cable, which does not hamper their use. Besides offering a choice of motors, many units also allow you to change the tool-holding part of the handpiece. Accessories available with the

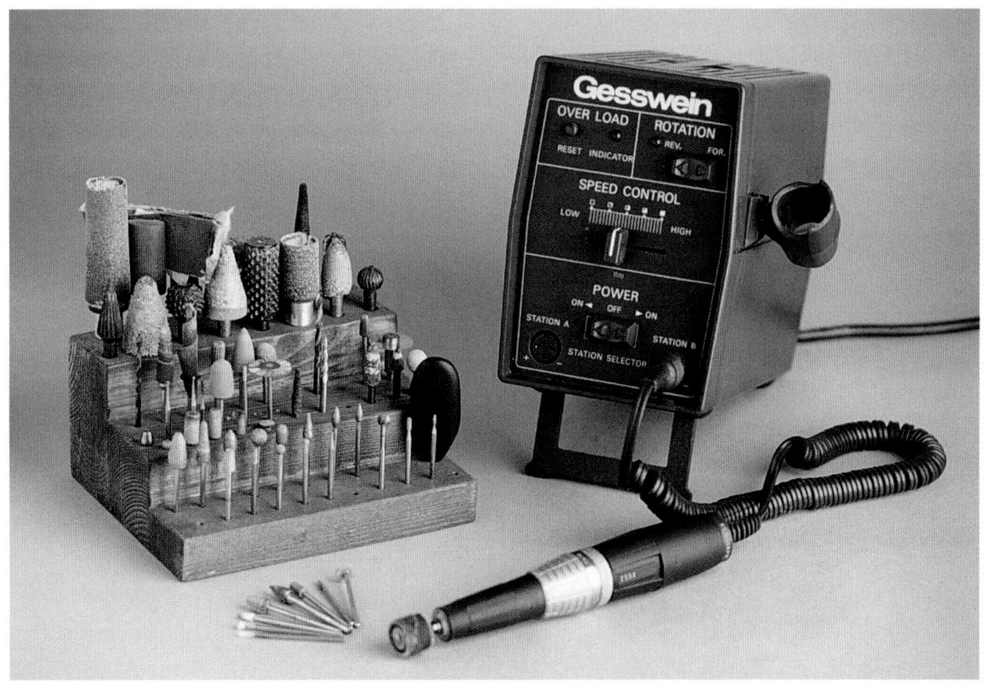

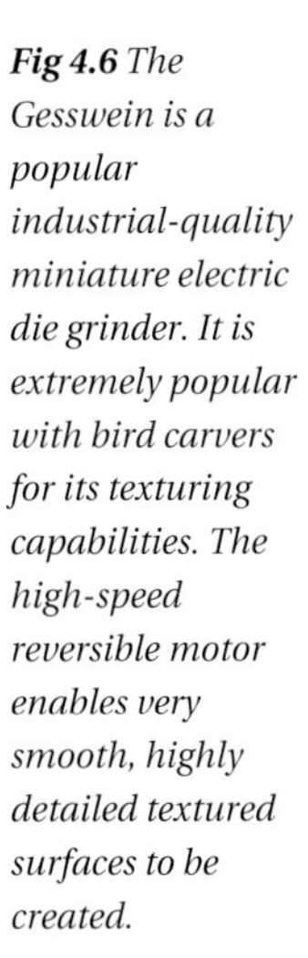

Fig 4.6 *The Gesswein is a popular industrial-quality miniature electric die grinder. It is extremely popular with bird carvers for its texturing capabilities. The high-speed reversible motor enables very smooth, highly detailed textured surfaces to be created.*

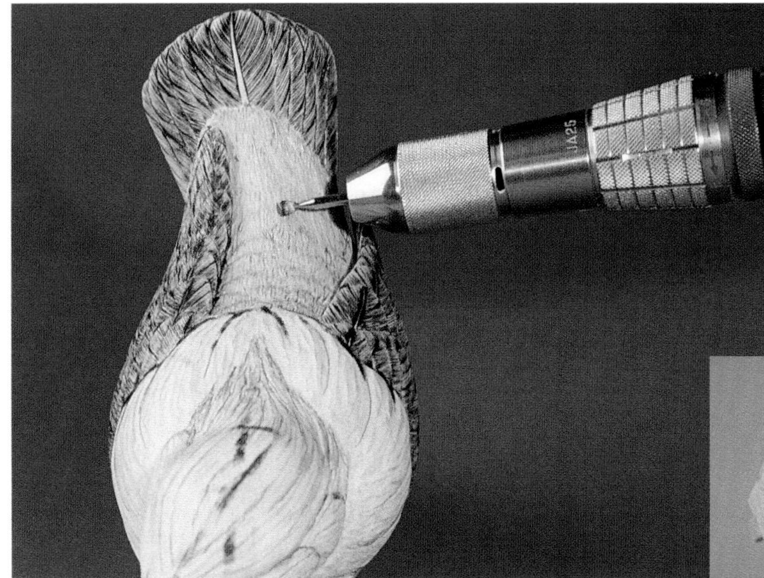

Fig 4.7 (Left) *This Gesswein model blows air forward to remove dust.*

Fig 4.8 (Below) *The high-speed die grinder can be used for actual carving too, but because of the high cost of replacement parts I mainly use the cheaper flexible-drive machine for the carving, reserving the die grinder for texturing.*

SUPPLIERS

Pintail
Foredom
RAM Products
NSK
Skillbond
Calder Polishing Company

Gesswein include a long-reach, narrow-nosed tool holder, and another which blows air forward to move dust (Fig 4.7). These are expensive machines to purchase and service, so I would not recommend using them for heavy work (Fig 4.8). I only use mine if a flexible-shaft machine will not perform the task adequately, as by comparison flexi-shafts are uncomplicated machines, and very cheap to maintain.

Safety

Again, very well-fitting eye protection is essential. Care must be taken to ensure that any tooling used in such high-speed handpieces is suitable for the high revs.

Miniature industrial die grinder (electric)

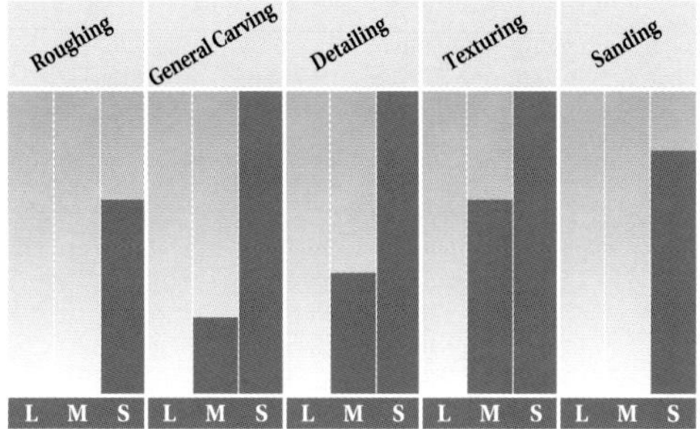

Unbalanced tools can cause damage to handpieces, and tool shanks can break if out of balance at such high speeds – especially those with the larger cutting heads.

Air-turbine grinders

Very high-speed grinders are one area in which air power is prevalent, and air-driven versions of the miniature die grinder are available if you have access to a good-quality compressed air supply. Companies like NSK and Foredom have air-driven units of similar specification to their electric units, discussed above. However, if you want really high speeds of 300,000rpm or more then air or gas power is the only answer. Everyone will have come upon one of these high-speed air turbines, when they last sat in the dentist's chair. They have virtually no torque at all and usually use

Fig 4.9 *Air turbines are very light and offer virtually no restriction to your hand movements, which makes them suitable for the most delicate operation.*

$\frac{1}{16}$in-shank burrs and stones with very small cutting heads. The tools are a push fit into a friction collet, and a knob and ramrod arrangement passing through the handpiece is used to eject them.

The handpieces are small and light, with only a small-diameter, flexible airline connected to them (Fig 4.9). Mine weighs just a few grams, about the same as a pencil, so you can work with one for long periods. They give you the ultimate in control, when doing minute detail work, and are often used for glass engraving, egg carving, working gems, etc.

Except for the lightness and ease of use, I think they offer little advantage to the woodcarver over a professional miniature die grinder, but they are popular with some carvers.

Although they are generally run on compressed air, and only require a very small compressor of about 1 cubic foot per minute (cfm), I run my Ultra Speed Products Turbo Carver (Fig 4.10) from a carbon-dioxide bottle of the type used to dispense beer. For occasional use, this

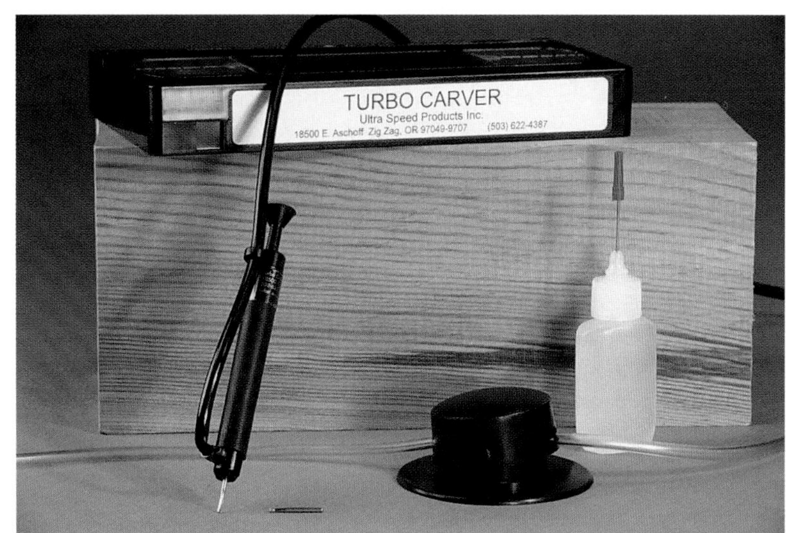

Fig 4.10 *The Turbo Carver is typical of the small and light very high-speed air-turbine handpieces popular with carvers in the USA.*

SUPPLIERS INCLUDE:

Ultra Speed Products
SCM Enterprises
Foredom

Fig 4.11
Lubricating oil in the exhausting air can prove a problem at a later stage, especially when applying finishes to the carving. The finger from a cotton glove provides a cheap, washable oil filter.

works quite happily. The Turbo Carver is much cheaper than the other turbines I have seen. It is an all-plastic, almost 'disposable' turbine, with a complete kit selling for about $140 US.

Air turbines usually require some lubrication in the air, and this oil can be exhausted onto your carving, although some makes have exhaust tubes. Cutting the finger off a cotton glove and fitting it over the handpiece is a cheap and effective way of stopping any oil getting onto the carving (Fig 4.11). The other snag with turbines is that they tend to have a rather annoying high-pitched whine, though some makes are equipped with silencers.

- **Make sure that the tooling used is suitable for the high speeds attained by these machines. Do not exceed the manufacturer's maximum recommended speed for the cutter.**
- **Keep collets clean, and insert the tool shanks fully in the collet before tightening. Don't use the wrong size collet for the tool shank, or be tempted to insert only a little of the tool shank into the collet to improve the tool's reach. Discard any tools which are damaged or do not run true.**
- **These machines are only suitable for small-scale work – consider a flexible-shaft machine for heavier work, as the maintenance costs are much lower.**

Miniature air-turbine grinder

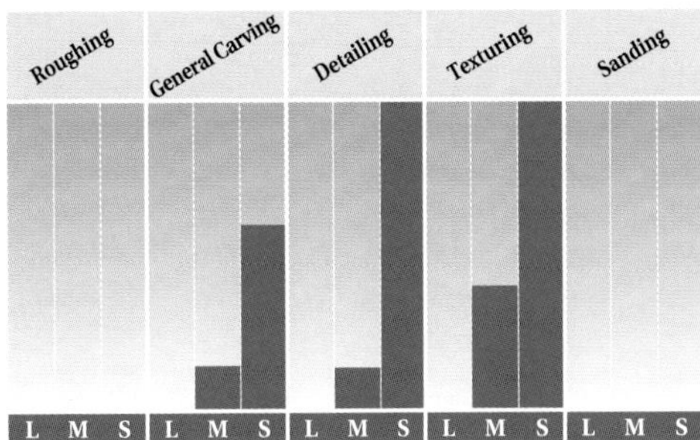

CHAPTER FIVE

Power Chisels

Reciprocating chisels have been around for a long time. I remember having some small chisel bits for my Burgess engraving machine when I was a teenage model-maker. Similar ones are still available from Record Power, and although they are not particularly powerful, they can be used successfully to apply surface textures to carvings (Fig 5.1). As power chisels they were of little use on carving projects of any size, and seemed intended for model-making and lino-print block cutting.

This has all changed now, and several very useful reciprocating chisels are available, in both professional and home-workshop varieties, with sufficient capacity to make them of interest to the woodcarver. The self-contained types intended for the home workshop are the most common, but those I have used do not work very successfully on very dense or tough timbers. Here they can only remove very small slivers of wood and carve fine details, but they come into their own when working with softer materials. If you can knife-carve, or use gouges with hand pressure only to work the timber, it is likely that it is a suitable candidate for one of the reciprocating chisels.

The big advantage of these over rotary tools is the complete lack of dust, and with it the need for masks and extraction (Fig 5.2). The downside of this type of tool is the noise and vibration. This is a fairly inevitable by-product of changing rotary motion to reciprocating movement, but

Fig 5.1 *Engravers can be used to create texturing, but are not very efficient when fitted with chisels.*

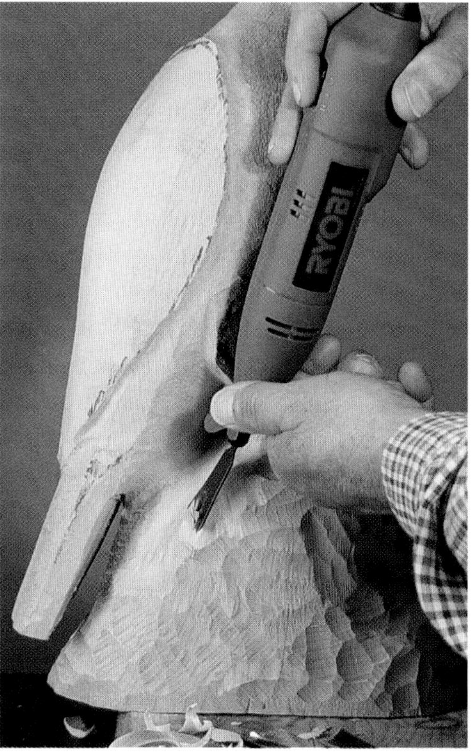

Fig 5.2 *Power chisels are ideal for those who want a degree of mechanization without clouds of dust – although you still get more noise and vibration than when working with traditional tools.*

Fig 5.3 *A sandbag can provide a firm but easily adjusted aid to holding work where a more permanent mount is difficult or undesirable.*

the amount of both vibration and noise varies from tool to tool.

Power chisels can take much of the physical effort out of carving, leaving you to concentrate on controlling the cutting edge, which is a much easier task than when using a mallet. Using a power chisel is more like cutting with a gouge by hand pressure, and they have a delicacy of touch which will enable them to cut right up to the edge of a thin area without break-out, where there would normally be great danger of damage. The machines are very suitable for people who find difficulty in controlling a gouge and mallet properly, or applying sufficient hand pressure to a gouge, as well as being a useful tool for carvers in general.

Just as when using a gouge and mallet, the importance of fixing the work as solidly as possible is soon realized. Unlike rotary flexible-shaft carving machines, you cannot really hand-hold the workpiece. Timber doesn't cut well when just hand-held, as the force of the hammer action is cushioned. It can be worked much better if fixed firmly in a vice on a solid bench, leaving both your hands free to control the tool better. Having said that, if you have a very solid bench then there is a quick and reasonably secure way of 'hand-holding' medium-sized carvings for some roughing-out operations. I use a sandbag on my bench to seat the carving, which can then be jammed firmly in place and held with one hand, while the other holds the carving tool (Fig 5.3). This speeds up some tasks by avoiding the constant readjustment of the carving vice or clamp.

Three styles of reciprocating chisel are available:

1 An accessory handpiece to fit the end of a normal flexible-shaft carving machine.
2 A dedicated machine with a flexi-shaft and a carving-tool handpiece.
3 A self-contained motor unit with the chisel mounted directly on the end of it.

Accessory handpieces for flexi-shaft machines

I have come across several power-chisel handpieces to fit existing rotary flexible-shaft carving machines. The heavy-duty Moviluty Movix flexible-drive carving system has a reciprocating chisel handpiece available. Although I have not tried this, it is made for their heavy-duty professional machine and sold as being suitable for wood and stone carving, so should be well constructed. A shaft and reciprocating handpiece are also available for their Minyflex unit.

I have used a number of different Far Eastern models of reciprocating chisel handpieces (Fig 5.4). Some were accessory handpieces with the standard American-style snap-on connector which will fit the Dremel, Foredom, and Pfingst carving machines; others came complete with their own flexible shafts. These could be run at slower speeds from a drilling machine, or connected to the handpiece of a flexi-shaft machine to run at higher speeds. Although they worked reasonably well, the user's hand took as much hammering as the chisel bit – which can be blamed on Newton's Law and on the small mass of the handpiece, which absorbs little of the vibration. I quickly ended up with pins and needles in my hand, and the handpiece soon became quite hot too. I am not very happy about the long-term effects of using a machine with such high vibration levels, as the effects of vibration can lead to long-term disabilities, so I no longer use one. If you do buy one, it is advisable to fit a heavy-duty inner shaft to your flexible-shaft machine, and I would advise fitting some rubber or foam over the handle to help cut down on the amount of vibration being absorbed directly by your hand and wrist. The cheap handpieces work, but are suitable for only occasional use.

Dedicated flexible-shaft power chisels

An American company called the Sugino Corporation sells a range of power chisels under the Auto Mach name which includes the heavy-duty Woodcarver flexible shaft with reciprocating chisel handpiece. This can be supplied as a shaft and handpiece only, to fit to your own motor, or as the Pro Woodcarver model, with its motor mounted in a metal transport case, with space for additional tool storage. This is a heavy-duty machine which could be used all day. In the UK, Avery Knight and Bowlers and Craft Supplies sell the Bordet flexible-shaft

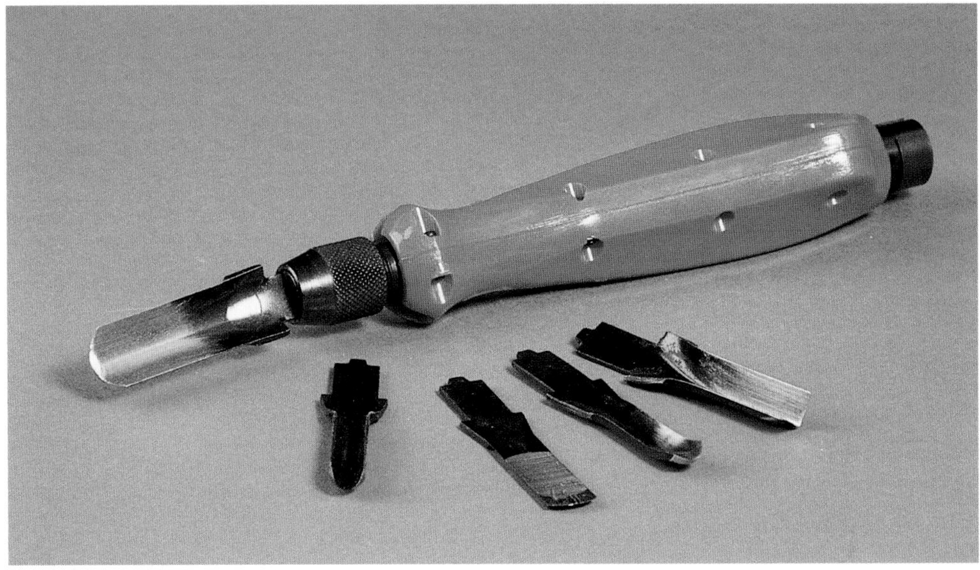

Fig 5.4 *An imported chisel handpiece which will snap on to a flexible shaft.*

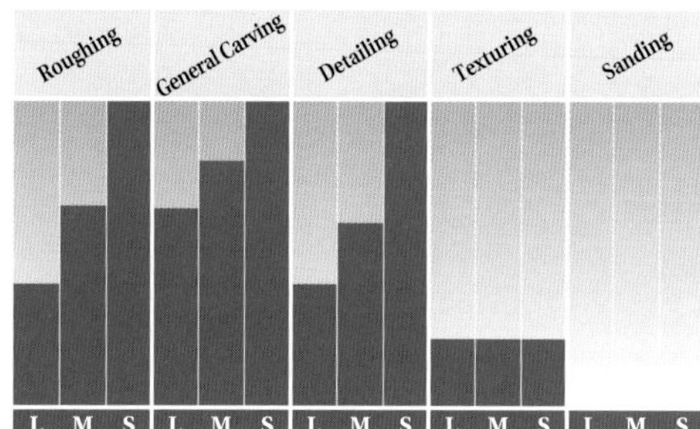

Fig 5.5 (Above and Left) *The Bordet carving machine, a dedicated flexible-shaft power chisel. (Photos by courtesy of Craft Supplies Ltd)*

reciprocating chisels (Fig 5.5). Again, these are heavy-duty machines which could be used to carve wood, marble, or stone, and would be perfectly at home in a professional workshop. Three models are available: one rated for continuous use, one for slightly less arduous conditions, and the cheaper option of a shaft and handpiece which can be fitted to your own high-speed motor.

Dedicated flexible-shaft machines with large continuously rated motors are the only ones that would really be suitable for uninterrupted use in the workshop.

Dedicated flexible-shaft power chisel (suitable for wide range of timbers and stone)

Roughing | General Carving | Detailing | Texturing | Sanding

L M S | L M S | L M S | L M S | L M S

Self-contained units

Many carvers will not be able to justify a professional-standard flexible-shaft power chisel for their workshop, but would like to make use of some of the advantages of a power chisel, and for them the one-piece self-contained units will probably be the answer. They are mainly lighter-duty machines, and it should be borne in mind that they are *not* suitable for hour after hour of continuous carving.

Ryobi produce what is probably the best-known self-contained unit on sale in the UK. It is available with a good range of carving chisels and gouges in the smaller sizes (Fig 5.6). Bosch produce a multi-purpose scraping tool, which like all the Bosch machines is easily and widely

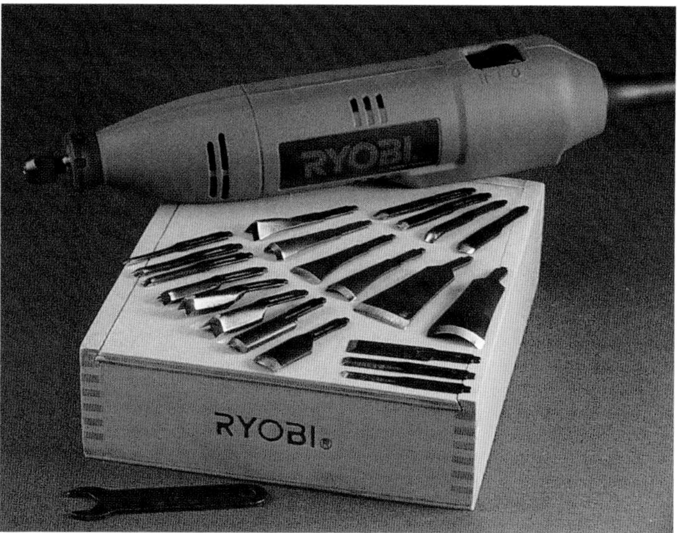

Fig 5.6 *Ryobi make a popular unit which has a wide range of available tooling. This style of tooling is common to several makes of power chisel.*

Fig 5.7 (Left) *The Bosch machine is basically a mechanized scraper for the DIY market. Although the range of tooling available is limited, it is a heavier, more powerful machine than most of its rivals. The tools available for the Bosch are not for detail carving – they come only in larger sizes.*

available through the general DIY outlets (Fig 5.7). It must be said that, at first glance, its value to the woodcarver seems extremely limited. There is only a very restricted range of chisels and gouges available for it, but you can adapt them and make further ones (see page 49).

I have used both these machines extensively in my workshop and find both fairly good, although they are only DIY machines and are not suitable for long periods of continuous use. The power and mass of the 180W Bosch unit make it suitable for quite heavy roughing out, and I have made some tools for it myself, including a large gouge which I made from their 60mm carbon steel scraper (Fig 5.8). This is very efficient on soft timbers, and the Bosch supplies enough power despite the large size of the blade. Of course, both these machines are more suitable for carving soft, easily worked timbers, and I use a lot of yellow pine (*Pinus strobus*). I particularly like the Bosch's push-button tool change, which is much easier than other units which require a spanner (Fig 5.9). If you have any

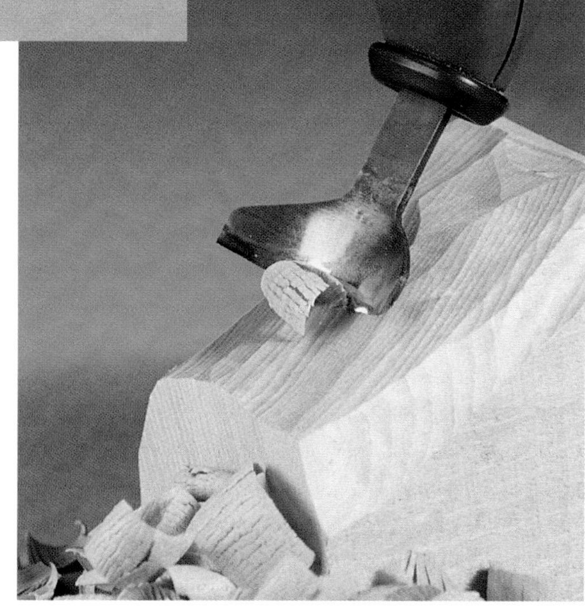

Fig 5.8 *A 2in (50mm) gouge made from a carbon steel scraper blade; the Bosch has plenty of power to cope with large tools.*

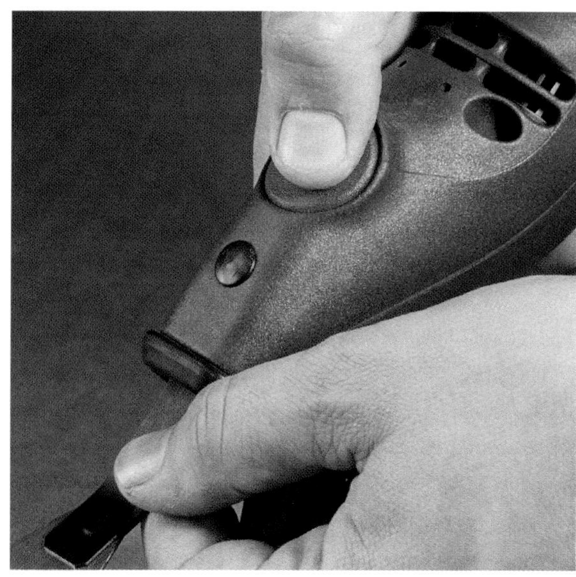

Fig 5.9 *All the other power chisels I have seen, even the professional ones, require a spanner or other tool to change gouges; with the Bosch you just push a button.*

Fig 5.10 (Right) Ryobi's extensive range of tooling is complemented by some excellent chisels made by Flexcut.

Fig 5.11 (Above and Right) Existing Bosch chisels and gouges can be adapted in the home workshop using only simple tools.

engineering skills and can modify their existing tools, you can greatly increase the usefulness of the Bosch machine. By making an adapter to take the smaller tools used by the Ryobi, Proxxon, Auto Mach, and other small power chisels, you could increase its usefulness still further. The Ryobi's motor is not as powerful as the Bosch, and I use it more for detailing work. It is also not as heavy, which means that less of the vibration is damped by the machine, especially if you fit larger gouges such as the ones made by Flexcut (Fig 5.10).

There are also some smaller mains-powered and low-voltage machines about, but the two I have tried fitted into the operational range of 'poor' to 'useless', along with my old engraving machine. They may be suitable for model-makers, but their potential use in general woodcarving is extremely limited, so try before you buy.

Auto Mach make both a hobby and a professional-quality self-contained carving machine. They are available from major US tool suppliers, but they are not distributed through any UK suppliers that I know of, and our protectionist CE regulations will probably ensure that they never are.

Self-contained power chisel (soft timbers only)

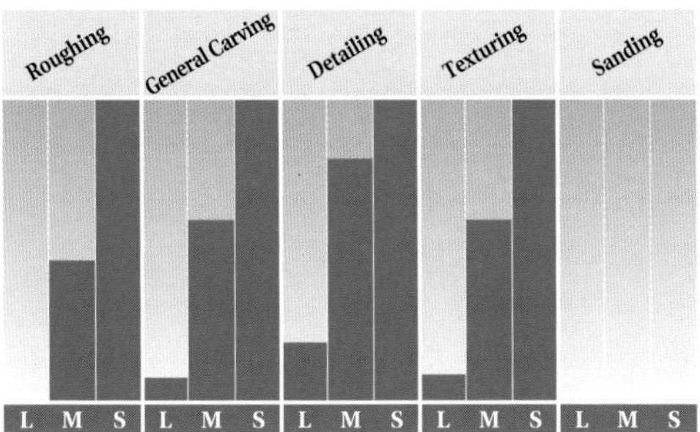

Extending the tool range for the Bosch carver

The small range of carving tools available for this machine does limit its usefulness, but with a little ingenuity – and a grinder or sander – it is possible to extend the range by modifying what is already available (Fig 5.11). The 10mm (⅜in) V-tool is easily modified to form a 6mm (¼in) or even smaller one; similarly, the gouge can be reduced in width to form a 6–8mm no. 5 sweep gouge.

The bevel-edged chisel can be reground to form a 9mm straight carving chisel or skew chisel. The sharp 40mm (1½in) carbon steel scraper supplied with the machine will sharpen and hone to make a fine chisel for removing corners and creating flat planes.

I used a belt sander with a 40–60 grit belt to modify the tools, as I find that this produces very little heat build-up in the tool. I keep my fingers on the back of the tool I am reshaping, and when they start to feel uncomfortable with the temperature, I cool the tool in water before carrying on.

After experimenting with it for a while, I decided that with a machine this powerful I didn't have to use only small tools. I took my remaining 60mm (2⅜in) carbon steel scraper from the box, heated it, and re-formed it into a 57mm (2¼in) no. 6 sweep gouge, then rehardened and tempered it. You might think that 2¼in was a bit ambitious – well it is, but in yellow pine you could happily use up to around 38mm (1½in) of the gouge's cutting edge, so I have now produced other gouges from about 1½in wide down, using the 40 and 60mm carbon steel scrapers, which are relatively cheap to buy.

I used a gas torch to heat the scraper and tapped it into shape over a piece of steel bar. Heating to bright red and quenching in water hardened the tool, and it was tested with a file to make sure it really was hard. The tool was then polished, and tempered by heating with a hot-air paint stripper until it turned a pale straw colour, before quenching in water again.

Smaller tools can be made by similar means from 15mm x 2.5mm (⅝ x ⅒in) ground flat stock (also referred to as gauge plate), available from an engineers' merchant's. This is a carbon tool steel, supplied in a soft state for easy working, which can be shaped first, before being hardened and tempered.

With greater engineering skills it would also be relatively simple to fabricate a tool holder to accept the range of small tools that are available for other machines on the market.

Safety

There is both noise and vibration associated with using any reciprocating chisel. The noise level from most tools is not exceptional, being similar to that of a small electric drill, but it can become a bit tiresome, and hearing protection would certainly be needed for prolonged use.

The effects of vibration are becoming a much greater concern to many informed woodworkers, who are now taking on board many of the safety concerns expressed in industry. According to the laws of Newton, there is a force equal and opposite to the one being applied at the cutting edge. The smaller and lighter the tool is, the more this opposing force (vibration) has to be absorbed by you (or by more sophisticated and expensive tool design, as in the SDS hammer drills). Larger machine mass helps dampen this vibration; however, I would not consider any of the machines that I have in my workshop to be suitable for many hours of continuous carving, but only for intermittent use. It would be nice to see manufacturers pay more attention to the vibration problem when designing tools which people may wish to use for long periods. Of course this would inevitably lead to an increase in price, and the market for carving tools is very small and probably not worth the investment. Most workshop power tools like drills and routers are only used very intermittently, so that the vibration is not too great a problem, but the temptation with a carving tool is to run it almost constantly, carving away for lengthy periods, which, without vibration damping, may cause long-term problems for the user.

The reciprocating action on the tools I have used only works when pressure is put on the cutting edge – the chisel doesn't move until you put it to the work and apply some pressure. The more pressure you apply, the harder the chisel cuts. It is all too easy to stick a cutter into yourself, though, so, as when using conventional unpowered edge tools, keeping both hands fully occupied *behind* the cutting edge is the best policy when working.

Tooling

Most manufacturers supply a range of tooling to fit their own machines, and, with the notable exception of the Bosch SDS cutters, most manufacturers of the small self-powered machines seem to use a similar tool shank. Flexcut, who make the innovative flexible carving gouges, also manufacture a range of high-quality gouges which fit the more common machines such as the Ryobi, Auto Mach, and Proxxon. They are of high quality, and I have found them to be better shaped and ground when they arrive, and to hold their edges better, than the cutters supplied with the machines. Flexcut have extended the range of cutters to include gouges and chisels up to 1in (25mm) wide.

Dedicated machines like the Bordet, or the Movix accessory handpiece, use chisels of a much more conventional design. They look like woodcarvers' gouges without a handle, and the tang is modified to a straight shank, which fits into the handpiece. Apparently it is possible to fit many ordinary woodcarving gouges, by removing the handle and making minor alterations to the tang.

- **Keep the gouges and chisels razor-sharp, especially when using the smaller machines.**
- **Select suitable timber for your carving – the smaller units can be ineffective on very hard or tough woods.**
- **Make sure the work is rigidly held and supported so that the impact of the chisel's action is not absorbed.**

SUPPLIERS OF MACHINES AND TOOLING:

Sugino Corp. (Auto Mach)
Rod Naylor
Craft Supplies (Bordet)
Falls Run (Flexcut)
Bosch
Ryobi
Hegner (Moviluty)
Avery Knight & Bowlers (Bordet)
Stretton (Flexcut)
Record Power (Proxxon)

CHAPTER SIX

Power Files

PORTABLE belt sanders with 3 or 4in (75 or 100mm) belts, looking similar to electric planes, are commonly used in general woodworking, but unless you carve on a monumental scale they will be of little use (Fig 6.1). If you are creating a big carving with large flat or convex surfaces then you may find them useful, but for most carvers a belt filing machine of the Powerfile style would be more suitable.

Powerfile is the name used by Black & Decker to describe their smallest abrasive-belt sanders, which, unlike the usual woodworking design, have most of the top and bottom surface of the belt exposed, like a file with a moving cutting face (Fig 6.2). Several manufacturers produce belt filing machines, which all have in common the file-like arm and substantially smaller belts than the usual 3in or more single-sided belt sanders generally used in woodworking. Belt sizes start at around 30mm (1¼in) wide, going down to 9mm (⅜in) or less.

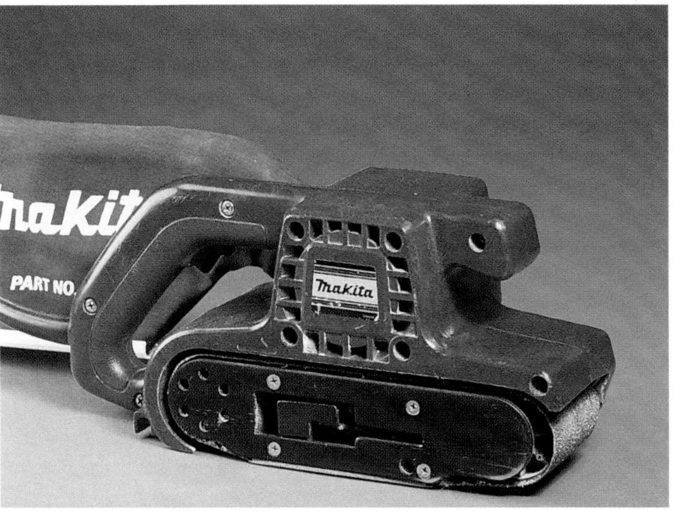

Fig 6.1 *My Makita 3in (75mm) belt sander, only of much use on very large carvings with convex areas.*

Fig 6.2 *The Powerfile's narrow, finger-shaped belt arm.*

Besides the B&D offerings there are a couple of other easily found belt files. Makita make a reasonably priced, 30mm wide industrial model, dubbed a multi-purpose sander, and Bosch have recently introduced an interesting variation on the belt sander, a cross between a conventional sander and file. The Bosch is a neat and compact wedge-shaped machine with a 40mm ($1\frac{9}{16}$in) belt. The wedge shape gives good access, but the exposed length of belt is short and a little wide for doing much carving.

Probably the most commonly available but useful models are the budget-priced Powerfiles from Black & Decker (Fig 6.3). They have been available for many years, in both single-speed and variable-speed versions, and are often heavily discounted and sold to the 'DIY present' market. Far from being 'the tool that does nothing for the man who has everything', these can be extremely useful for a carver.

I first tried one after talking to carver Brian Faggetter about a 30in-long (760mm) hammerhead shark carving he had done in yew (Fig 6.4). It had plenty of knots and interesting grain, and I was surprised to hear that most of the shaping and sanding had been performed not with an Arbortech, but with a B&D Powerfile and some special Hermes abrasive belts that he had found. I had to try this for myself, and got my hands on the single-

Fig 6.3 *The Black & Decker Powerfile, a cheap and useful power carving tool.*

Fig 6.4 *Hammerhead shark in yew by Brian Faggetter. (Photo by courtesy of Brian Faggetter)*

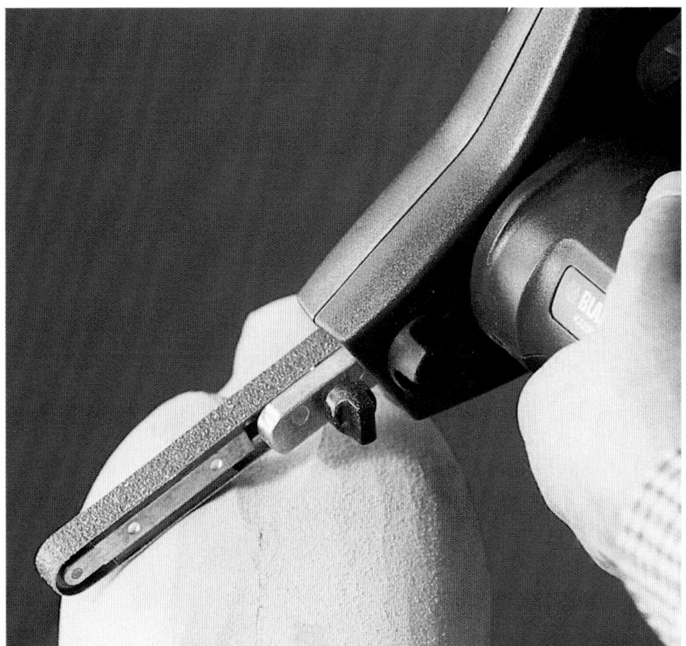

Fig 6.5 *The Powerfile is a versatile and easy-to-use carving tool, shaped to give you maximum access to all areas of the carving.*

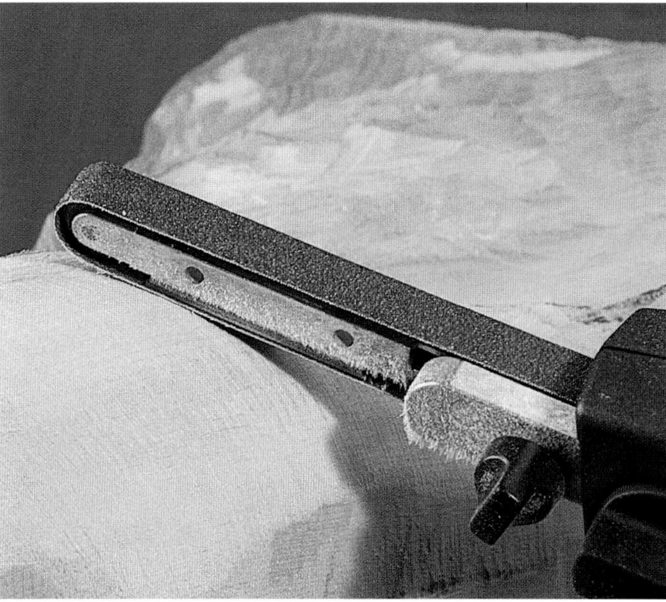

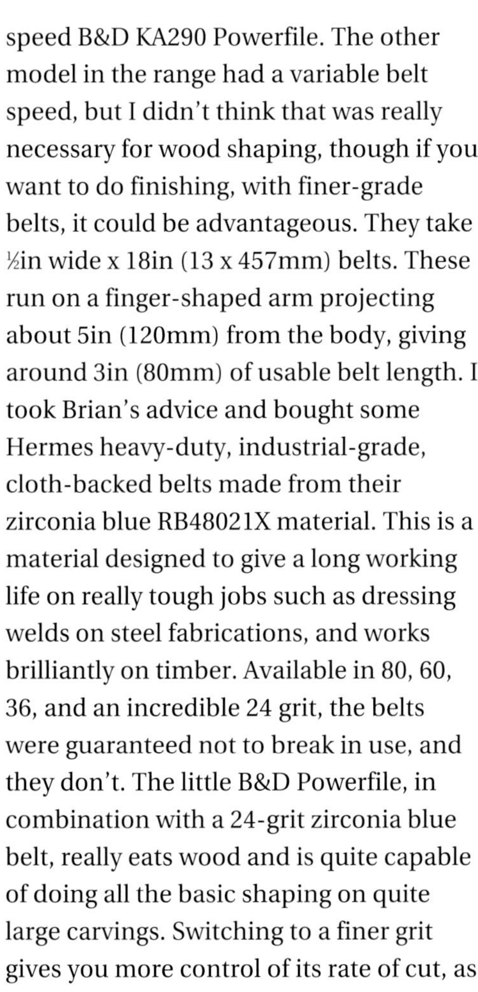

speed B&D KA290 Powerfile. The other model in the range had a variable belt speed, but I didn't think that was really necessary for wood shaping, though if you want to do finishing, with finer-grade belts, it could be advantageous. They take ½in wide x 18in (13 x 457mm) belts. These run on a finger-shaped arm projecting about 5in (120mm) from the body, giving around 3in (80mm) of usable belt length. I took Brian's advice and bought some Hermes heavy-duty, industrial-grade, cloth-backed belts made from their zirconia blue RB48021X material. This is a material designed to give a long working life on really tough jobs such as dressing welds on steel fabrications, and works brilliantly on timber. Available in 80, 60, 36, and an incredible 24 grit, the belts were guaranteed not to break in use, and they don't. The little B&D Powerfile, in combination with a 24-grit zirconia blue belt, really eats wood and is quite capable of doing all the basic shaping on quite large carvings. Switching to a finer grit gives you more control of its rate of cut, as well as removing the marks left by the very coarse abrasive, which leaves a rather rough, rasped finish. I was also impressed by the way that the belts stayed clean and unclogged, while I worked on a wide variety of timbers. I can use the roller tip of the sander to carve, as well as the flat of the belts, and with light pressure I get good control and sensitivity from the tool (Fig 6.5).

The belt-tensioning device is poor and does not have a very positive action, and the dustbag doesn't really work; but don't let this put you off. The machine is definitely DIY, but does the job, and at the price, even a fairly short working life could be tolerated.

I have cut down the dust emission to a very acceptable level by throwing away the dustbag and making a vacuum-cleaner adapter from a 4in (100mm) length of 1¼in (30mm) plastic waste pipe

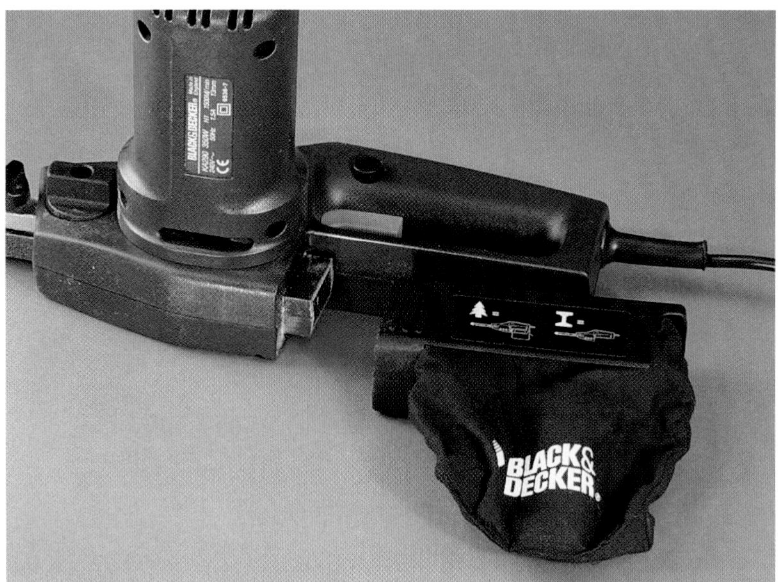

Fig 6.6 *The dust bag supplied ceases to work after a minute or so.*

(Figs 6.6 and 6.7). I softened this in boiling water, before forcing it over the rectangular duct and allowing it to cool. My vacuum-cleaner hose plugs into the other end, and the adapter is held in place on the Powerfile with a couple of spots of hot-melt glue.

I like the B&D because it is cheap and compact, and, although not of professional build quality, mine has done a lot of work and is still going strong.

Besides the Makita 30mm belt filing machine, there are other heavier-duty industrial machines on the market, but unfortunately they tend to come with fairly expensive industrial-sized price tags too. For the professional carver, or the amateur who uses a belt file extensively, they could still prove a very good investment, though. Flex Porter

Fig 6.7 *When fitted with an adapter to my workshop vacuum cleaner and a plastic flap to seal the side, dust extraction is extremely effective. The belts are the coarse zirconia ones I use for roughing out.*

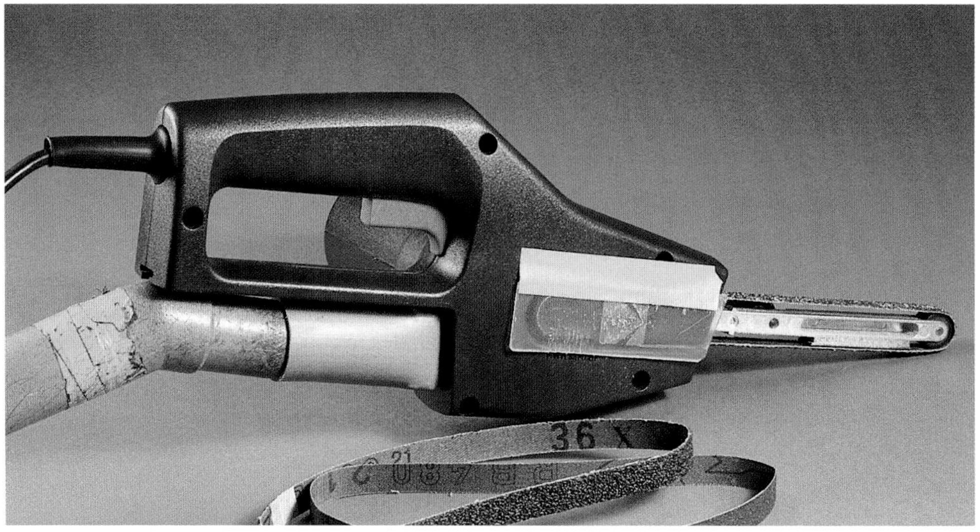

SUPPLIERS:

Makita
Bosch
CSM
Black & Decker
Hamilton Power Products (Flex Porter Cable)
SECO (Belt It)

Cable abrasive-belt files are available with both 9mm and 30mm-wide belts. Unlike the B&D and the Makita machines, the belt arm can be swivelled in relation to the motor, to increase access and usability. The most flexible of the belt filing systems available is the British-built Belt It abrasive-belt grinding machine. This has a complete range of over 100 quick-change belt arms, giving a variety of sizes, shapes, end-roller diameters, and working areas. The arm's position can be altered in relation to the motor, and they are available in both electric and compressed-air-powered versions.

Although all the machines mentioned are dedicated belt filing machines, in the past I have also seen an attachment to fit an electric drill or angle grinder. This took the same belts as the B&D Powerfile, but I am not sure that it is still available.

3–4in belt sander

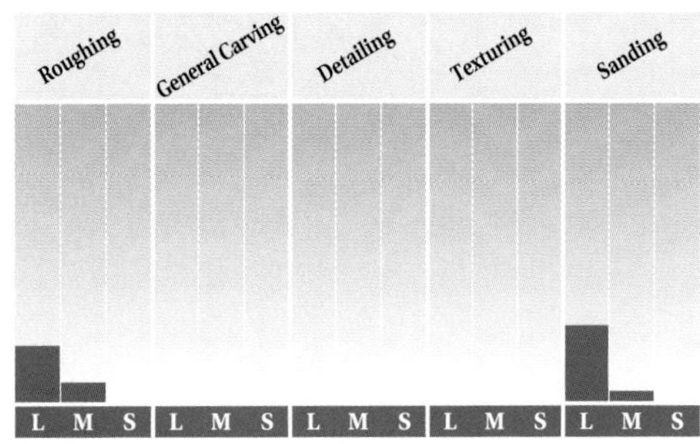

Power file

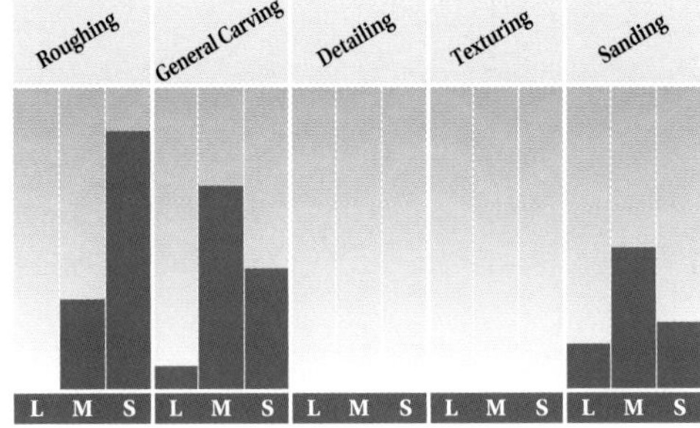

Tooling

Most of the manufacturers of belt sanders supply branded belts to fit their own machines; however, they are available from numerous other independent sources. I buy my Hermes zirconia blue belts from CSM, who bring a full range of interesting, trade abrasive products within reach of the home workshop.

- **Carve with only a slight pressure on the belt to avoid forcing it off track.**
- **Investigate different abrasive materials for carving and finishing. The blue zirconia abrasives in coarse grits such as 24 or 36 are remarkably fast and effective for roughing out. Aluminium oxide belts of 80 grit and finer will refine the finish, and non-woven abrasive belts like Webrax can create a silky finish.**
- **Clamp the work securely, leaving both hands to control the machine. Make sure your dust extraction is working effectively.**

CHAPTER SEVEN

Angle Grinders

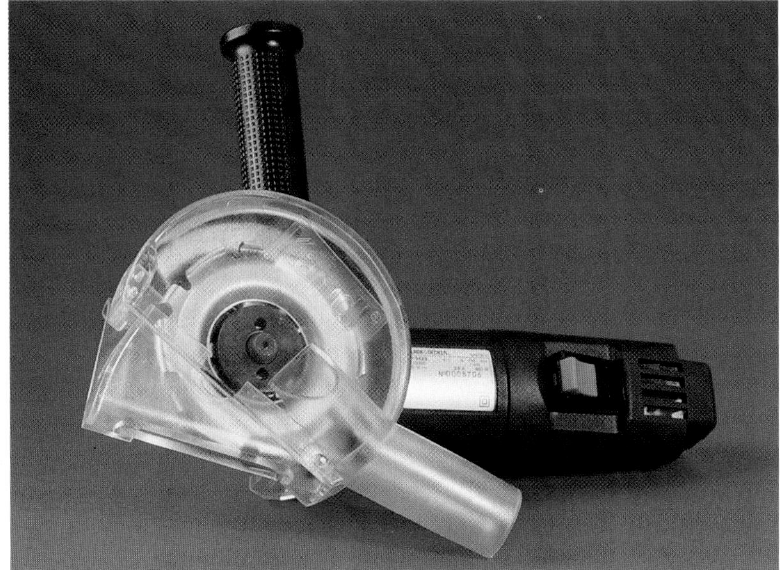

Fig 7.1 Angle grinders have become popular carving tools for medium-to-large work.

THE angle grinder has become a popular tool with those producing larger carvings, and on all but the largest work it has probably replaced the rather more dangerous chainsaw (Fig 7.1). Carving at any scale from moderately large to gigantic requires you to remove vast quantities of waste timber before you get near to your final goal. Once, this could only be achieved by the use of an axe or adze, followed by hours of chiselling with a large gouge and mallet. Something which requires less 'elbow grease', like a chainsaw or an angle grinder, is a very attractive proposition to most carvers, but many are rightly wary of chainsaws. This leaves angle grinders as a popular choice, even for work of more moderate scale, which many more carvers aspire to.

An angle grinder can easily benefit people working on carvings of a cubic foot or less, and it will find applications in many workshops for roughing out and general shaping. They are suitable for carving, sanding, and polishing, saving a lot of physical effort on large work. Their use can easily be justified in terms of time and effort saved, especially if you carve to sell your work. They generally have plenty of power available to tackle large work, but suffer from being rather noisy and from a lack of suitable safety clothing.

Any tool that devours wood so readily can also wreak havoc on you. Using an angle grinder requires caution, and I would dispute whether angle grinders and carving discs are as safe a tool as many would like to believe.

Angle grinders consist of a motor driving a gearbox, the output from which is at right angles to the motor axis. The cutting disc can also be presented at a shallow angle to the work, allowing more control over the cutting action than cutting discs mounted on the end of a motor shaft. There is also a reasonable range of tooling available for them, which has helped increase their popularity.

Unfortunately, the gearbox adds considerably to the noise generated by the machine, making hearing protection essential and giving you the opportunity to really fall out with your neighbours.

Angle grinders come equipped with a metal half-guard and a side handle, which is the standard arrangement for their normal role of grinding and cutting metal using flexible bonded abrasive discs. The guard is designed mainly to cope with grit and sparks from the flexible cutting and grinding discs, which don't possess quite the same potential for snagging clothing, cables, etc. as the saw-profile teeth of carving discs. The metal guarding can be adjusted, but should never be removed except when using polishing mops; when carving discs are fitted, some additional guarding is very desirable. The side handle is essential to the proper control of the machine and should not be removed. The angle grinder requires both hands to hold and control it, and the side handle makes its operation much safer. It will prevent the

Angle grinder

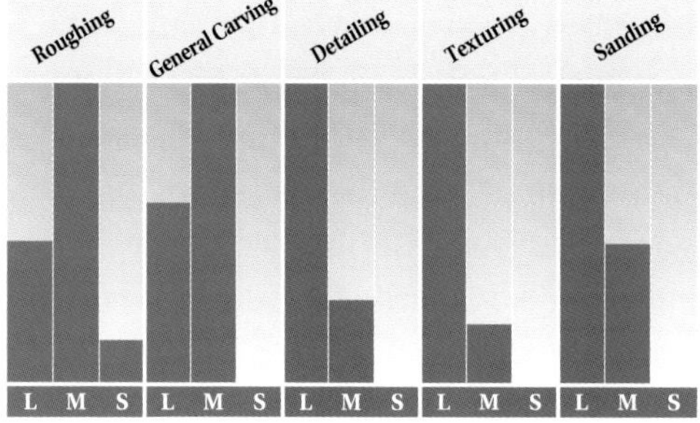

Fig 7.2 *The chainsaw provides the basic tooth design concept for most angle-grinder carving discs; many, like these from King Arthur's Tools, actually utilize circles of saw chain. (Photo by courtesy of King Arthur's Tools)*

grinder being wrenched from your grip if a dig-in occurs while you are carving.

Angle grinders can be bought for as little as £30, although an industrial-quality machine with a long working life is likely to cost up to four or five times as much. Carving discs start at around £20, so angle-grinder carving can be approached on a fairly tight budget.

As with all machines, 'you get what you pay for'. Professional machines will have many refinements, such as stronger motor armatures, better bearings, spindle locks, less vibration and noise; buying cheap can work out to be expensive in the long run.

Angle-grinder carving discs

By far the most common angle-grinder carving discs have some form of saw tooth, to give rapid stock removal on as wide a range of timbers as possible (Fig 7.2). They

SUPPLIERS INCLUDE:

Bosch
Stayer
Black & Decker
Draper
Metabo
Atlas Copco
Makita

Fig 7.3 *Arbortech took the basic saw chain idea, but formed the teeth in the periphery of a steel disc. The cutter shown here, very similar in design to the Arbortech, is no longer available in the UK; I preferred this design of guard.*

are mainly manufactured for use in conjunction with 4in (100mm) or 4½in (115mm) grinders, although at least two companies make larger discs.

Chainsaw teeth

The Arbortech carving discs from Australia have been around for about ten years, and were one of the first available (Fig 7.3). Most carvers are familiar with the design which consists of a pressed metal disc, with half a dozen teeth in the outer edge. The tooth form is similar to that of a chainsaw, but the teeth are cut into the edge of the tough steel disc. The solid rim between the teeth regulates the chip size, creating a more controllable cutter which is capable of greatly reducing the effort required to rough out large carvings. This was the first angle-grinder cutter that I came across and I was very impressed by its performance on all but the very toughest timbers.

Its successful design was soon copied by another company. These discs, although cheaper, were made from an inferior grade of steel which did not hold its cutting edge so well, making them a much less attractive proposition. Due to litigation, this product seems to have disappeared from the market, but you might still find the odd example around.

The idea of using a cutter in an angle grinder to create a heavy stock removal tool was taken up by several other manufacturers, and so other designs of cutting disc can be found, mainly based on chainsaw-style teeth. The chainsaw tooth features literally in the American-made Lancelot carving discs from King Arthur's Tools (Fig 7.4) and in the Supercut discs which are sold by Rod Naylor. The Lancelot has a circlet of saw chain, clamped between two stainless steel discs to form a cutter which effectively has its own built-in anti-kickback clutch. If the chain jams in the work or hits a nail, the chain will slip, helping to prevent the grinder being wrenched from your hands. The discs are slotted to add a little flexibility and to create a 'cooling-fan' effect. King Arthur's Tools make a range of cutting discs for

Fig 7.4 *The Squire and Lancelot carving discs from King Arthur's Tools can be mounted together on one spindle to give a very efficient carving tool. (Photo by courtesy of King Arthur's Tools)*

Fig 7.5 *With teeth more like a circular saw, and made of tungsten carbide to keep its edge and work difficult materials, the Power Gouge was the first alternative to the chainsaw style of cutter.*

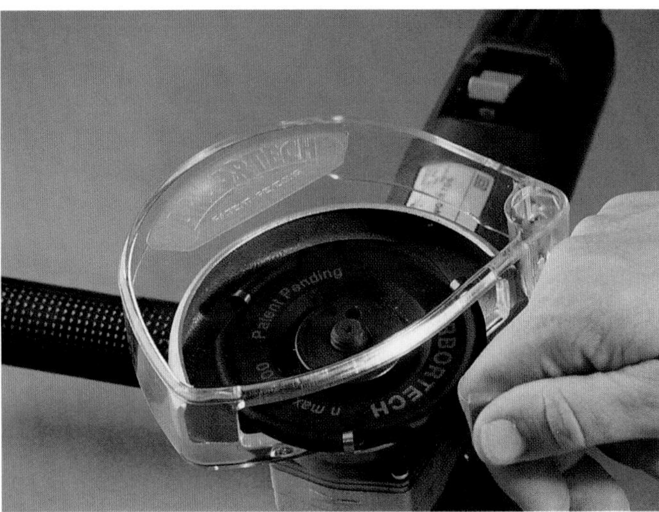

Fig 7.6 *Arbortech make this heavy-duty industrial cutter which has easily replaceable tungsten carbide teeth, an improvement on brazed teeth that cannot easily be replaced.*

small angle grinders, and you can get versions of the Lancelot disc with 14 or 22 teeth, for roughing and finishing.

Saw chains are manufactured from very tough steel, but are readily sharpened with the correct saw file or with special abrasive stones fitted to a small drill or grinder. When the chain finally needs replacing, a replacement chain circlet can be bought for around half the price of a complete carving disc, which is a useful saving.

A slightly smaller version called the Squire, with either 12 or 18 teeth, can be bolted to the side of the Lancelot to enhance its capability to create smooth, sweeping cuts.

The Supercut disc is very similar to the Lancelot, but is only made to fit 4½in (115mm) angle grinders. The slipping clutch effect means that the chain circlet cutters are not as efficient on very hard materials as carving discs with fixed teeth: they are prone to slipping when they come up against the extra cutting resistance offered by tough materials.

Carbide teeth

The original Arbortech used teeth formed from the steel disc, but for tougher materials tungsten carbide teeth can be more effective, and they now make an Industrial Pro version with three replaceable carbide tips.

Another company, Bowman Innovations, manufactures a carving disc which looks more like a circular saw and is called the Power Gouge (Fig 7.5). Unlike a circular saw blade, these steel discs only have from three to six teeth attached to their circumference, the rest of the disc being left plain to control the cutting action of the teeth. They are made in a variety of sizes from 100 to 230mm (4–9in) in diameter. They are long-lasting and relatively cheap, but I prefer the cutting action of the Arbortech Industrial and Vortex discs for general carving.

The Arbortech Industrial Pro is a solid, machined steel disc and uses three replaceable circular tungsten carbide cutting tips (Fig 7.6). It doesn't have as many teeth as many other cutters, but the cutting speed and finish are very good and it performs well on a wide variety of woods. The rim of the tool between the teeth limits the depth of cut, keeping the cutting action very controllable. This is a particularly sturdy and well-made cutting head which deserves the title 'Industrial Pro'. Its replaceable, circular carbide teeth can be rotated to allow for wear, and may also be removed and sharpened on a small diamond slipstone to prolong their life. Like all carbide tooling, the cutting edge has a very long life unless chipped by careless handling. This is an especially useful tool when working in tougher timbers, and worth the additional outlay.

Rod Naylor has recently introduced the Vortex angle-grinder carving disc to his range (Fig 7.7). This is based on the interchangeable carbide-tip tooling he uses with the smaller Tungsten Tornado.

Fig 7.7 *Vortex, a six-tooth carving disc with replaceable tungsten carbide teeth, from Rod Naylor.*

Saw-toothed carving discs

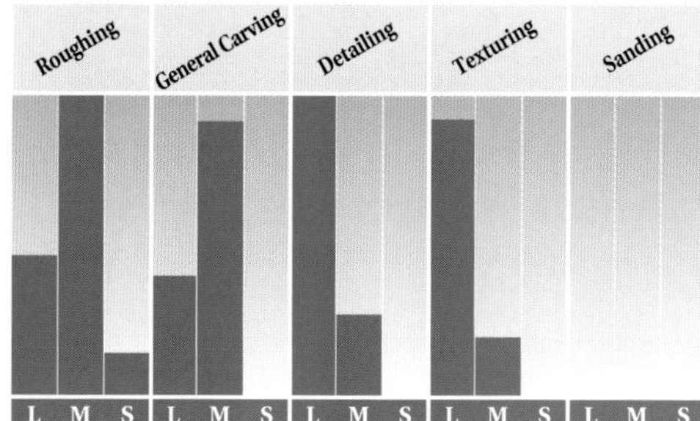

Looking a little like the Arbortech Industrial, this stainless steel disc cutter has six tungsten carbide circular cutting tips attached to its double-rimmed periphery, giving a faster, smoother, and wider cut. He also supplies replacement tips for both cutters which are suitable for carving stone.

Not all carving discs are a variation on the saw blade, though. The American company L. R. Oliver, who make the well-known Karbide Kutzall carving burrs, so successfully used by many carvers in flexi-shaft machines and die grinders, also manufacture an interesting alternative to the saw-toothed carving disc (Fig 7.8). The Karbide Kutzall carving disc has the same

Fig 7.8 (Right) *Karbide Kutzalls are usually thought of in terms of rotary carving burrs, but they also have angle-grinder tooling in their range.*

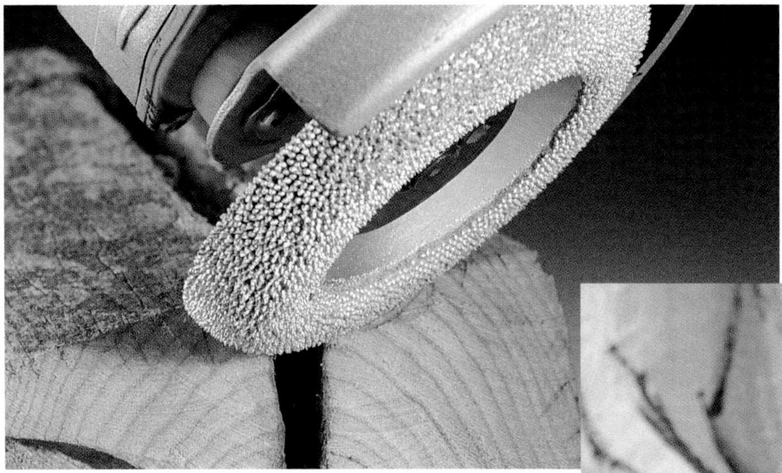

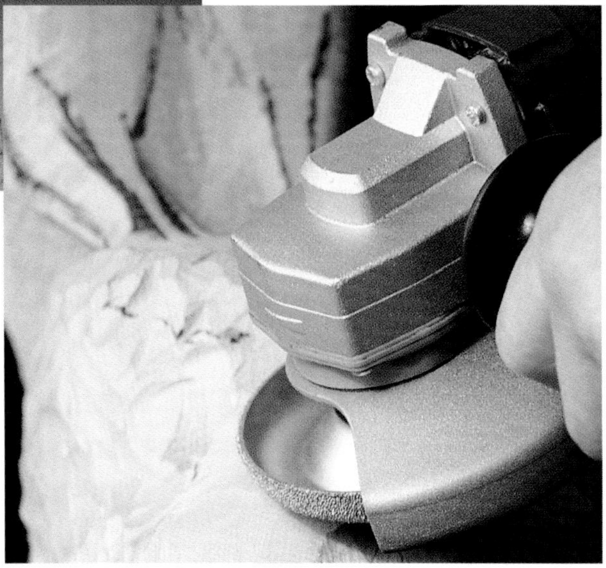

Fig 7.9 (Left and Below) Kutzall carving discs are more like heavy-duty sanding pads, and won't remove as much stock as a toothed carving disc. They are also limited to working seasoned timber.

structured tungsten carbide tooth form that is used on the rotary burrs, giving the tool an aggressive abrasive action, rather than a true cutting action. This makes it a good second tool for removing the tooling marks left by chainsaws and toothed angle-grinder carving discs, whilst it is still aggressive enough to perform much more carving than could be done with a disposable sanding disc (Fig 7.9).

The Karbide Kutzall discs are made for the 4in (100mm) angle grinder, in both a doughnut shape and a flatter sanding-disc style, and they are available in two grades. Additionally, the sanding-disc style is available to fit a 7in (180mm) grinder.

The small discs come with only one size of fixing hole, to suit 4in grinders, but I have increased the bore of mine with a taper reamer so that they will fit my 4½in (115mm) machine. Most manufacturers supply their carving discs with different bore sizes, or with an oversized bore and adapter washers. Unfortunately Olivers don't, but the modification was simple.

The cutting performance of these abrasive discs varies according to the wood being worked, and how well it is seasoned. Because the material is really being sanded away, rather than removed as chips, the cutting action is more affected by the moisture and resin content of the timber, or by difficult areas like knots and burrs. These discs are more prone to clogging when working with some materials, and some experimentation is necessary. The cutting action doesn't seem to slow down badly until the cutter is very well clogged, though. Clogged discs can be soaked in paint stripper to loosen the timber debris, then rinsed and brushed clean with a wire brush, although regular brushing lessens the need for soaking. PTFE cutter spray might make them easier to keep clean with just a wire brush, but I have yet to try it.

I quite like using the Kutzall discs, and they perform very well on the varieties of seasoned timber I usually carve. If you work your wood green, then I think you would find them much less useful, but this would apply to any other form of sanding disc too. I often appreciate the slower stock removal rate they give, as it gives me more time to think about shaping.

The Kutzall discs are faster-cutting than the flat, flap sanding discs supplied for grinders, or conventional sanding discs used with a backing pad. One advantage of them is that, unlike toothed cutters, the abrasive action of these discs allows the work to be carried out with almost complete disregard for grain direction. You can concentrate more on the shape and less on the grain of the timber. Although the cutting action is not as aggressive as the saw-tooth discs, the Kutzall carving discs neatly span the gap between saw-toothed carving tools and coarse abrasive discs or flap discs.

They will not remove the material as quickly as a toothed cutter, and seem expensive for a glorified sanding disc, but

Abrasive carving/coarse sanding discs

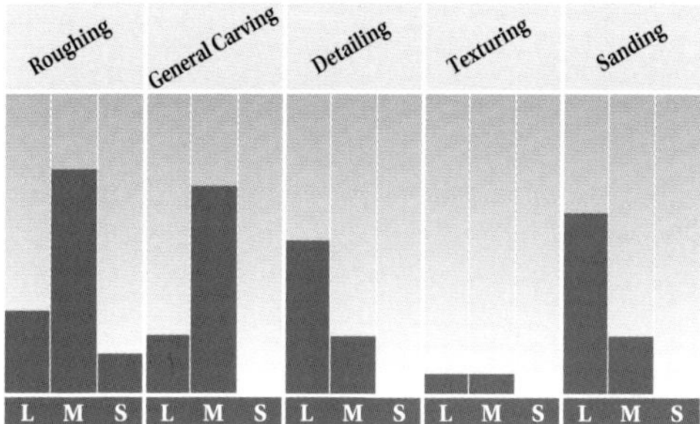

disposable abrasives only have a short life compared to tungsten carbide tooling and, as 4in flap wheels cost around £5 each, a Kutzall disc, with a lifespan measured in years, would soon justify itself.

Arbortech have added to their range a small carving adapter for the angle grinder, which uses a disc about 2in (50mm) in diameter (Fig 7.10). The Mini Arbortech consists of a plastic housing which mounts on your angle grinder, with the small cutting disc at the end. It is driven by a small, rather flimsy-looking vee-belt from the spindle of the angle grinder. The extended housing

Fig 7.10 (Above and Right) *The Mini Arbortech is a carving adapter which mounts on the angle grinder.*

gives the smaller cutter much better access, but when I tried one I found it was fiddly to set up properly and not as well constructed as I had hoped. The small disc was not as efficient as I would have liked either, and I much prefer to use small chainsaw cutters like the Tornado in my long-nosed die grinder. I cannot present the cutter to the work in the same way as with the Arbortech, but the cutting action is more efficient and the die grinder much quieter than my angle grinder.

Fig 7.11 *A wide variety of sanding accessories is available for angle grinders.*

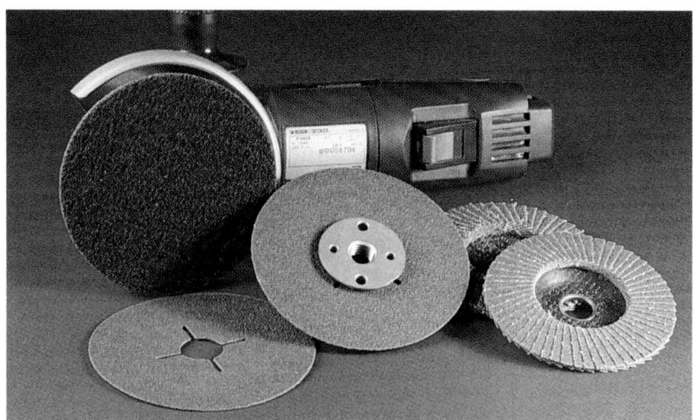

Mini Arbortech

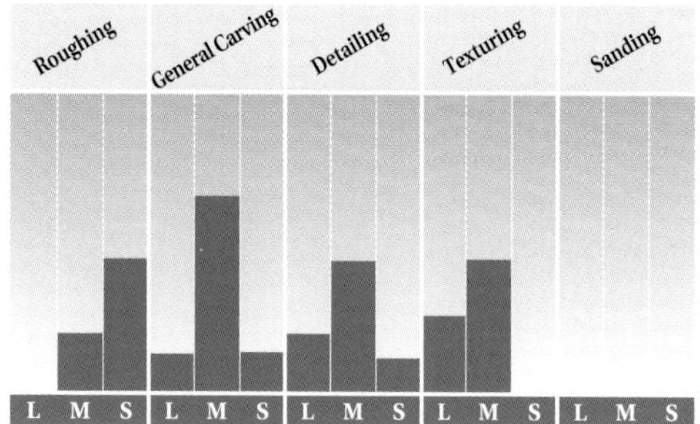

Sanding and polishing

Large carvings can also have much of their sanding completed using the angle grinder, and polishing bonnets and brushes can be fitted to them (Fig 7.11). When using polishing bonnets, the metal guarding is usually removed.

Flapdiscs

Heavy sanding and shaping can be performed using flapdiscs, which were originally designed for dressing welded seams (Fig 7.12). They are made up from a

Fig 7.12 (Above and Right) *Flapdiscs are designed for cleaning up welding, so are quite capable of carving, but work out expensive in the long term.*

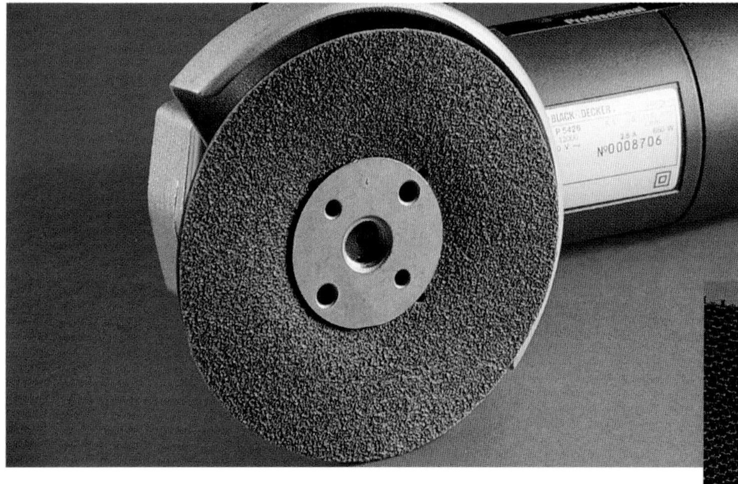

Fig 7.13 (Left) Various grades of sanding disc, used in conjunction with a flexible backing pad, can be used to carve and sand timber.

Fig 7.14 (Below) Norton non-woven abrasives are quickly attached or changed by means of a special spiked-grip backing pad.

series of overlapping flaps of tough zirconia abrasive, fastened to the surface of the disc. Available in grades of around 40 to 120 grit, they are capable of removing a lot of timber, carving as well as sanding. As they wear, fresh abrasive is revealed, so they have a reasonably long life, but are not as economical as the Karbide Kutzall discs.

Sanding discs

By fitting a flexible backing pad to the grinder you can use the tough, fibre-backed sanding discs (Fig 7.13). Both the backing pads and the discs are relatively

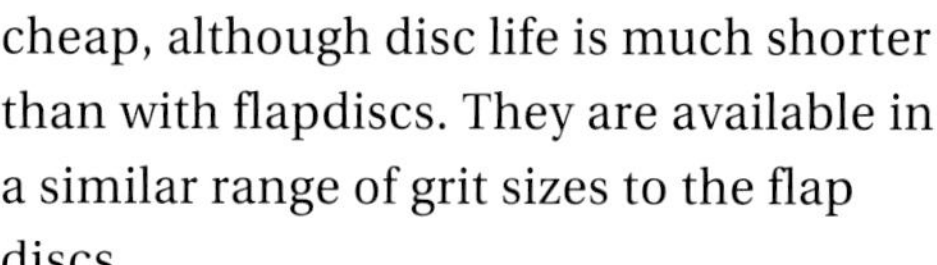

cheap, although disc life is much shorter than with flapdiscs. They are available in a similar range of grit sizes to the flap discs.

Non-woven abrasives

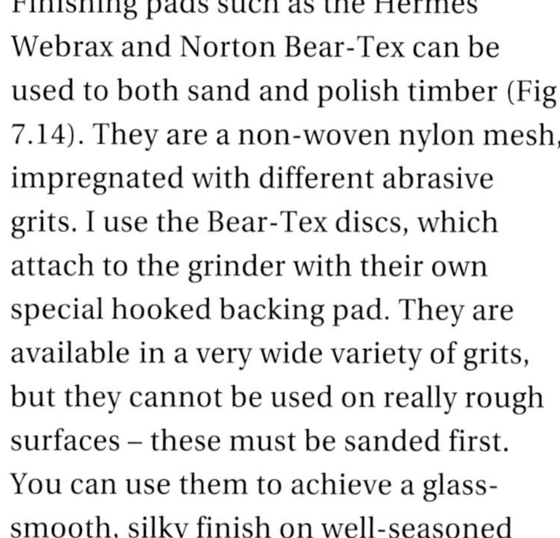

Finishing pads such as the Hermes Webrax and Norton Bear-Tex can be used to both sand and polish timber (Fig 7.14). They are a non-woven nylon mesh, impregnated with different abrasive grits. I use the Bear-Tex discs, which attach to the grinder with their own special hooked backing pad. They are available in a very wide variety of grits, but they cannot be used on really rough surfaces – these must be sanded first. You can use them to achieve a glass-smooth, silky finish on well-seasoned timber (Fig 7.15).

Fig 7.15 Non-woven abrasives are capable of achieving excellent surface finishes after initial coarse sanding.

Fig 7.16 *Lambswool bonnets and finishing sponges can be used to polish finished carvings.*

Polishing

CSM sell compounding sponges, which are used in the car trade to polish waxed bodywork, and you can easily buy lambswool polishing bonnets to use on large polished work (Fig 7.16).

Safety

Angle grinders and carving discs are much cheaper to buy than a chainsaw with all its associated safety equipment, but the dangers of using angle grinders and carving discs are often underrated. Precautions should be taken to protect yourself, your clothing, and the electric cable from coming into contact with the carving disc.

Earplugs or defenders to protect your hearing from the scream of the grinder, and goggles or other eye protection, are both essential; and an RCD trip should be fitted to the power supply (see pages 12–13). Work clothing should be snug-fitting and as difficult to snag as possible. Chainsaw protective clothing is *not* effective against these cutters, and wearing it would give you a false sense of security. The fibres in chainsaw clothing are designed to jam the chain and drive sprockets – an angle grinder is not so easy to stop. There is no specific protective clothing designed for the job; a partial solution is to wear a long, thick, leather welder's or blacksmith's apron; this will give only limited protection, but more than jeans or cotton workwear. Cutters do not tend to snag the leather as easily as cloth overalls: they will scuff the surface if just lightly touched, which is one reason why leather is used for motorcycle clothing. The leather apron affords good protection against the cutting action of Karbide Kutzall carving discs and conventional sanding discs, though, making them an attractive and safer proposition to use. There is no really good protection available that I know of against a toothed carving disc. A leather welder's apron costs between £10 and £20, and will also provide protection against the abrasive carving burrs used in conjunction with flexible-shaft machines and die grinders. To a lesser extent, it offers some protection against knife cuts when whittling hand-

Fig 7.17 *Carving discs are dangerous and extra guarding is really essential.*

held items, too. I have glued in two additional pieces of leather to reinforce my apron in vulnerable areas. The extra thickness will give more reaction time in the event of accidentally coming in contact with the cutting disc.

Wearing protective clothing can give you a false sense of security. It doesn't make you impregnable – it can only reduce the risk to an acceptable level.

Guarding

The angle grinder with a toothed carving disc has only slightly less potential for perpetrating terrible damage on the operator than a chainsaw. Toothed carving cutters are more efficient at catching clothing and ripping flesh than the grinding discs for which these machines were originally designed. The standard guarding fitted to the grinders leaves much of the blade unprotected, and does not allow you to adjust the amount of blade exposed, as you can on a circular saw, for instance. So supplementary guarding of these carving discs is highly desirable to make their use safer (Fig 7.17). Extra guarding cannot always be used, however, and there are times when you might want to remove the additional guarding; but great care should then be exercised to ensure safe working if you do so.

Arbortech and Kaindl both make special guards for use with carving discs, addressing their particular safety hazards. Both guards are manufactured in a tough, clear plastic and easily bolt on to a standard grinder using the spare side-handle mount. They will fit most 4in or 4½in grinders.

The Arbortech version (Fig 7.18) is heavier and more strongly constructed, but leaves the disc protruding all the time by a controlled but variable amount. This gives you some control over the depth of cut being made, but the blade is not covered when you put the grinder down, and the guard does not have an extraction point.

The Kaindl version is of a different design, which, though of lighter construction, completely encloses the cutting disc when it is not cutting. It does this by having a sprung guard to cover the

Fig 7.18 *Arbortech make a heavy-duty polycarbonate guard which easily attaches to the grinder, using the spare side-handle thread.*

SUPPLIERS INCLUDE:

Rod Naylor
Pintail
CSM
L. R. Oliver
King Arthur's Tools
Craft Supplies
BriMarc
Norton

blade when it is not in contact with the work, similar to the guarding on a portable circular saw. Because the carving disc is completely enclosed, the waste wood needs to be removed – hence the extraction point.

Like all machine guarding, both models can be restrictive at times, but you should own one and use it wherever possible. Whichever you choose, if it is fitted and adjusted correctly it will greatly cut down the risk of snagging yourself, cables, or clothing.

Atlas Copco produce two Multi Carver kits, industrial-quality angle grinders already fitted with their own-badged Arbortech Industrial discs and ready fitted with guards. These are available with either the standard Arbortech-style plastic guard, or an adjustable guard with a dust extraction point, similar to, but heavier than the Kaindl guard.

Side handles should *not* be removed, even if they seem to get in the way occasionally. The handle is essential for keeping a firm grip and maintaining good control of the machine; otherwise you may find the grinder being twisted from your hands by the cutter.

The grinder's own metal guarding should *only* be removed when the machine is being used with a polishing bonnet.

- **If you are going to use a grinder for a lot of work, buy a good-quality professional model.**
- **Don't remove the metal guarding, or the side handle, which is essential for proper control of the tool.**
- **Tungsten-carbide-toothed carving discs perform better on tough timber than steel-toothed models, and don't need sharpening as often.**
- **Toothed cutters are equally at home on green and seasoned timber, but the abrasive discs and cutters are best used on seasoned timber.**
- **All workpieces need to be held securely whilst you work.**

CHAPTER EIGHT

Die Grinders and Routers

THE use of a router in carving is mainly limited to making signs and to preparation for relief carving, where it can be used to establish quickly the background and the different levels within the carving. The die grinder, which uses a similar motor, is a hand-held machine and a much more flexible tool, with the potential to be used in similar applications to the flexible-shaft carving machine. Carvers who do large work and use angle grinders extensively will find a die grinder is possibly better suited as a partner to their angle grinder than a flexi-shaft. It is a more robust machine, and can be used in conjunction with mini-chainsaw cutters like the Tornado where rapid stock removal is required.

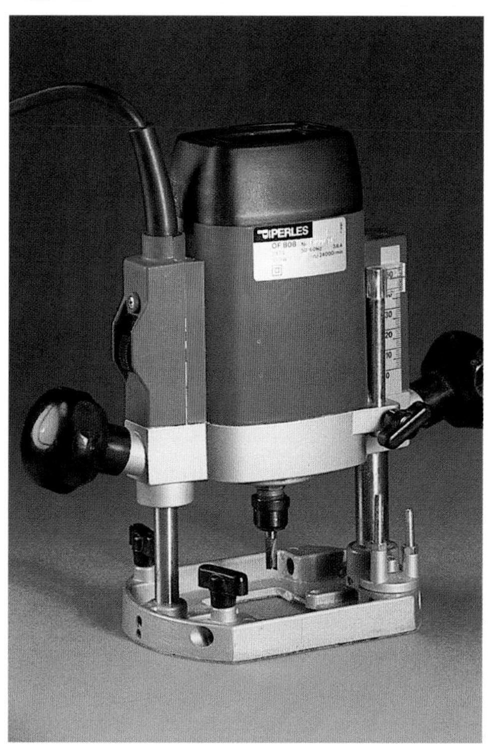

Fig 8.1 *The plunging router can be usefully employed to remove the background areas in relief carving.*

Routers

Die grinders and routers are very similar in many ways, the basis of both being a powerful motor with a collet on the end of the motor shaft to hold the tooling, and strong front bearings. The plunging router is probably the most revolutionary woodworking power tool of the late twentieth century. It is so versatile that with a good range of tooling and some homemade jigs, it forms almost a complete power workshop. Although it has revolutionized cabinet work, it has not made much impact on woodcarving as its only real use is in forming the background and blocking out the various levels of a relief carving (Figs 8.1 and 8.2). Use of the router will enable carvings in deep relief to be quite quickly and accurately roughed out. To prevent the router base tipping as the background is removed, the panel being worked on should be surrounded by a frame of waste wood of the same thickness, and 'ski bars' used on large items. If you are carving relief panels to be fitted into doors or furniture, this extra support can be the

Fig 8.2 (Left and Below) *The router can be used for sign-carving too. Waste pieces of wood are used to support the router and prevent its base tipping when near the edge of the work.*

edge of the panel which will later be fielded to fit into the frame.

Ski bars are fitted to the router so that it can be supported over a much larger area, which prevents the base tipping through lack of support. Trend make ski bars for some models of router, but they are a simple accessory to make yourself. They consist of two rectangular metal or hardwood bars, with two holes drilled in each so that they can slide on to the router's side fence bars (Fig 8.3). The skis can be made to any size to suit the carving you are working on, and held in place with clamp screws which grip the fence rods. The router can now be used to remove waste from the carving, setting the cutter to various depths as required.

Fig 8.3 *A router fitted with home-made ski bars for additional support. (Photo: Anthony Bailey)*

SUPPLIERS INCLUDE:

Bosch
Black & Decker
DeWalt
Makita
Ryobi
Stayer
Hitachi

Router and baseplate (sign and relief carving only)

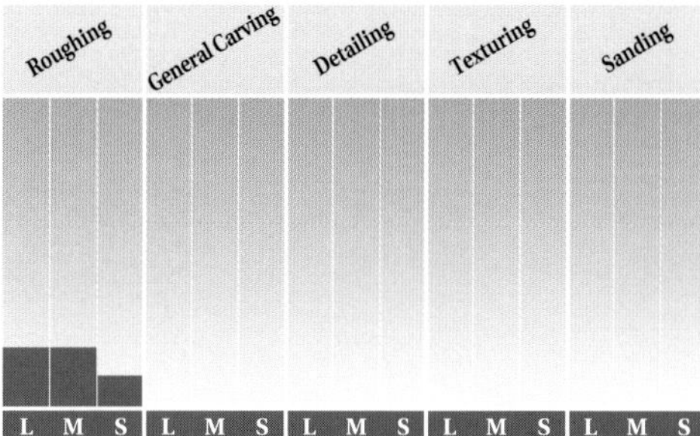

The router can also be fitted to a pantograph arm to create a 2D copying and sign-carving machine. Both Trend and Micom make sign carvers to take basic plunge routers.

Many routers are now fitted with a variable speed control, which is a useful option to look out for because with some timbers it can help to prevent burning. Additionally, electronic soft-start and braking is available on some models, which is advantageous on machines with powerful motors.

Tooling

Standard two-flute router cutters of various sizes can be used, and both carbide-tipped and HSS cutters are suitable. If you are creating very deep relief, you should use a router which will take cutters with larger shanks than the commonly used ¼in (6.4mm) ones. Trend list single- and double-flute pocket cutters up to 95mm (3¾in) long (overall) with ½in (12.7mm) shanks, 75mm (3in) long with ¼in shanks, which would allow you to rough out relief panels nearly 4in (100mm) thick. Great care must be taken to avoid cutter breakage when cutting deeply: many passes should be taken with a maximum depth of about half the cutter diameter. Instead of square-ended cutters you can use radius cutters, which are less likely to leave tool marks where you have strayed too close to the margin of the finished carving. Of course, it is also possible to use the same style of sintered carbide carving burrs that are employed in flexible-shaft carving tools, which can be useful if the timber is prone to splintering.

SUPPLIERS INCLUDE:

Trend
Titman
Wealden
BJR

Die grinders

In a router, the addition of a baseplate to the basic motor unit allows a controlled depth of cut to be maintained, whilst keeping the cutter perpendicular to the surface of the work. The die grinder is simply a router motor with no baseplate or plunging mechanism. Most routers combine the baseplate and motor assembly into an integral unit, but a few of the smaller 500–600W units – such as the Bosch POF 500 and 600 and the small Black & Decker and Stayer routers – have motors which can be removed, turning them into hand-held, short-nosed die grinders. Some manufacturers, such as Makita, also make laminate trimmers which are basically a specialized baseplate fitted to a die grinder, and laminate trimming attachments are an option from some other manufacturers such as Bosch.

Die grinders are usually found in the industrial tool ranges of manufacturers, and are used for more delicate grinding, deburring, and polishing operations than can be carried out with an angle grinder. In addition to the short-nosed models, which are similar to those used as routers, some die grinders come with an extended, slender nose, which makes them easier to hold and gives them better reach. These long-nosed versions are much better for woodcarving use, because of the increased access which

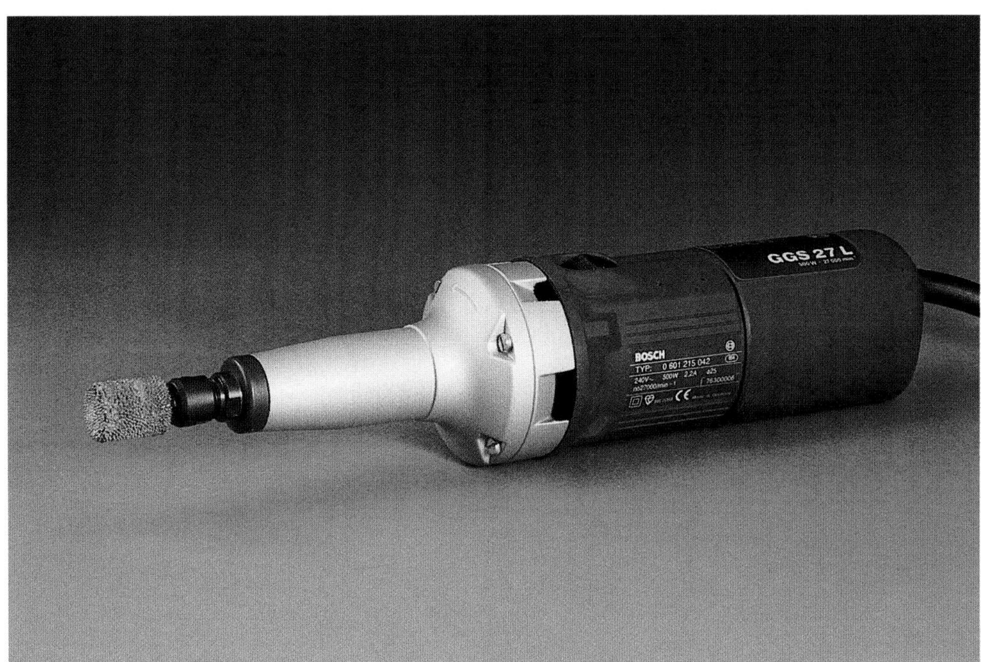

Fig 8.4 *My Bosch long-nosed die grinder, used for heavier jobs than I would tackle with my flexible-shaft machines.*

the long reach and slender nose give you.

Again, as with the routers, some models are available with electronic speed controls, soft start, etc.; a speed control can be a very useful addition to prevent burning when working with some timbers.

The die grinder is a much more versatile carving tool than the dedicated router, and will carry out the same sort of carving functions that you would expect of a flexible-shaft carving tool fitted with a large handpiece. The flexible shaft is the weak link of the flexi-shaft tool, and can be damaged or broken fairly easily when doing heavy work with large burrs and cutters. The die grinder does not suffer from this disadvantage, so is a very good option for the carver who always wants to use large burrs, and a good companion to the angle grinder for larger sculpture. The die grinder has the further advantage of being rather quieter than an angle grinder.

I have been using the long-nosed Bosch GGS-27L (Fig 8.4) for heavy roughing out on larger carvings, where I might have used my flexi-shaft and a large cutter and handpiece before. At 27,000rpm it beats my fastest large flexi by 5,000rpm, making a noticeable difference in cutting rate when using structured carbide burrs. It works especially well with the new Karbide Kutzall mushroom-shaped cutter, which has a 2in (50mm) diameter head. The arbor is supplied separately, allowing the head to be fitted either way round, which increases its versatility. (The arbor has also been pressed into service with an Arbortech mini-cutter.) With no shaft to break on the Bosch machine, I can afford to be a bit more heavy-handed, but at over 1.5kg (3.3lb) it requires both hands on the tool, so I tend to lose some of the flexibility I normally get when I can hand-hold a carving. As most of the carvings that I would use this tool for are either too big, or just on the limit of size, to hand-hold anyway, this is not a major problem. The weight is noticeable if the tool is in use for a long period, though, especially

SUPPLIERS INCLUDE:

Bosch
Atlas Copco
Black & Decker
Makita
Stayer

Die grinder

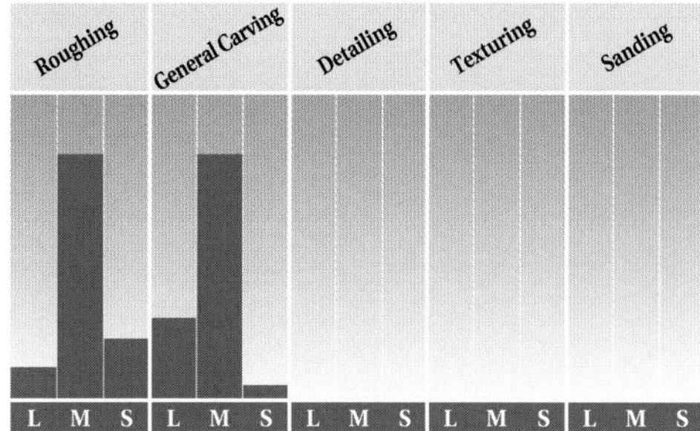

when you are used to a flexible-shaft handpiece weighing about 100g (3½oz). I have often felt that a speed control would be advantageous, so if you are contemplating buying one it is an option worth looking for. I have now bought a separate speed control to use with all my portable power tools.

If your carvings are at the larger end of the scale, this is a tool well worth considering, and the long-nosed models definitely have the edge in terms of access when carving. The cheapest way to get a die grinder is to purchase one of the routers with removable motors, but of course you will only be getting the short-nosed version. If you use one of these with King Arthur's Tools' Percival cutter, then depending on the model used you will have a reach of 4 or 6in (100–150mm); but the body will get in the way when using structured carbide burrs. There are no DIY versions of the long-nosed die grinder that I know of, so you will have to buy the more expensive professional-specification machines if you want to enjoy the advantages of increased access with all cutters.

Tooling

The most suitable tooling for carving with the die grinder is probably the structured carbide burr (see pages 30–1), and this is what I mainly use and would recommend (Fig 8.5). Other cutters can be used too, and my long-nosed die grinder is particularly good when used in combination with Rod Naylor's Tornado cutters and an angle-grinder-style side handle.

The Tornado is basically a circle of chainsaw blade clamped between two discs, and is a very efficient cutter (Figs 8.6 and 8.7). The newer Tungsten Tornado is slightly smaller, giving better access to carvings (Fig 8.8). It has replaceable

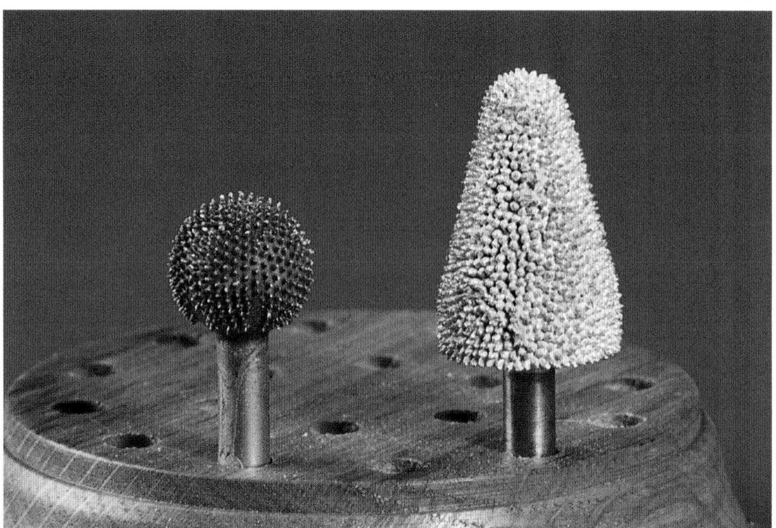

Fig 8.5 *The large carbide burrs used with a flexible-shaft unit are just as good when married with a die grinder*

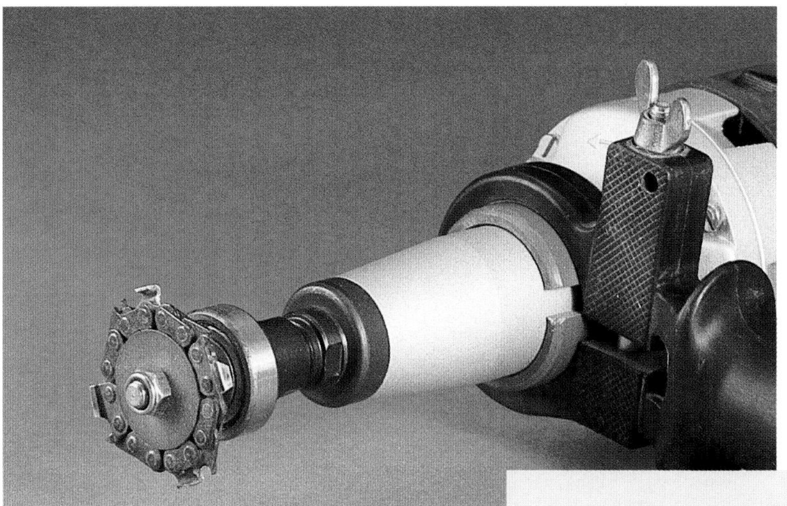

Fig 8.6 *Rod Naylor's Tornado cutter, which is similar to the Percival ones.*

Fig 8.7 *Both the original Tornado and the Percival cutters use circlets of chainsaw chain like this. (Photo courtesy of King Arthur's Tools)*

tungsten carbide tips, like a miniature version of the industrial Arbortech, and performs well with even the toughest timbers.

I could not find a proprietary side handle to use with my die grinder's 35mm (1⅜in) nose, so I made a split plastic adapter to use with the standard 43mm (1¾in) side handle from my Bosch electric hammer drill. The side handle (Fig 8.9)

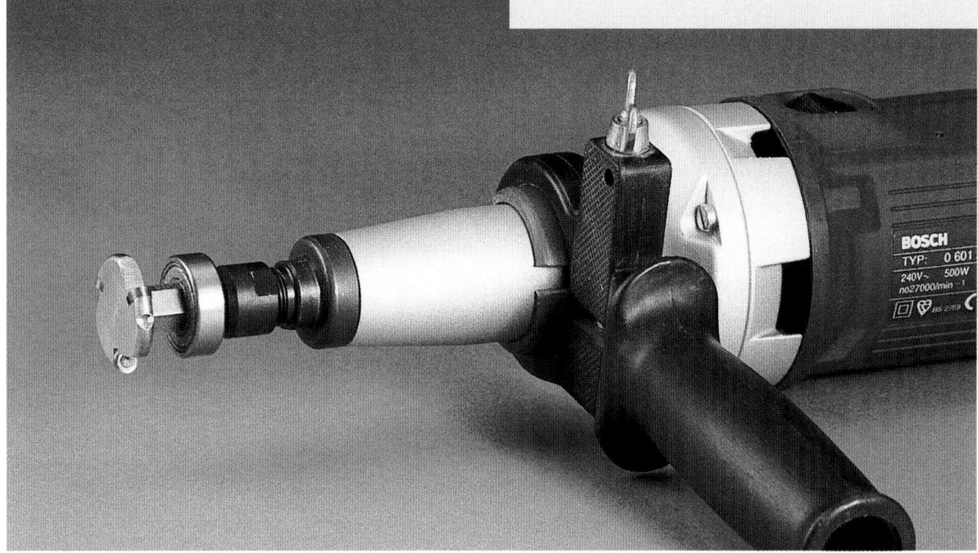

Fig 8.8 *The Tungsten Tornado is the professional replaceable carbide-tipped version. It is smaller in diameter and will work well on tougher timbers than its chainsaw counterparts.*

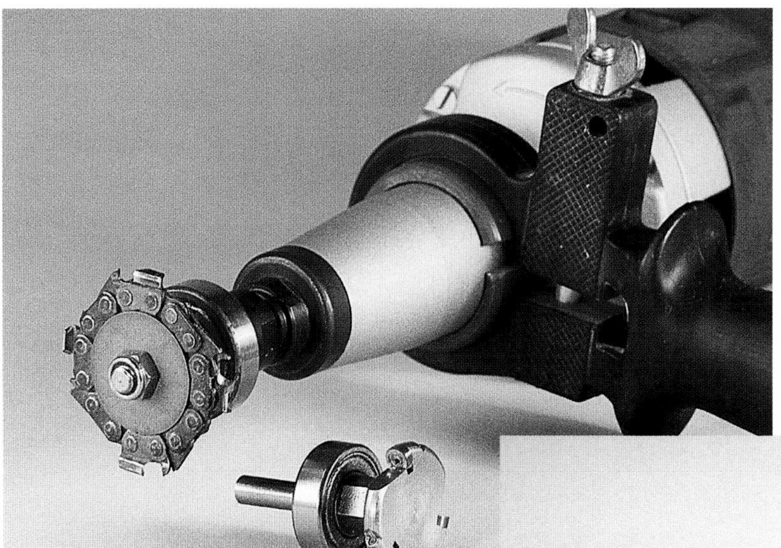

Fig 8.9 (Left) The side handle fitted to the die grinder gives you better control when working with these fairly voracious cutters.

Fig 8.10 (Below) The Percival Plus cutters have multiple rings of chainsaw teeth. (Photo by courtesy of King Arthur's Tools)

gives more control of the cutter, and makes it an excellent carving tool for larger-scale carvings which really aren't big enough to warrant using my Arbortech.

King Arthur's Tools' Percival cutter is similar to the Tornado. It is sold in the UK by Craft Supplies, and is available in 4 or 6in (100 or 150mm) long versions. Percival Plus has three circlets of chain clamped side by side for more rapid working (Fig 8.10).

See Chapter 3, Flexible-Shaft Machines, for further information on tooling.

SUPPLIERS INCLUDE:

Rod Naylor
Craft Supplies
King Arthur's Tools
Pintail
Shesto
L. R. Oliver

- **Used with the same range of cutters as the flexi-shaft, there is usually more power available and no relatively weak shaft to restrict you, but the condition of the cutters is still important. Abrasive cutters should be kept clean and toothed cutters sharp, and allowed to work at their own rate, without straining the motor.**
- **Keep collets clean, and insert the tool shank fully in the collet before tightening. Don't use the wrong size collet for the tool shank, or be tempted to insert only a little of the tool shank into the collet to improve the tool's reach.**
- **Clamp the work securely, leaving both hands free to control the machine properly.**
- **Fitting a side handle assists with the control of the more voracious cutters.**
- **Do not exceed the manufacturer's maximum recommended speed for the cutter.**

CHAPTER NINE

Chainsaws

An essential everyday work tool for the forestry trade, chainsaws have gained some popularity as a carving tool, but for many carvers the angle grinder has now usurped their place. Most people are justifiably wary of chainsaws, and they are crocodiles in careless and unskilled hands. Injuries caused by them can be horrific and even fatal, the stuff of tabloid news headlines. You can no longer easily go along to a tool hire shop and borrow one, but anyone can go out to the nearest 'DIY Super Shed' and purchase one. The correct safety equipment is often not even available, and you are unlikely to receive any guidance. Since the development of angle-grinder carving discs, the necessity of using a chainsaw on many large carvings has greatly decreased. An angle grinder and carving disc is more than capable of the scale of work most carvers undertake and, although still a dangerous tool, most carvers will feel more in control and at ease using one.

I would not suggest that anyone should embark lightly upon chainsaw ownership unless they really need to, but if you decide to – and there are large-scale tasks for which they are particularly useful – then seek guidance in selecting a suitable machine and equipment (Fig 9.1).

Purchase and use all the safety equipment from the outset, and make sure you enrol for at least a basic course in chainsaw maintenance and use.

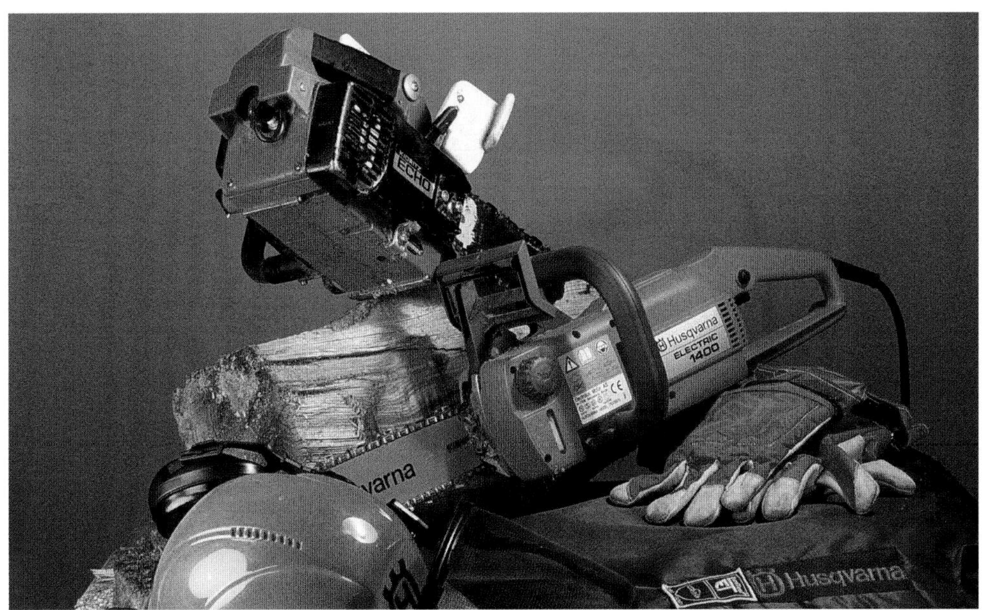

Fig 9.1 *Small electric and petrol chainsaws can be useful for large carvings and for timber conversion, but the safety equipment necessary adds considerably to their expense.*

Large petrol-driven chainsaws can be used to convert freshly felled logs into planks and carving blocks, which can be used green or stored and seasoned. To convert tree trunks to planks, a chainsaw mill is often used, the simplest type consisting of a roller fitted to a long chainbar. The roller can be adjusted to set the thickness of plank being sliced off. Very powerful motor units and special saw chains are required to rip down the grain and make planks, and often a motor is fitted to each end of the chainbar. These saws are too large and heavy to be of any use for carving, even if they have short chainbars fitted; smaller units are needed.

The chainsaw was probably the first powered roughing-out tool to be utilized for carving. In skilled hands they are capable of blocking out carvings, rapid shaping, and even adding details on large work. Chain bars and chains have evolved over the years to give greater control, and are much refined from the original basic tool. In America you can even buy miniature chainsaw carving bars, which are little bigger than a large breadknife and are intended for carving, but I cannot find anyone in the UK who sells or has come across them.

To really benefit from using a chainsaw as a carving tool, you need to be creating very large-scale work containing many cubic feet of timber – sculpture of the scale and type seen in public places. If you don't do this type of work regularly, then the expensive and relatively dangerous chainsaw is probably best avoided.

Electric or petrol?

Chainsaws are available in numerous makes, models, and sizes. The large petrol-engined ones are used to fell and log timber, but are too heavy to be of much use in carving, where the smaller, lighter models used for trimming and limbing trees are much more appropriate. Whether you require a petrol or an electric model mainly depends on where you intend to use it. Petrol-engined saws are unsuitable for use in the average workshop, because of the dangerous fumes, but are more suitable for outdoor work, where the damp British weather can render the use of an electric model dangerous. Many manufacturers make petrol-engined saws, but often they don't have even a token electric model in their range, so the choice of electric models is limited. For workshop or occasional outdoor use, the electric chainsaw is probably your best choice. They are lighter, quieter, and don't produce dangerous exhaust fumes or use highly flammable fuel. If you work mainly outdoors, then a petrol-engined saw may be a better choice; it should not be used indoors.

The large and powerful saws used for felling and converting timber are expensive; but it is the smaller, lighter machines which are used in carving, and they are generally the cheaper models. Although price might be a big consideration – especially when you consider the necessary extra outlay on safety equipment and training – choose a manufacturer who offers good back-up and local service. Examine and handle the machines first if you can, checking the weight, balance, and feel of each machine. It is important that you are comfortable with a machine that you are likely to use for many hours. Ensure that spares and servicing are available easily and locally.

I have two small chainsaws in my tool collection: a 12in (305mm) bar petrol version made by Echo, which I have had for many years, and which is mainly used for chopping up firewood; and a 14in (355mm) bar Husqvarna electric model, which I use

SUPPLIERS:

Electric chainsaws are not as popular as petrol ones, so you are most likely to come across machines from Stihl, probably the best-known in the UK, who include a heavyweight 2kW electric model in their range; or Husqvarna, who make the 1.4kW model 1400 EL which I use in my workshop. Other makes you may find include:

Partner
Jonserad
Makita
Black & Decker
Bosch
Stayer
Allen Power Equipment (Echo)

in the workshop and occasionally outdoors (Fig 9.2). The Husqvarna is a well-balanced, quiet, and surprisingly powerful machine which easily tackles large jobs, whilst being light enough to use comfortably for quite long periods.

Tooling

Saw chain is available in various types, with different cutting characteristics, from the larger manufacturers, but they are not all suitable for use on small saws. The use of a chainsaw for carving is likely to increase the risk of kickback, so the choice of a chain which is designed to minimize kickback is recommended. A guide bar with a small nose also reduces the risk of kickback, but most chainbars on small saws fit into this category. If you are

Chainsaw

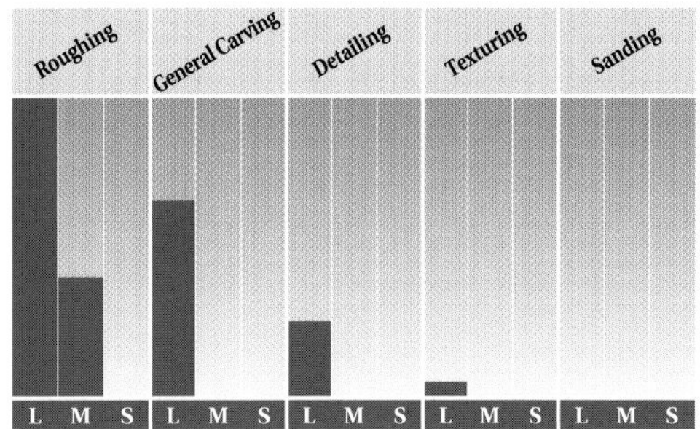

unsure, seek advice from the manufacturers or talk to carvers who use one regularly.

If you want to see chainsaws in action, one of the best carving events in the UK is the Husqvarna-sponsored annual Sculptree event. This is held at Westonbirt Arboretum in Gloucestershire, where a team of carvers use chainsaws and various other means to convert large lumps of damaged, diseased, or fallen tree into sculptures to be auctioned for the charity Tree Aid. Of course you can find chainsaw carving at other events such as county shows, but Sculptree is the only event where you will find a whole team of professional carvers working in the one place and see some inspirational carvings.

Training

It is essential that you get proper training in the use and maintenance of the chainsaw before you start using one. If you are lucky enough to know a professional user who already holds certificates of competence, then they may be able to give you the basic training you need to use one at home. Anyone using a

Fig 9.2 *The electric chainsaw is best suited to workshop use and will quickly cut away waste, plane and shape large carvings.*

chainsaw in their business, though, either as an employee or self-employed, should have certificates of competence covering the use of the chainsaw in all relevant areas, showing their compliance with the Health and Safety at Work Act (in the UK), or equivalent regulations in other countries. It is most important that you are shown how to maintain and use the saw safely, even if you do not actually require a chainsaw certificate to use one.

Individual hobby users who have not undertaken any training and do not use safety equipment may find their insurers less than helpful if they have an accident. Your local professional chainsaw sales and service shop should be able to advise on what colleges or other providers of chainsaw training are available in your area. Ideally you should find a course that will give you a nationally recognized certificate in chainsaw maintenance and crosscutting, the two areas of standard training which are of relevance to the woodcarver. In the UK, these are available from various colleges around the country as well as from a network of independent trainers. The National Proficiency Tests Council, based at the National Agricultural Centre at Stoneleigh in Warwickshire Tel. 01203 696 969), runs suitable courses, and agricultural colleges and some colleges of further education run similar ones where there is a local need. Independent trainers can often tailor courses specifically for chainsaw carving, rather than forestry work, which would be very useful.

Unless you need a National Proficiency Tests Council certificate and identity card for your business (which costs extra), try and find an instructor who will give you a FASTCo Record of Training Achievement, a simple certificate to show the training you have undertaken. If you cannot find any training in your immediate area, contact the Forestry and Arboriculture Safety and Training Council (FASTCo), 231 Corstorphine Road, Edinburgh, EH12 7AT (tel. 0131-314 6247), who will provide you with the name of a suitable training company or person.

Safety equipment

Whether you are using a small electric unit in the workshop or a more powerful petrol-engined saw outside, a full kit of safety clothing is absolutely essential (Fig 9.3),

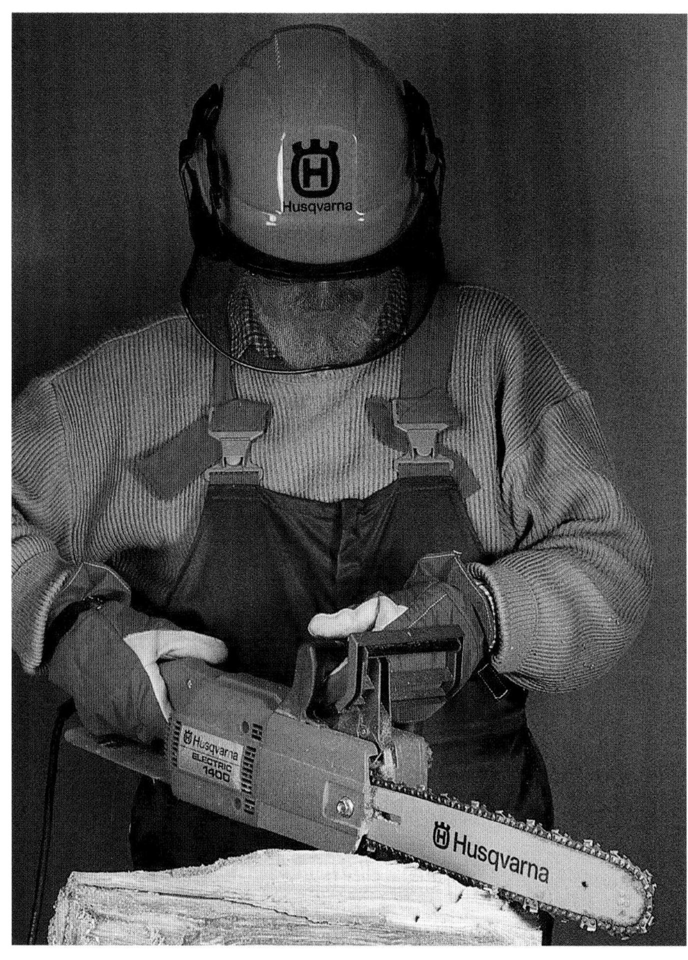

Fig 9.3 *Full safety chainsaw equipment is as essential for carving as for forestry work, even though you may feel overdressed for the workshop!*

and it may cost as much or even more than the average small chainsaw. Ignore the advertising photos seen in general power-tool catalogues, of people operating chainsaws wearing only lumberjack shirts, jeans, rigger gloves, and goggles – these will offer you virtually no protection at all.

The *minimum* protection recommended by the Health & Safety Executive in the UK for casual chainsaw use is:

1. a protective helmet to BS 5240 with mesh visor and ear muffs fitted;
2. chainsaw mittens with cut-retardant padding;
3. protective leggings with all-round blocking material;
4. protective gaiters worn over industrial steel-toecapped footwear or chainsaw boots.

A package containing a complete basic kit contained in a holdall is available from several suppliers, or you can purchase the items separately. Of course, forestry is an outdoor occupation, and the clothing manufactured reflects this. The main drawback I find with chainsaw clothing is that it is fairly bulky and warm to wear – however, getting used to that is preferable to horrific injuries. There are several types of trousers available besides leggings, and I prefer a bib-and-brace style for comfort when working, although leggings are probably cooler to wear. Jackets are also available to give upper-body protection.

Electric chainsaws, whether used indoors or out, should always be used with an RCD circuit-breaker (see pages 12–13). These are cheaply available (£12–15) in the form of a 13-amp socket adapter, and provide additional safety when using any portable electric power tool.

Finally, remember that no amount of safety clothing provides total protection against an accident – training and safe working practices are still very important too.

● Work must be very well secured: large pieces may have enough mass to sit securely while being worked on, but sandbags and ratcheted hold-down straps of the type used with trailers are useful to secure work.

CHAPTER TEN

Other Portable Power Tools

VARIOUS other portable power tools can find occasional uses in carving too, including the orbital sander, jigsaws and their variants, and that old faithful basic power tool we all own, the electric drill.

Portable planers

SUPPLIERS:

All power tool manufacturers seem to have at least one model in their range, including:
Bosch
Black & Decker
Ryobi
Makita
Atlas Copco

Unless you are going to carve very large objects with flat planes and large convex surfaces, an electric planer (Fig 10.1) is not the most useful carver's tool. However, if you don't own a planer-thicknesser or jointer, a planer will take the hard work out of squaring up blanks before marking out and bandsawing. They are useful for planing up plinths for carvings, too.

Portable power plane

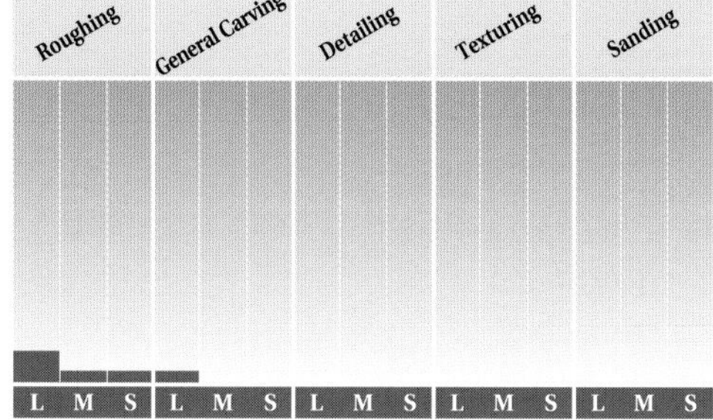

Orbital sanders

The standard ½- or ⅓-sheet orbital sander, and even a palm sander, will prove to be of little use unless you are making large sculpture with smooth flat or convex faces. However, the latest additions to

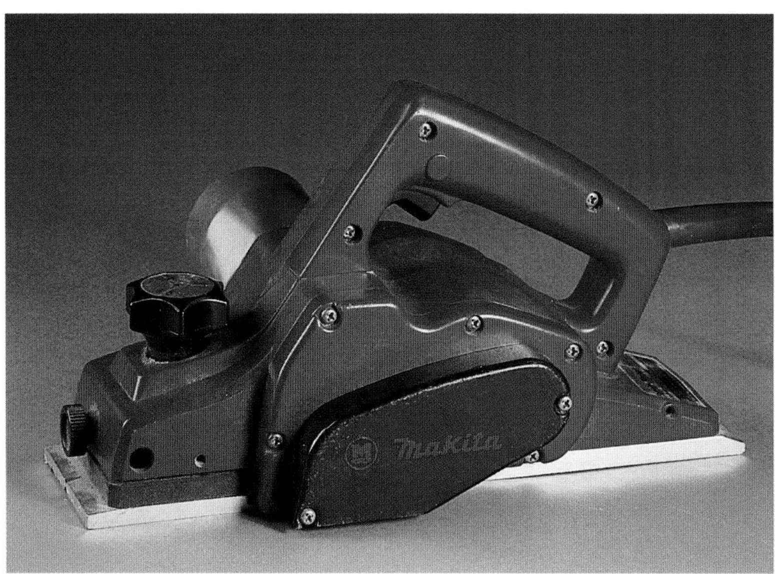

Fig 10.1 *A Makita planer takes the 'elbow grease' out of squaring up blanks for accurate marking out and cutting.*

SUPPLIERS INCLUDE:

Bosch
Fein
Ryobi

power tool manufacturers' ranges include a new style of mini-orbital sanders with a small triangular head. This is ideal for sanding nooks and crannies (if you carve them!), and will be able to sand many areas on larger carvings. I have a Ryobi machine in my workshop, which, although it is not in constant use, certainly saves my fingertips from wear at times and cuts down on the 'elbow grease' required (Fig 10.2).

⅓ and ¼ sheet orbital sander

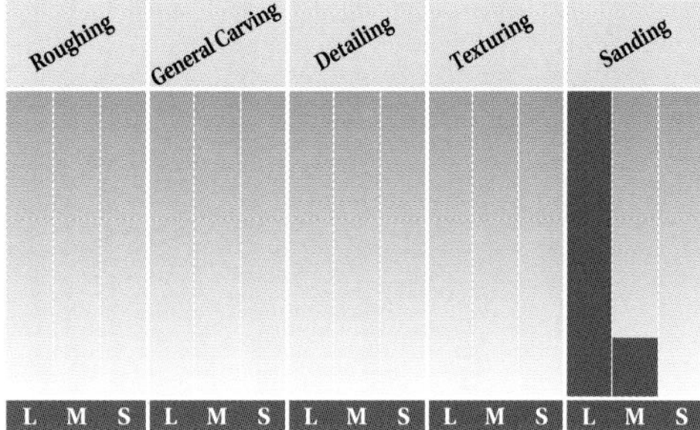

Detail sander

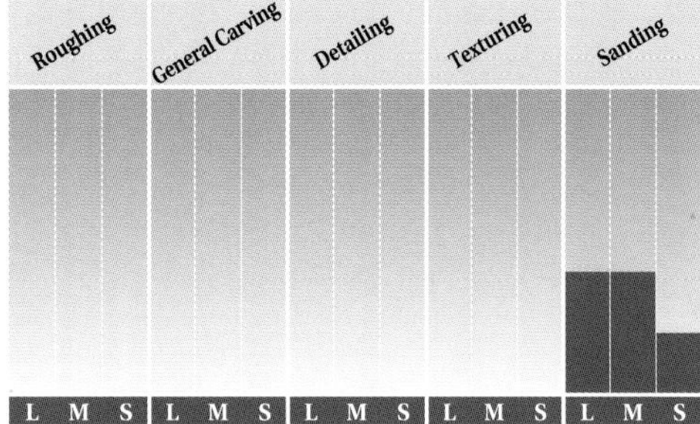

Electric drills

The portable pistol drill has found its way into most households, and comes in dozens of guises from the simplest hole driller through the screwdriving and hammer-drilling variants to the pneumatic hammer drills which drill the hardest of materials with ease.

Drills are very useful for removing waste and creating holes or hollows in a carving. They have the great advantage that they can be brought to the work easily when needed, and their use does not need any pre-planning: if you need a hole, you drill it.

You don't need a very specialized machine for it to be useful when you are carving, but variable-speed trigger controls enable you to start drilling holes

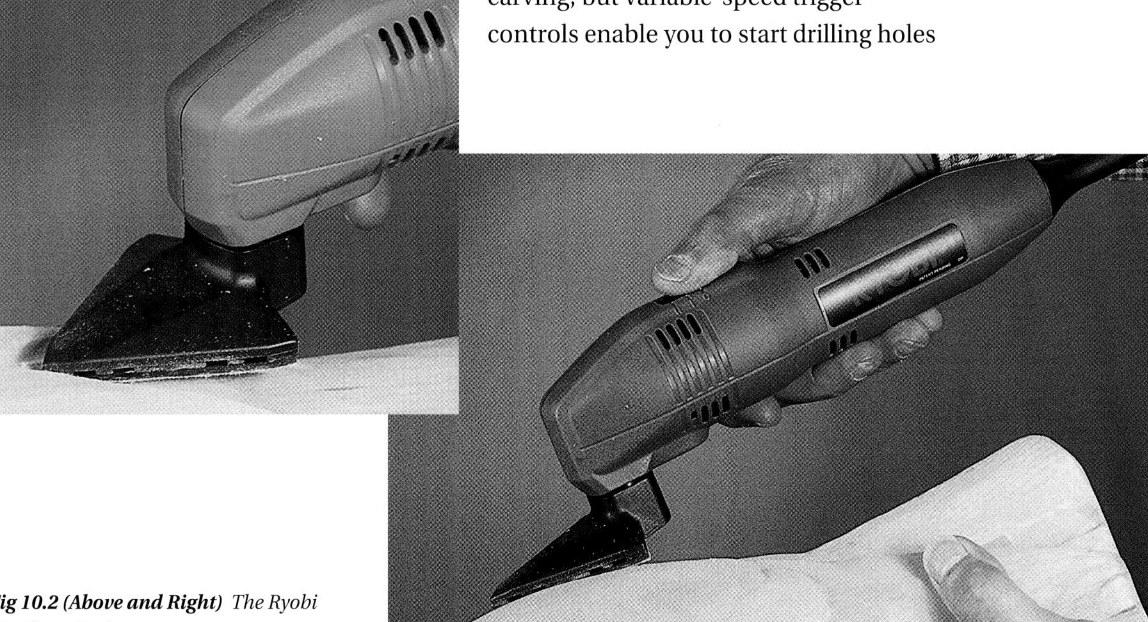

Fig 10.2 (Above and Right) The Ryobi detail sander in use.

SUPPLIERS:

Bosch
Stayer
Black & Decker
Draper
Metabo
Atlas Copco
Makita

All the major power tool companies make a wide range of drills.

with more precision on uneven part-carved surfaces. Prices vary not only with the machine features, but also with the build quality: a professional power tool is likely to cost two or three times its DIY equivalent, but with DIY-type usage it should last your lifetime.

Accessories and tooling

Drill bits

Of course, you can use just about anything which will drill holes (Fig 10.3), but for small holes I prefer the 'brad point' or lip-and-spur drills rather than the engineers' 'jobber' pattern. Where larger holes are needed, flat bits, Forstner bits, and saw-tooth machine bits are all useful. Flat bits are not as good at drilling overlapping holes, and can rip lumps out of the work. They also tend to have very long points, which you have to make allowance for when drilling blind holes. I prefer the saw-tooth machine bits, which are very good at drilling overlapping holes. The best ones I have used are those manufactured by Clico, which seem to be designed with better clearances and do not tend to jam as much as others when used in a hand-held drill.

A Swedish company has made a virtue out of a drill bit which won't drill straight holes. This latest innovation is called the 3D bit and is distributed in the UK by TCL Supplies. It is rather like a combination of drill and router, and once it has cut into the timber surface and stabilized, it will then cut in all directions, including backwards. This makes it possible to drill curved holes and make pockets, which you couldn't do with any other conventional bit. It is ideal if you want to remove waste from between an animal's legs or other areas enclosed by the carving, allowing you to create holes following the carving's required contours. These bits are very well made and similarly priced to saw-toothed bits but, unlike them, are widely available from tool stores.

Flexible shafts

One of the most useful jobs for your electric drill is to assist you when sanding up a carving; certainly the larger sanding devices are better suited to the speeds at which an electric drill runs, rather than the very high speeds attained by flexible-shaft carvers.

The bulk of the drill and chuck will make access difficult to many areas of a carving, so it is worth investing in a

Fig 10.3 *Suitable bits for removing waste and generally drilling wood. From left to right: the TCL 3D Bit; a lip-and-spur bit; and a Clico saw-toothed machine bit.*

Fig 10.4 *Drill clamp and flexible shaft is a useful combination for sanding.*

flexible shaft to improve matters (Fig 10.4). You can buy very cheap shafts, but these have plain bearings which soon get sloppy and are rather a false economy. I would go for a better-quality one with proper roller bearings fitted at each end, and if you find a choice go for the one with most flexible outer shaft. I mainly use one which is made by Foredom, the flexible-shaft carving machine manufacturer, which will accept the same snap-on handpieces I use on my carving machines; but I also have a larger, heavier one which will accept up to a $\frac{3}{8}$in (10mm) tool shank.

Drill stands and clamps

If you use your drill with a flexible shaft, you need to anchor the drill in some way: the simplest way for occasional use is probably to grip the side handle in a vice. If you are going to use it regularly, it is much more convenient to fit your drill into a proper stand or clamp, and various manufacturers supply them. In my workshop I use a particularly solid and well-made drill clamp by Carroll Tools, who manufacture sanding drums (Fig 10.5). I can use it either with the flexible shaft, taking the sanding drum to the work, or as a fixed drum sander, as appropriate. I also use it with a honing

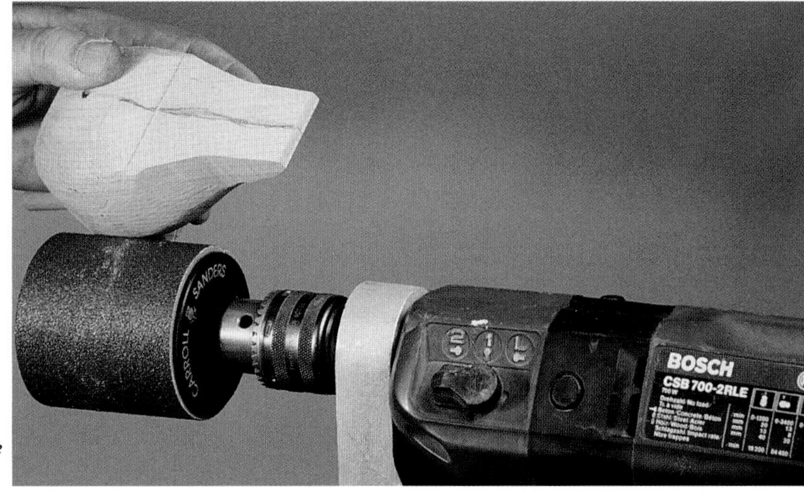

Fig 10.5 *A drill fixed in a strong bench-mounted clamp from Carroll Tools leaves both hands free to manipulate the work.*

Drill with flexible shaft

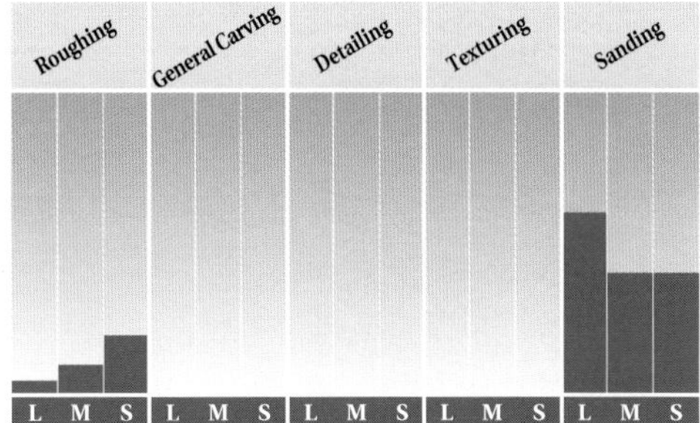

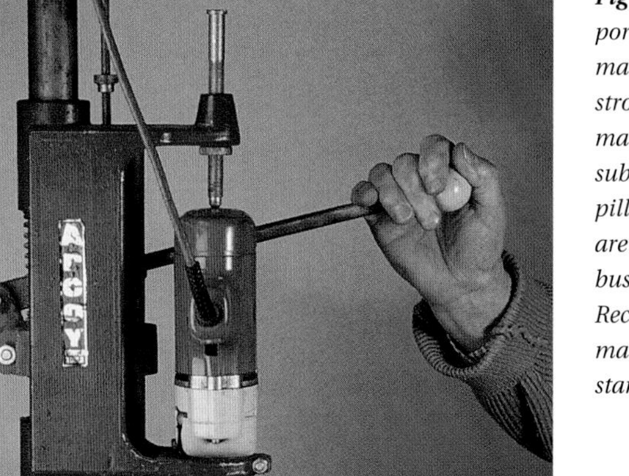

Fig 10.6 *My portable drilling machine in a strong drill stand makes a good substitute for a pillar drill. Arcoy are no longer in business, but Record Power make a similar stand.*

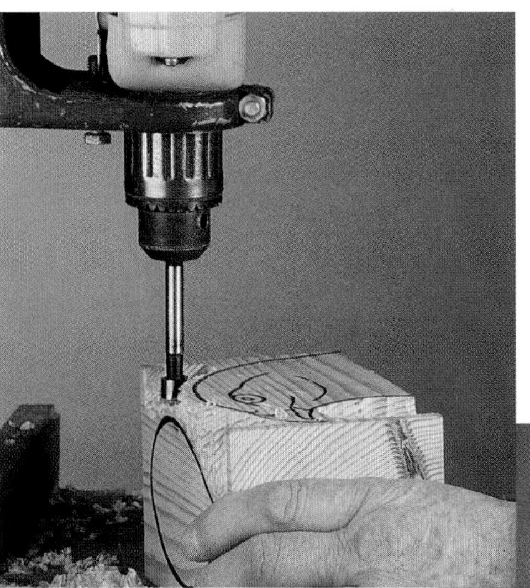

Fig 10.7 (Above) *Using the drill stand and a suitable saw-tooth machine bit to remove waste in the early stages of carving. Make sure enough scrap wood is left to support the blank adequately.*

Fig 10.8 *A wide variety of sanding accessories is available: these are just a few, including one of the original cushioned sanders, a large-diameter foam sanding drum.*

wheel to keep my edge tools sharp when carving, which is much cheaper than a dedicated honing machine.

Several well-made drill stands are available which will also turn your drill into a useful bench drill. I use a very substantial and sadly obsolete model by Arcoy (Figs 10.6 and 10.7), but was glad to see that Record Power include an almost identical model to my 'old faithful' in their range.

SUPPLIERS INCLUDE:

Axminster Power Tools
Carroll Tools
Clico
Record Power

Sanding accessories

I have only ever come across one person who said he really enjoyed sanding! Fortunately for the rest of us who wish the process to be as painless as possible, a plethora of sanding attachments has sprung up, some being more useful than others (Fig 10.8). Below I have looked at the main ones that you are likely to find.

Orbital sanding pads

Several small orbital sanding systems are available (Fig 10.9), and are much favoured by woodturners. The small abrasive pads are usually attached with Velcro or are self-adhesive, and to my mind the ones with a cushioned foam face are the best. They work especially well on concave surfaces, but as you can never sand with the grain you have to beware of leaving the small circular scratches which are the hallmark of the orbital sander.

Rigid abrasive sleeve sanding drums

The drum sanders that I would recommend using all allow for some degree of conformance to the surface being sanded, but this type (Fig 10.10) uses a hard rubber expanding drum and rigid, spiral-wound, card sanding sleeves, and has virtually no 'give'. These are the sanders which are often included in budget-priced kits containing a variety of sizes. These rigid drums work well enough on a flat surface that is already smooth, but if you try to sand away imperfections with them they bounce on the surface, making matters worse rather than better. Curved surfaces are marred by the series of facets which these drums tend to create. They can have their uses where you wish to preserve sharp edges, and fitted with a coarse-grade sleeve they become a useful carving tool, which will rapidly remove timber.

Foam drum sander

The large, approximately 4in (100mm) foam drum sander often found in DIY stores uses a soft, cloth-backed sleeve like a small linisher or belt-sander belt. The medium-density foam allows the drum a much greater degree of flexibility, conforming to the surface being sanded and preventing bounce. Its size makes it more suited to substantial flat areas and large-radius curves, though, and it is more useful to the

Fig 10.9 (Above) *Orbital flexible sanding pads are favoured by woodturners, but can be equally useful on carvings.*

Fig 10.10 (Right) *Rigid-sleeve rubber sanding drums can be used for carving, but are not so good for sanding because they bounce.*

Fig 10.11 ***(Left)*** *Carroll Tools make a wide range of well-engineered foam-cushioned sanding drums.*

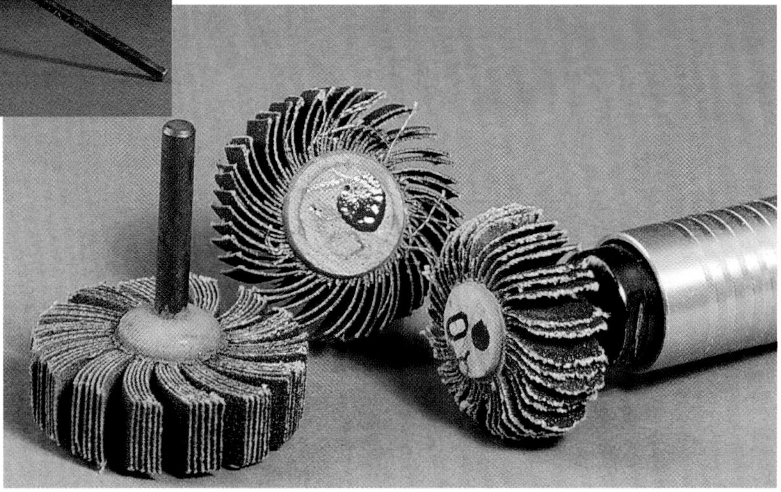

Fig 10.12 (Right) *A selection of abrasive flap sanders.*

cabinetmaker or the carver who works 'big'. Because of the large diameter it needs to be run slowly, making the drill the ideal power source.

Foam-covered sanding drums

The first versions of these that I saw were for use on a spindle moulder, converting it for use as a bobbin sander. They were too large and heavy to be used by hand, but I have since found that smaller versions are available. I have used some American ¾in (20mm) diameter soft sanders, but now use some nicely engineered small drums made by Carroll Tools (Fig 10.11). These are all 2in (50mm) long and are available in ½, ¾ and 1in diameters (13, 19, and 25mm).

All these sanders are cushioned with a covering of thin foam, and loose abrasive sheets are held in place with a cam locking bar. The big advantage of these drums is that any type of abrasive material can be cut to fit, although I normally use thin cloth-backed abrasives because they last longest. The cushioning allows the drum to adjust very well to variations in the surface being sanded, with little tendency to bounce and hardly any faceting of curved surfaces. These are the most versatile drums that I have found for use on carvings.

Flap sanders

Flap sanders consist of strips of abrasive attached to a core. They conform fairly well to curved surfaces and don't bounce at all, but some are a bit stiff, especially the smaller ones (Figs 10.12 and 10.13). Their softness and ability to conform to surfaces can be improved still further by removing every other flap and splitting

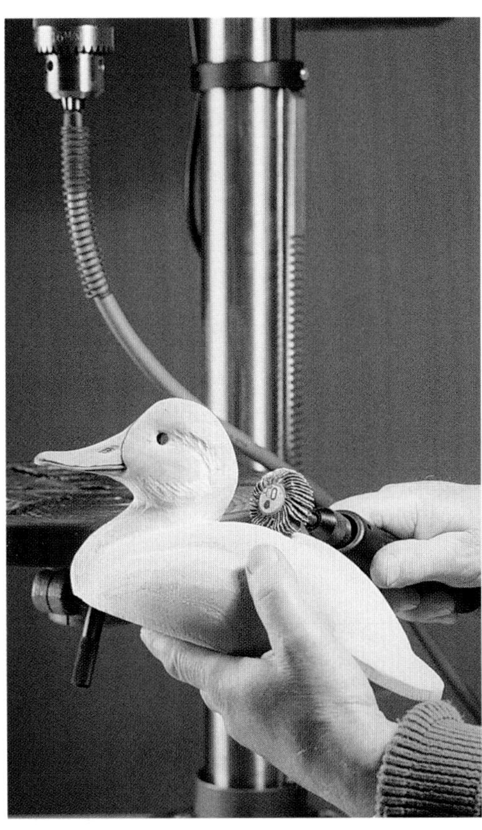

Fig 10.13 *Abrasive flap sanders are useful on carvings with soft curves and no sharp edges.*

the remaining ones into ¼in (6mm) strips. This will allow the sanding of more intricate areas without undue softening of details. Commercial versions made in this style can sometimes be found, but are often hard to source.

Flap sanders are fairly expensive to buy and have a relatively short life, especially when modified as I describe. Some industrial flap sanders are available that have replaceable abrasive strips, and there are some designs which alternate abrasive strips with brushes, but the ones I have seen were intended for the professional and were very expensive for home workshop use. You may also come across flap sanders with the abrasive cloth strips interspersed with non-woven nylon abrasive material.

Non-woven abrasives

Scotchbrite is a familiar product, manufactured by 3M, and used by those of us who wash dirty pots and pans. Most other abrasives companies make similar non-woven nylon abrasive materials, with names such as Hermes Webrax and Norton Bear-Tex. I use this type of material in the form of rotary flap wheels or brushes to finish-sand carvings: the ones I usually use (Fig 10.14) are supplied by Norton Abrasives, or by

Fig 10.14 *Non-woven abrasive wheels can quickly bring a pre-sanded surface to satin smoothness. Some wheels are interleaved with flaps of cloth abrasive.*

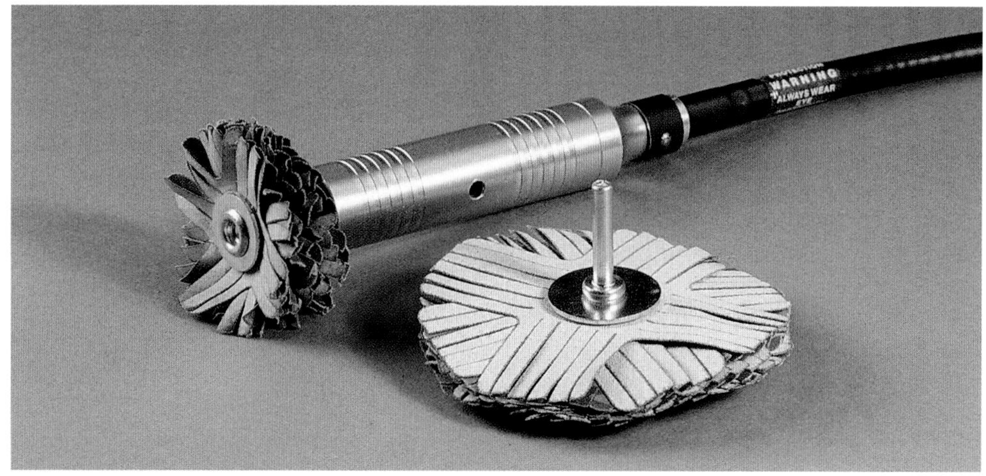

Fig 10.15 *Sanding stars are made from cloth-backed abrasive and will sand complex contours.*

CSM, who sell various industrial abrasive products to the home user. If you pre-sand the surface to about 80 grit first, these wheels will quickly convert it to a silky-smooth finish, conforming well to the surface and details of the carving.

Small 'defuzzing' pads are available in the USA, and they are used extensively by decoy carvers to remove wood fibres from fine texturing. They are simply circles cut from the non-woven sheet material and mounted on a small mandrel. You can easily make your own sander for final smoothing, which will conform extremely well to irregularities in the surface being sanded and give a silky, almost burnished finish. Scotchbrite and similar non-woven abrasive pads are available in several grades, and circles of these can be cut and mounted on a commercial arbor (of the type designed for cutting or grinding wheels) to fit into the chuck of your drill or flexi-shaft.

Sanding star wheels

I found these interesting abrasive mops in the CSM catalogue, tried them, and like them very much. Circles of abrasive slashed into strips are mounted on an arbor, and when they are 'run in' they form a soft, gentle abrasive mop, which works well on carvings and shaped mouldings (Figs 10.15 and 10.16). They are available in up to 600 grit, which is gentle enough for sanding any carving. These wheels, and the non-woven abrasive flap wheels, can save you hours in the sanding of complex carvings.

Fig 10.16 *The action of a fine-grit sanding star is very gentle, and ideal for sanding awkward areas.*

Fig 10.17 Pneumatic sanding drums, like these from Sandboss, are the ultimate in cushioned sanders.

Pneumatic drum sanders

Until I received a small Swedish pneumatic drum sander for review, the only pneumatic drums that I had heard about were very large fixed machines used by makers of hunting decoys in the USA. Small pneumatic drums are now available from two manufacturers: Kirjes, a Swedish company, and Sandboss from the USA (Figs 10.17 and 10.18). Both these brands are available in a variety of sizes, and the sanding sleeve is held in place by an inflated rubber drum. They are simply blown up with a bicycle pump, and the pressure, and hence the drum's firmness, is easily adjusted (Fig 10.19). They are the ultimate in cushioned drums, and the only real drawback is that ready-made

Fig 10.18 (Left) *A large pneumatic sanding drum, in conjunction with an electric drill and bench clamp, can be used for general shaping and sanding, leaving both hands free to manipulate the carving.*

Fig 10.19 (Right) *The firmness of a pneumatic sanding drum is controlled by adjusting the air pressure within the rubber bulb. A bicycle pump supplies the air.*

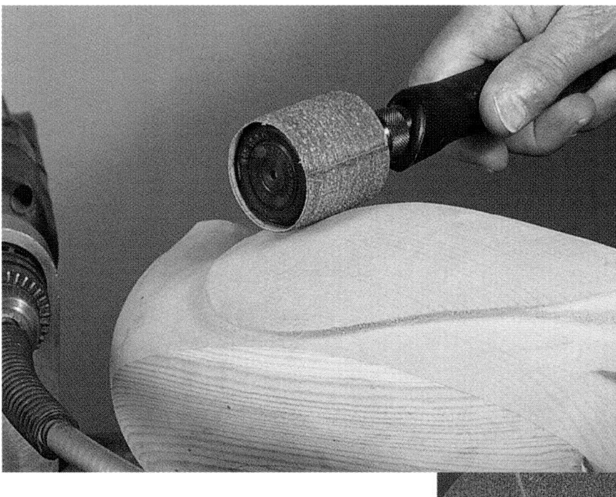

Fig 10.20 *Kirjes make well-engineered pneumatic sanding drums for smaller work.*

Fig 10.21 *Sandboss produce lambswool polishing sleeves for their pneumatic drums, allowing them to impart that final polish to your work.*

sanding sleeves need to be purchased for them. I particularly like the smallest Kirjes drum (Fig 10.20), which I use frequently, although I would have liked it with a 2in (50mm) wide sleeve to give it more reach and better access to carvings, like the small Carroll Tools drums.

Polishing carvings

A drilling machine can also be used to take some of the hard work out of tasks such as buffing up wax. CSM sell car-body compounding sponges to fit drills, or you can fit a backing pad and use a lambswool polishing bonnet. The Sandboss pneumatic sanding drums can be fitted with lambswool sleeves and, with low air pressure in the drum, they will conform well to the surface being polished (Fig 10.21). My favourite tool for buffing up the oil and wax finishes that I tend to use on carvings is a 4in (100mm) diameter soft, natural-bristle brush from Liberon. Wax is applied in the normal way: I use a non-woven abrasive pad which also denibs the surface and doesn't leave bits snagged on the carving as wire wool does. When the wax is dry the brush is run lightly over the surface, bringing it to a deep, rich shine, which I complete by rubbing with a soft cloth. I get lovely results without too much of the traditional elbow grease.

SUPPLIERS INCLUDE:

- CSM
- Norton Abrasives
- Pintail
- Carroll Tools
- Done to a Turn
- Canland
- Clico
- TCL Supplies
- Liberon

Jigsaws and reciprocating saws

The use of a jigsaw (Fig 10.22) is probably limited to preparing blanks for relief carving or laminations for shaped carving blocks. A variant on the jigsaw, sometimes referred to as a 'Sabre' saw, has the blade in line with the motor

Fig 10.22 *The jigsaw has only limited uses for the carver.*

Fig 10.23 *Sabre saws are the larger cousin of the jigsaw.*

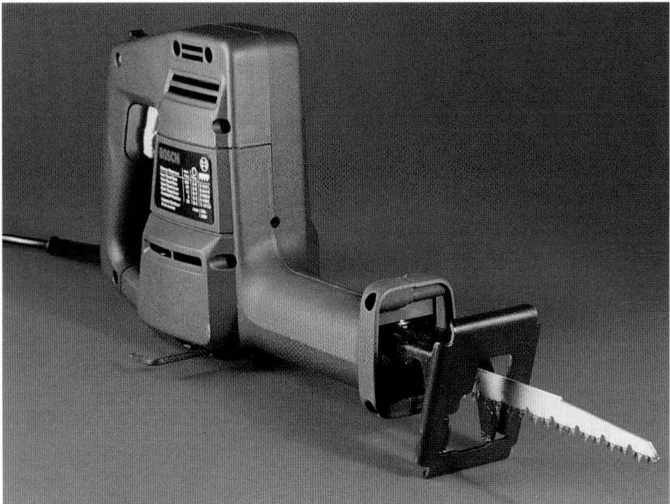

instead of at right angles, and could be used to cut away areas of waste (Fig 10.23). This will take a long blade similar to a padsaw, but I have not found it ideal, and certainly wouldn't suggest getting one especially for carving. If you are not careful when using one, the blade can more or less stand still while the body hammers into the work; although they do have many other uses, such as when you need to do some plumbing.

'Alligator' and similar saws are like giant electric carving knives, with two rather expensive, contra-reciprocating blades (Fig 10.24). They are a safe workshop alternative to a chainsaw for cutting off lengths of thick timber; however, a bow saw is cheaper, and just as fast, if not so accurate. They come into their own for softwood joinery, cutting purlins and floor joists, but are no real substitute for a chainsaw in other circumstances, such as carving or converting large timbers.

Fig 10.24 *Tyrannosaw has contra-moving blades like a bread knife and is a safer bet than a chainsaw for cutting the odd blank, but no substitute for many other chainsaw tasks.*

Reciprocating saw

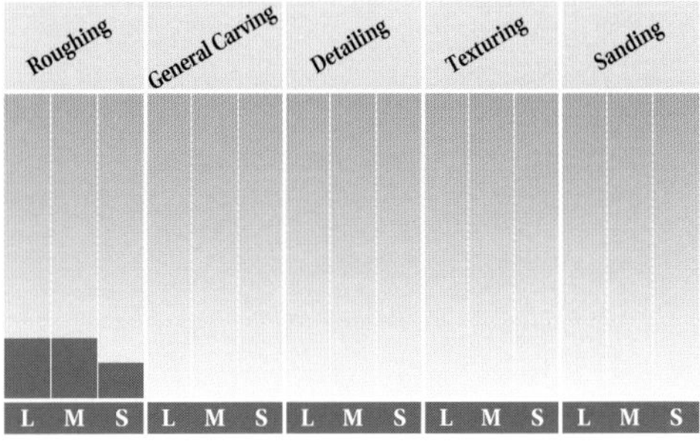

SUPPLIERS INCLUDE:

Bosch
Stayer
Black & Decker
Draper
Metabo
Atlas Copco
Makita

All the major power tool companies make a wide range of reciprocating saws including jigsaws, 'Sabre', 'Shark', 'Alligator', 'Tyrannosaws', etc.

CHAPTER ELEVEN

Fixed Workshop Machines

FIXED workshop machinery can play a very useful part in preparing timber for carvings, and most serious carvers will eventually acquire at least a bandsaw, probably the most versatile workshop machine for preparing carving blanks. Other non-portable workshop machines can also be put to use for various carving tasks, and although perhaps not considered essential to the woodcarver, if you already own them they may as well earn their keep. The bandsaw is probably the most useful machine tool for the carving workshop, but I also put my pillar drill, belt and disc sander, and planer-thicknesser to good use. Other fixed machines are of less general use, although some may find them useful for particular applications. Copy-carving machines are really the province of the commercial woodcarver – although when two members of your family both have their eyes on your latest carving with a view to adorning their mantelpiece with it, it would be very nice to own one!

Surface planers and planer-thicknessers

Although the planer or planer-thicknesser (Fig 11.1) cannot in any sense be judged a carving tool, it is a great asset to start work with an accurate, square-edged blank. This is particularly necessary if you are going to use a machine to remove the initial waste from the blank, using for instance a drill, circular saw, or bandsaw. Bandsawing the top and side profiles of a pattern from the block will only give accurate, undistorted results if the faces of the blank are truly at right angles to

Fig 11.1 *A typical workshop planer-thicknesser.*

SUPPLIERS INCLUDE:

Record Power
Elu
Kity
Sheppach
Sedgwick
Axminster Power Tools

begin with. Planing up your stock before carving also enables you to see the grain and figure in the timber, as well as making faults easier to spot. You can then more easily plan how your carving will fit on the blank to its best advantage.

If you need to laminate timber to produce large carving blocks, then the accurate, well-finished flat surface provided by a planer is essential if your glue lines are to be almost invisible on the finished work.

To get good square blocks, make sure that the side fence is set at a true right angle to the machining table before you start. Then plane two adjacent sides, using the side fence to ensure that the second side is at right angles to the first (Fig 11.2). If you have a thicknesser, use this to finish the other two sides; this is more accurate than trying to use the planer, which may give you a tapered blank, even though the faces are at right angles.

Safety

Make sure that the blades are sharp and correctly set, and that the cutter-block guard is adjusted to suit the width of the workpiece.

Never pass your hand over the cutter block, even with the guards in place: feed from one side to the other and use a wood or plastic push-stick.

Planer-thicknesser

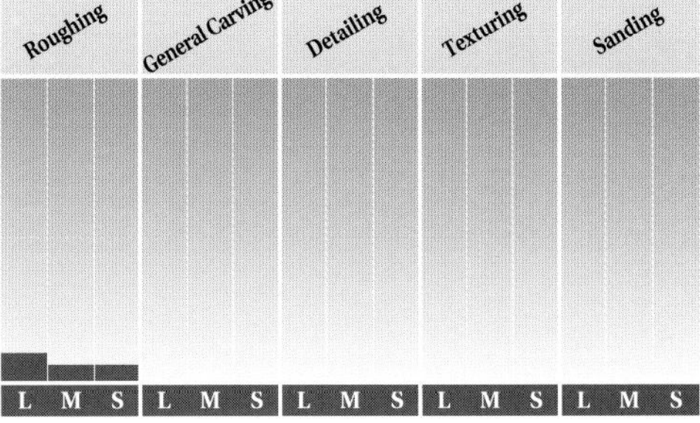

Fig 11.2 Squaring two adjacent edges of a blank before marking out and profiling on the bandsaw leads to much greater accuracy.

Bandsaws

Probably the most useful multi-purpose fixed workshop machine for the carver, once acquired it will find countless tasks around the workshop. I wonder how I managed without one – it saves me much time and energy, and when treated with respect it is probably the safest powered saw in common workshop use. Unlike some other machines, they are not liable to throw work across the room or drag you towards the blade; but extra care does need to be exercised when cutting uneven-shaped timber, and push sticks should still be used when working near the blade. Although relatively safe in use, bandsaws are not without some problems: blades are particularly slow to change and they can break unexpectedly, leaving you with a half-cut blank and no spare.

Bandsaws are available in two styles: two-wheel and three-wheel. The three-wheel models tend to be the smaller and

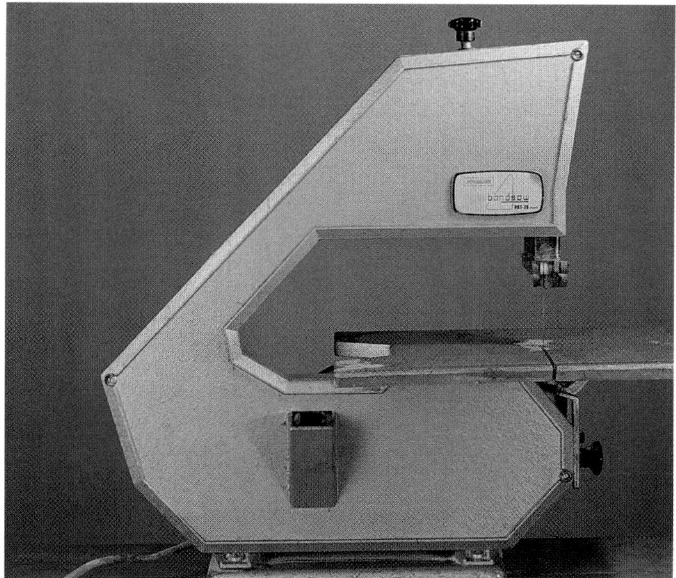

Fig 11.3 *A small three-wheel bandsaw. This was the first fixed workshop machine I bought, many years ago.*

Fig 11.4 *The three-wheel design gives the bandsaw a large throat, similar to that of a big two-wheel machine, but the depth of cut and available power of most such machines severely limits their usefulness.*

lighter of the two. The three-wheel design allows for a larger cutting width between the blade and the upright support of the machine's body, which is useful on small saws (Figs 11.3 and 11.4). Most three-wheel machines only give a cutting depth of 3–4in (75–100mm), although there are exceptions. Draper/EMCO produce an interesting-looking 'Swing' model with a 6¼in (160mm) depth of cut and an in-built 8in (200mm) sanding disc; and Inca produce the Expert 500 with a 7½in (192mm) depth of cut and large 20in (505mm) throat.

The smaller three-wheel models seem to be more prone to blade breakage than two-wheel machines. This could be due to the smaller wheel diameter causing more flexing and metal fatigue in the blade and its butt-welded joint, or to the quality of the necessarily thinner blade material, which often seems to be inferior to that used on two-wheel machines.

Besides accepting heavier, more rigid blades, two-wheel machines (Figs 11.5 and 11.6) generally have a much greater depth of cut than is available on three-

Fig 11.5 *A typical two-wheel workshop bandsaw, with a cutting depth of around 8in (200mm) and about a 12in (305mm) throat.*

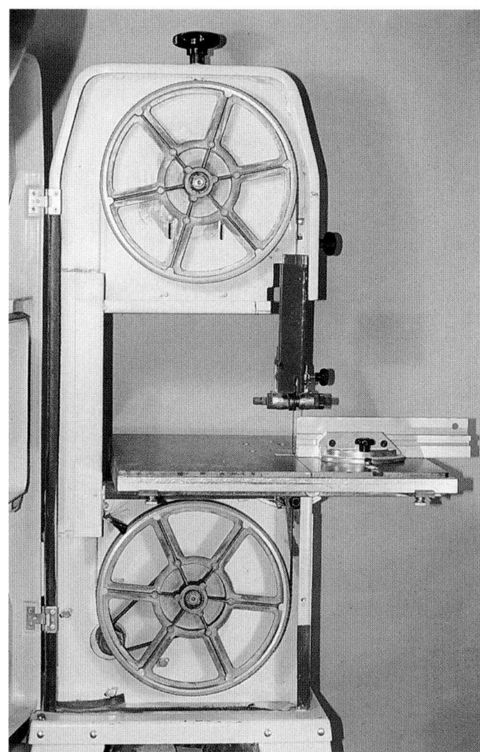

Fig 11.6 The large wheels of the two-wheel bandsaw give it a usefully wide throat.

wheel models. Most have cutting depths of 6in (150mm) or more, making them eminently suitable for the woodcarver's use. In my workshop I have used an 8in (200mm) Kity machine and a Far Eastern Multico machine, very similar to the Axminster Power Tools BS350CE. Both of these I found to be quite satisfactory for most carvings, although I sometimes wish for a 12in (305mm) model. Unfortunately, above an 8in depth of cut, the prices of machines rise very steeply, so unless you really need that extra cutting depth or can find a rare secondhand machine, a 6 or 8in machine is your most likely purchase. I think a 6in is the minimum you should contemplate, and an 8in machine would probably cover the work undertaken by most carvers – with careful planning, and some lamination of the carving blanks, I manage to carve full-size swans!

Timber conversion

The bandsaw's first use is to convert rough timber into square-edged carving blanks. Unless your carvings are always going to be small, it is advantageous to own as big a machine as you can afford (and fit in your workshop!) for timber conversion, and this is where I often wish for a 12in machine. Handling deep cuts in hard timbers requires a powerful motor and a sharp blade of suitable type. For rough-cutting timber and preparing blanks, a wide, heavy blade with large teeth that give plenty of swarf clearance is necessary. Without this, the blade will tend to 'run off' during the cut, leading to blanks with wavy sides that require planing.

I use a ¾in (19mm) wide skip-tooth blade with only 4 teeth to the inch (25mm) when preparing rough timber. These heavy blades are large enough for you to be able to extend their lives by sharpening and setting the teeth. I leave the blade on the machine and use a small low-voltage mini-grinder with a grinding or sanding wheel to sharpen the teeth, and an ordinary Eclipse-style saw-setting tool.

Profiling

The most important use of the bandsaw in actual carving is for the profiling of carving blanks. If you meticulously plan your carvings – creating drawings from various viewpoints, making maquettes, or working from published plans – then the bandsaw is probably the most important power tool you could add to your workshop. It will enable you to profile your carving blank accurately, removing a lot of the waste wood. You can accurately cut out both the side and top profiles from a well-squared carving

Figs 11.7–11.9 *Stages in profiling a carving blank on the bandsaw.*

blank, establishing the maximum extent of the carving's profile at the start (Figs 11.7–11.10). The table can then be tilted and further waste removed from the corners too, saving much time in roughing out the carving. Of course, the large blade used for preparing blanks is not very suitable for profile cutting as it will not negotiate tight curves. The best all-round blade that I have found for accurate profiling is a ¼in (6mm) wide skip-tooth blade with 6 teeth per inch (25mm). This will manage to negotiate

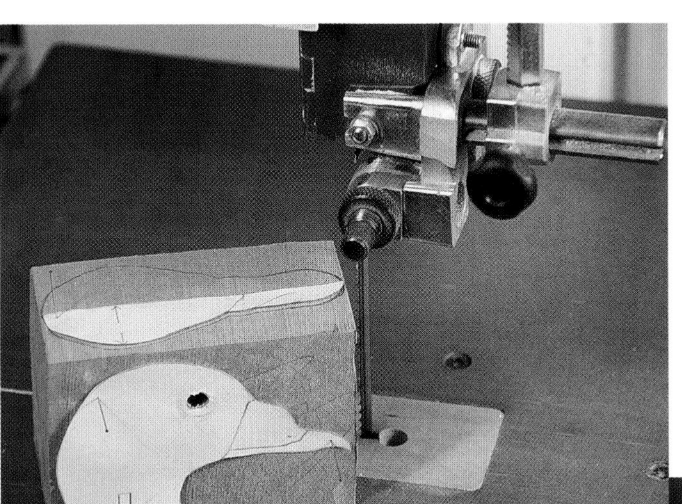

Fig 11.7 (Above)
Mark out the side and top profiles on a previously squared block of wood.

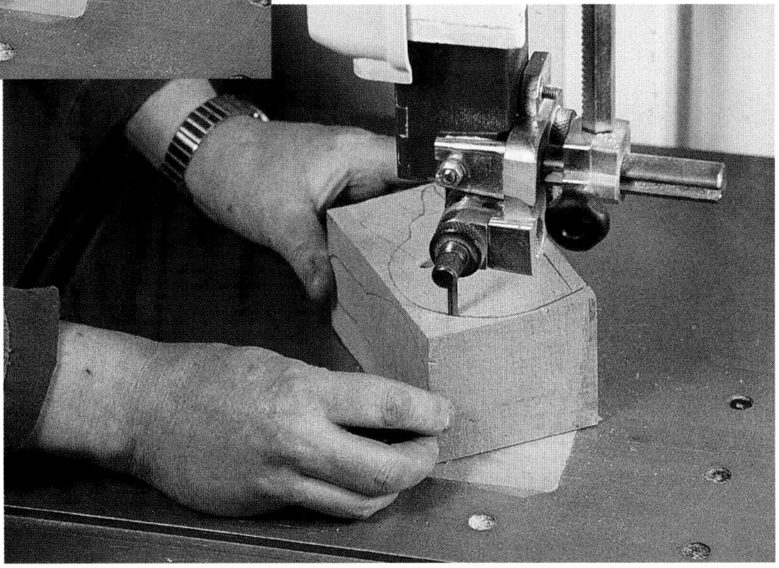

Fig 11.8 (Right)
Cut out the side profile, keeping the waste as intact as possible.

Fig 11.9
Reassemble the block with the waste pieces from the side profile before cutting the top profile.

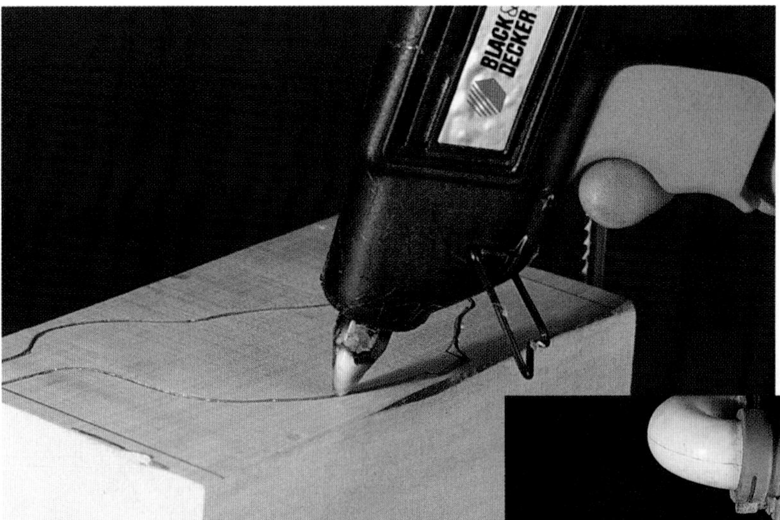

Fig 11.10 *To keep the reassembled block together while cutting, you can use tape or spots of hot-melt glue. The hot-melt glue gun is indispensable around the workshop for tacking things together and making temporary jigs and fixtures.*

quite tight bends, whilst still achieving a fairly accurate vertical cut. Accurately set blade guides and very sharp blades are needed, and the upper blade guide needs to be adjusted so that it just clears the top of the work, to give maximum support to the blade and safety to the operator.

I find the profiling blades cannot be satisfactorily sharpened, and on some timbers they can have a short life. Blades can be bought ready-made, but if you use quite a lot this can prove fairly expensive. The cheapest way is to purchase a 100ft coil of ¼in x 6tpi blade and make your own (Fig 11.11). In a couple of hours you

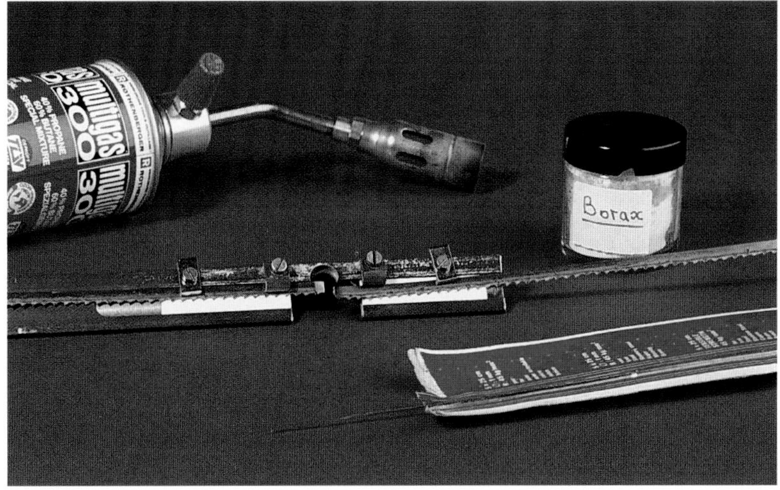

Fig 11.11 *Making or repairing bandsaw blades requires only a small range of equipment.*

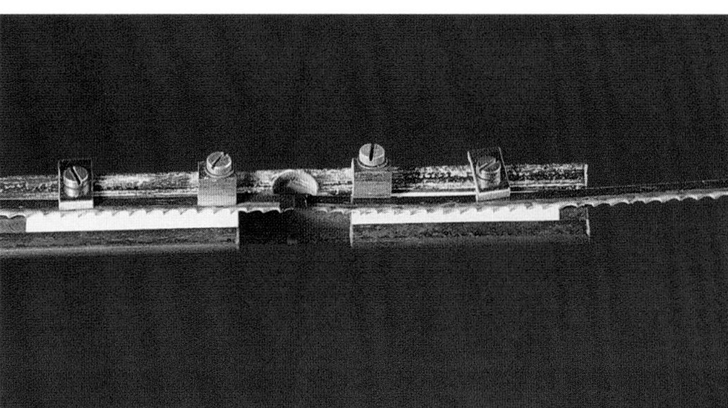

Fig 11.12 *A home-made jig to align the ends of the bandsaw blade.*

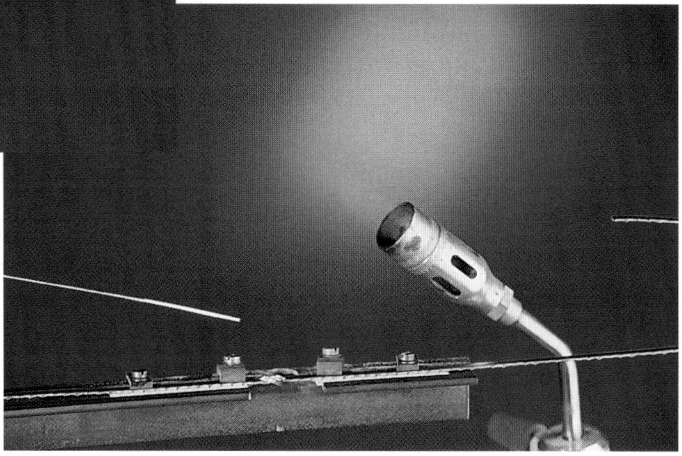

can produce a dozen blades, using a home-made or commercial jig (such as that supplied by BriMarc Associates), a gas blowtorch, and some silver solder (Figs 11.12 and 11.13).

Fig 11.13 *The blade ends are silver-soldered together, before allowing the joint to cool and cleaning it up.*

Blade breakages

Blades do break, but the occurrence can be minimized on all machines with a little care; to help diagnose problems, the most probable causes are listed here:

1. blade tension – too little or too much;
2. poorly dressed and levelled blade joints;
3. joint not properly welded (commercial) or soldered (homemade);
4. blunt blade, necessitating too much force to make it cut;
5. forcing the blade – usually a blunt blade, wet wood, or wrong type of blade;
6. blade jamming – not enough clearance, wrong blade type, or blunt;
7. badly adjusted guides, allowing blade to twist;
8. top guide not adjusted, leaving the blade unsupported above the work and dangerously exposed;
9. backing out of a cut, trapping the blade or pulling it out of the guides.

Limitations on curve cutting

There is a wide range of blade widths, tooth counts, and form variations available, but as blades take quite a long time to change most users stick to one favourite combination.

The blade width determines the minimum radius of curve that can be cut continuously without jamming and, to some extent, the accuracy of the cut (wide blades are much less prone to wander when cutting thick material). The tooth pitch and form determine the finish of the cut, but can also affect the accuracy if the sawdust is not removed fast enough to suit the feed rate. I use the ¼in skip-tooth, 6tpi blades for just about everything, only changing blades when really necessary for accuracy of cut or blade strength. It is a good general-purpose blank-cutting blade, which will allow cutting of quite tight curves. The blade width determines the minimum radius of continuous cutting, but of course it is possible to keep carefully backing the blade out to create more clearance, and negotiate tighter curves in a series of tangential cuts. This is all right for just the occasional tight curve, but it is difficult to cut accurately this way, and backing out of cuts can pull the blade out of the guides, increasing the risk of breakages.

I sometimes lubricate the blade by rubbing a candle against it when cutting tight curves, especially in damp or resinous timber, which tends to grab the blade. A small wooden wedge is kept by the machine and can be slipped into the cut to stop any tendency for it to close up and trap the blade. Rounding the back corners of the blade has been suggested as an aid to negotiating tight curves, but I have found it makes little difference.

Aside from the possibility of cutting tight curves as a series of short tangential cuts, the minimum *continuous* radius that can be cut with various widths of bandsaw blade is as follows:

Blade width		Minimum radius	
in	mm	in	mm
¼	6	¾	19
⅜	10	1½	38
½	13	2¼	57
⅝	16	3	76

Blade tension

Blade tension is important for accurate cutting; some stretching of the blade and settling of the machine under tension is bound to occur when a new blade is fitted, and this necessitates retensioning. It is often said that bandsaw blades should not be left tensioned for long idle periods, but should have the tension removed and then be retensioned before use. This is supposed to help keep the blade running true, but I leave my blades tensioned all the time and have noticed no problems. So, although initial retensioning of new blades is occasionally required, I think it is probably unnecessary, assuming the machine is well built and stable, to remove the tension when the machine is out of use. To do so will probably lead to variations in performance due to differing blade tensions being achieved each time.

Bandsaw

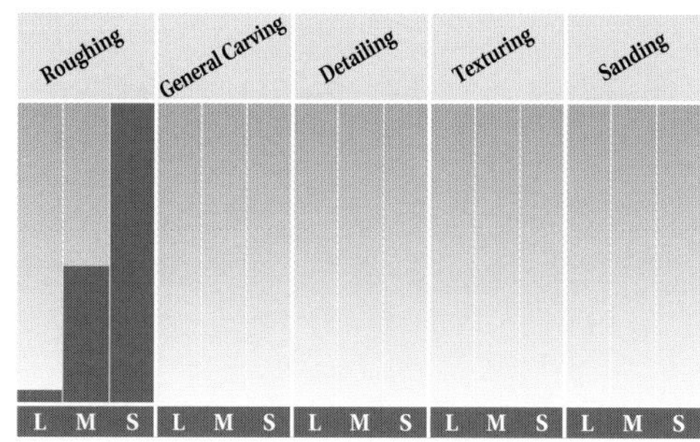

Maintaining an accurate cut depends not only upon blade tension, but on various other factors such as the sharpness and set of the teeth. An old saw-setter's handbook suggests that there are so many variables affecting the working of the bandsaw blades that tension should be 'just enough to enable the saw to cut straight'. You can't really argue with that!

Safety

Bandsaws are amongst the safest fixed machines to use, as the cutting action tends to hold the work firmly down on the table. However, when cutting blanks from logs, it is important that you prevent the timber from being snatched and turned by the downward pressure of the blade. This dangerous occurrence can kink or break the saw blade, but more importantly it can drag unwary fingers into the blade. Larger

Fig 11.14 *Converting the log to a usable blank. Scrap wood has been screwed to a waste area to stabilize the log while cutting, making the operation much safer.*

logs could be planed, or even split, to provide a flat surface, but another alternative is to temporarily nail or screw a piece of timber to the side of the log while you safely make the first cut to provide a flat surface for subsequent cuts (Fig 11.14).

When profile-cutting in two directions, reassemble the waste pieces from the first cut to support the blank while you make the second profiling cut. You can use spots of hot-melt glue or adhesive tape to help hold the block back together (see Fig 11.10 on page 97).

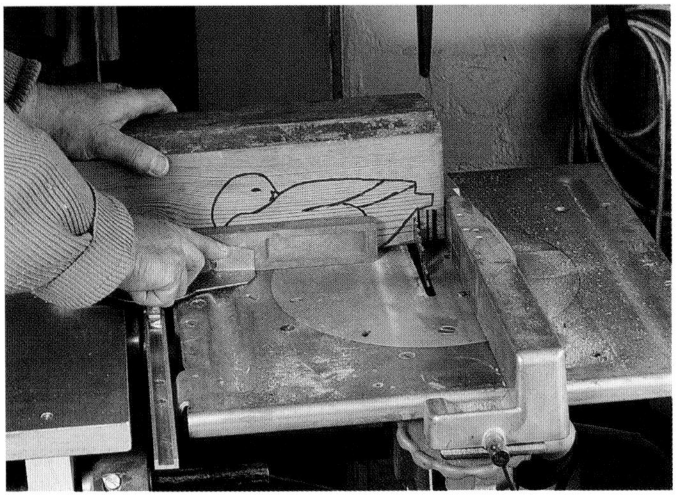

Fig 11.15 *A typical workshop sawbench.*

Make sure you set the top blade guide correctly: it should just clear the top of the work being cut. Always use wooden or plastic push sticks when working near the blade. The whirring wheels and blade of a bandsaw blow dust everywhere, so make sure the machine is connected to a working dust extractor to minimize this, and wear a dust mask as well.

Choosing a bandsaw

The rigidity of the machine's construction, the accuracy and degree of support given by the top and bottom blade guides, and the power of the motor are the three important areas to consider when choosing a bandsaw. If the body construction is not rigid and the guides are not accurate and correctly aligned, a bandsaw is unlikely to cut accurately with the thinner blades necessary for profiling. Add a blunt blade to a poor machine, and you are going to lose all the real advantages that using a bandsaw should bring.

Most manufacturers and importers of fixed woodworking machines include bandsaws in their ranges, so there are plenty to choose from. Unless you are only going to undertake small carvings, buy the biggest, best-constructed machine you can afford.

Circular saws

Although it is of very limited use in woodcarving, if you are by nature a methodical person then you can use a sawbench (Fig 11.15) to prepare a carving blank and to remove quite a lot of the

SUPPLIERS INCLUDE:

Elektra Beckum
Elu
Kity
NMA (Agencies) (Scheppach)
Startright
Rexon
Record Power
Draper
Axminster Power Tools

Blades, ready made-up or in rolls, are available from most large tool shops, and BriMarc Associates distribute a simple brazing-jig kit.

Fig 11.16 *Using a sawbench to remove waste in the early stages of carving. Great care must be taken, as a top guard cannot be used for this operation. A hold-down clamp or hold-down fingers should be used, positioned above the saw blade to provide some protection (these have been removed for clarity in Figs 11.15 and 11.16, but a home-made alternative is shown in Fig 11.17). Leave plenty of waste wood on the blank to keep it sitting solidly on the saw table, and don't work with very small blanks. The depth of cut of the saw blade is adjusted for each pass, and 'feathers' are left between the cuts for support, the waste being broken or cut off later.*

waste timber. It is a relatively slow process requiring great care, and it is essential that you use an accurately squared block of wood to begin with, just as it is when using the bandsaw.

Transfer the side and top profiles of your pattern to the block, then, by adjusting the depth of cut and the position of the side fence, make a series of cuts in the face of the block, up to the marked profile. By adjusting the side fence by twice the kerf or cutting width of the blade each time, and adjusting the cutting depth for each cut, the timber can be removed fairly accurately to the profile (Fig 11.16). The block can then be turned at right angles and the process repeated for the second profile. Leave supporting pieces at the ends of the block, and then you can remove some of the intermediate supporting 'fins' as you go. Alternatively, as the supporting wooden fins are only a saw blade's width (about ⅛in (3mm)), they are easily broken off or carved away afterwards. The result, once you have removed all the support fins, is very similar to that of using the bandsaw except for the slightly stepped surface.

The size of block you can prepare, and just how much of the waste you can remove by this method, depends upon the

Circular saw

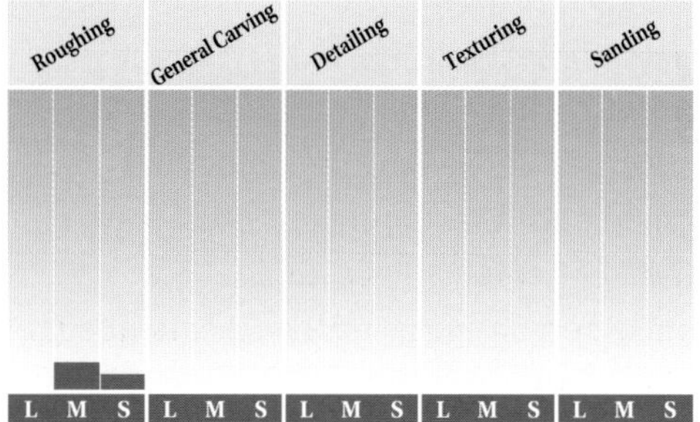

depth of cut of the sawbench. Sawbenches are available in a very wide variety of benchtop and free-standing styles with various capacities.

Safety

Great care should be taken when grooving on a sawbench, as the top guard has to be removed on most machines (those with riving-knife-mounted guards) to allow the timber to pass over the blade. If your saw has the facility to take a hold-down shoe, then fit one, as this will cover the top of the blade. Mine has sprung hold-down clamps, which were removed for clarity in Figs 11.15 and 11.16. If yours hasn't, make a flat plate guard to mount on the fence, which will cover the top of the blade whilst allowing the blank, but not your hand, to

SUPPLIERS INCLUDE:

Elektra Beckum
Elu
NMA (Agencies) (Sheppach)
Kity
Clarke
Draper
Startrite
Sedgewick
Al-Ko
Axminster Power Tools

Fig 11.17 A makeshift top guard to cover the blade on a saw bench when grooving; this is a necessary addition if hold-down clamps are not available.

pass underneath (Fig 11.17). Use the mitre-cutting guide to keep the blank square when feeding the timber past the blade. Don't try to prepare small blanks by this method.

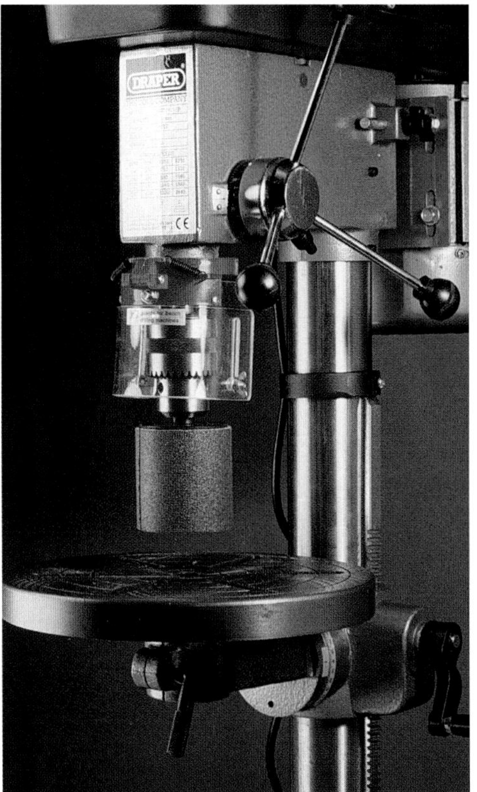

Fig 11.18 *A pillar drill is a useful workshop machine; it is seen here fitted with a Carroll Tools sanding drum.*

Pillar drills

These are very useful workshop tools: a pillar drill (Fig 11.18) can be put to use removing a lot of the waste from a squared block of wood, in much the same way as the circular saw or bandsaw. Again you will need to leave substantial ends to support the block, and possibly one or more intermediate fins too. The timber should be clamped whilst drilling, and using a saw-tooth machine bit will allow overlapping holes to be drilled. The method is not as tidy as using a saw, and you must make allowance for the centre 'pip' of the drill. Forstner bits, sharp flat bits, and the latest 3D wood bits are all suitable for drilling away waste material.

If you have prepared a maquette for your carving, a variation of this system will allow you to remove waste from the squared block and create a contoured surface which cannot be produced with the saws. Again this is a method suitable for the more meticulous carver, as a whole series of accurate measurements has to be taken (Fig 11.19). A suitably sized grid is drawn on the surface of the square-edged wooden blank. The maquette is temporarily attached to a square base of

Fig 11.19 *Using a try square to take measurements from a maquette. The base in this case is marked with ½in (13mm) squares.*

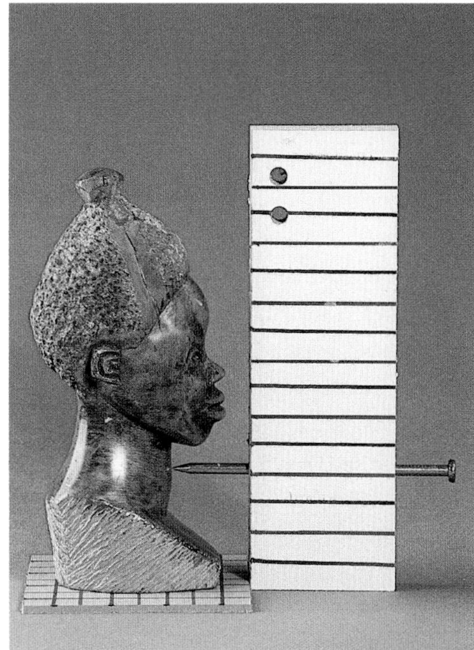

Fig 11.20 *This simple pointing device is drilled through at ½in (13mm) intervals, and the pointer is a 6in (150mm) nail.*

the same dimensions as the wooden block, forming a datum block. The edges of this block are marked in the same increments as the grid. A try square with a blade longer than the maquette is tall, also marked in the same increments as the grid, is offered up to the edge of the datum block. Measurements can now be taken at all intersecting points of the grid, from the edge of the try square to the maquette. The measurements can then be used to set the drilling depth of a series of small-diameter holes at each grid intersection. The waste timber between the holes is then removed using any suitable method, until the bottoms of all the drilled holes are joined up to form the basic contoured surface of the carving. An alternative to the try square is the home-made pointing device shown in Fig 11.20.

Pillar drills are also valuable when used with sanding drums, either as a fixed bobbin sander using a pneumatic or foam-cushioned drum, or in conjunction with a flexible shaft and various sanding attachments (Fig 11.21).

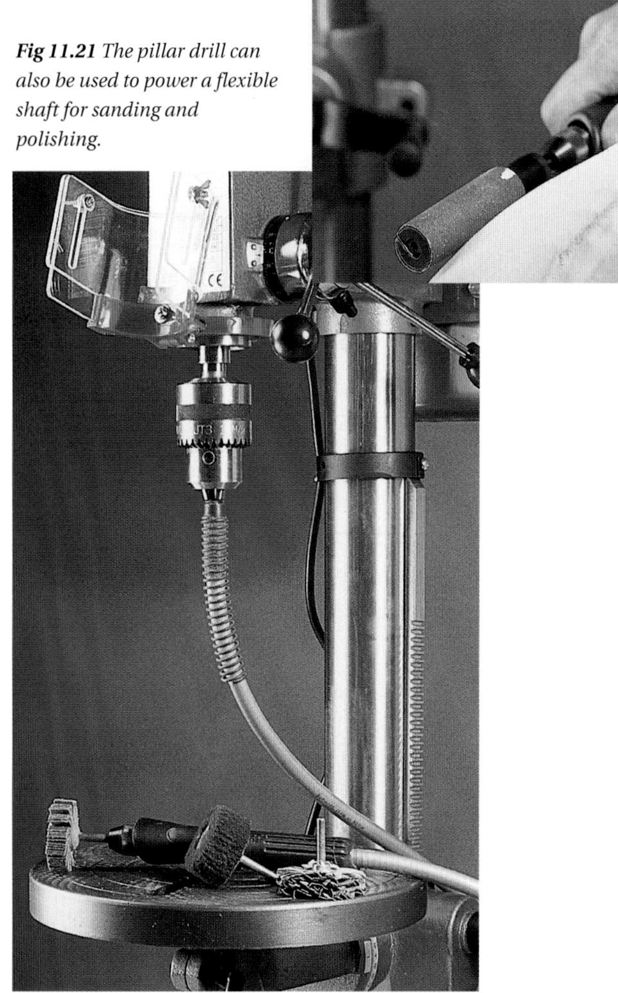

Fig 11.21 *The pillar drill can also be used to power a flexible shaft for sanding and polishing.*

Flexible-shaft drives are more versatile, relatively cheap, and can be used with a variety of small sanding devices. The relatively slow speeds available on pillar drills are ideal for sanding – in most cases they work much better than a high-speed flexible-shaft carving machine, where it is easy to run the sanding drum at too high a speed.

There is a wide variety of suitable sanding drums available (see pages 85–6 and 89–90), but the important point to watch is that the abrasive is cushioned. Drums which use rigid card sanding sleeves do not sand surfaces smooth, but skip over the surface and cause dents. They may be cheap to buy, but the finish you can obtain on carvings with rigid sanding drums is very poor, and their best use is for carving shapes rather than sanding smooth. I have a preference for two types: one is the pneumatic sanding drums, particularly the Swedish Kirjes drums, or the Canadian Sandboss pneumatic drums, which are not quite as well built but a little cheaper. The Sandboss range includes a large 4000 model, 5⅜in diameter x 11⅝in (137 x 295mm), which can be very useful when fitted to a lathe or pillar drill, leaving both hands free to manipulate the work. The other drums I particularly like are Carroll Tools' well-engineered range of cushioned sanding drums, which, unlike the pneumatic models, do not need expensive ready-made sanding sleeves. The Carroll sanders lock the abrasive on to the rubber-cushioned drum using a specially shaped key, so you can economically cut the abrasive from any of the wide range of abrasive papers and cloths available. They produce a wide range of drum sizes, from ½in (13mm) diameter to large units designed to fit spindle moulders.

Sanding is one area where flexible shafts of the rather stiff type intended for electric drills can be successfully used, as high speeds are unnecessary and even undesirable when sanding.

Pillar drill (with flexible shaft)

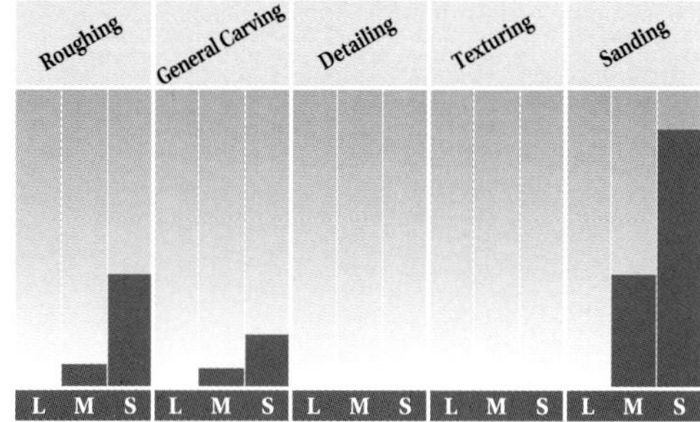

Safety

Clamp blocks of wood securely when drilling holes; a variety of vices and clamps is available, or you can construct your own. Don't hand-hold small pieces, as they can be easily ripped from your grasp, damaging your hands. The motors are powerful, so when using flexi-shafts, only fit the shaft finger-tight in the machine's chuck; it will then slip if you jam or snag the shaft. This particular tip stems from a frightening experience I had many years ago, from which I was lucky enough to walk away unscathed. I snagged the tool on my overalls, the flexible shaft tied itself in a knot, and I didn't dare let go my grip. Fortunately I hit the power-off button quickly, and the machine stopped before any serious damage was done to me. The flexible shaft was a write-off – so make sure your power switch is easily accessible, or better still have an auxiliary foot switch fitted in the feed to an NVR switch on the machine (see page 13).

When sanding, especially with larger drums, check the maximum speed recommended for the drum you are using and don't exceed it. Again, flexible shafts should only be fitted finger-tight when

SUPPLIERS INCLUDE:

Draper
Rexon
Record Power
Axminster Power Tools
Done to a Turn
Canland (Sandboss)
CSM
Carroll Tools

sanding, to allow the shaft to slip in the drill chuck if it snags.

Choosing a pillar drill

Drilling machines are very useful workshop tools and are available in a wide variety of sizes and specifications. I particularly like the Record machines, which, although lacking in one or two features found on imported machines, are well-made and solid.

Workshop sanders

Fixed sanding machines (Fig 11.22) can be used to pre-shape carvings, and are especially effective when fitted with very aggressive abrasives in the 24–40 grit range. Sanders are often found as combination machines, with both disc and belt sanders run from a single motor. These are useful general-purpose workshop machines which are relatively inexpensive. They can be used to 'knock the corners off' carvings, quickly removing waste material. Sanding is usually carried out using the section of belt between the two crowned (barrel-shaped) wheels, which is often supported by a table. If the table can be removed or dropped away, you can use this part of the belt to round corners off rather than create flats, and generally perform more shaping tasks.

Some belt sanders enable you to sand against the non-driven idler wheel, enabling concave surfaces to be reached too. This style of sanding is especially catered for in a new style of belt sander which has made an appearance in the USA, the contact roll sander. Here the undriven roller is interchangeable for different sizes, and is made from rubber. The sanding is done using this roller-supported area of the belt, which is not enclosed in any way, rather than the middle of the belt between the rolls; the effect is similar to using the tip of a large power file.

In the USA, large, motorized pneumatic sanding drums are available, which are popular with many commercial carvers of items such as decoys (Fig 11.23). I haven't come across these in the UK, but with a

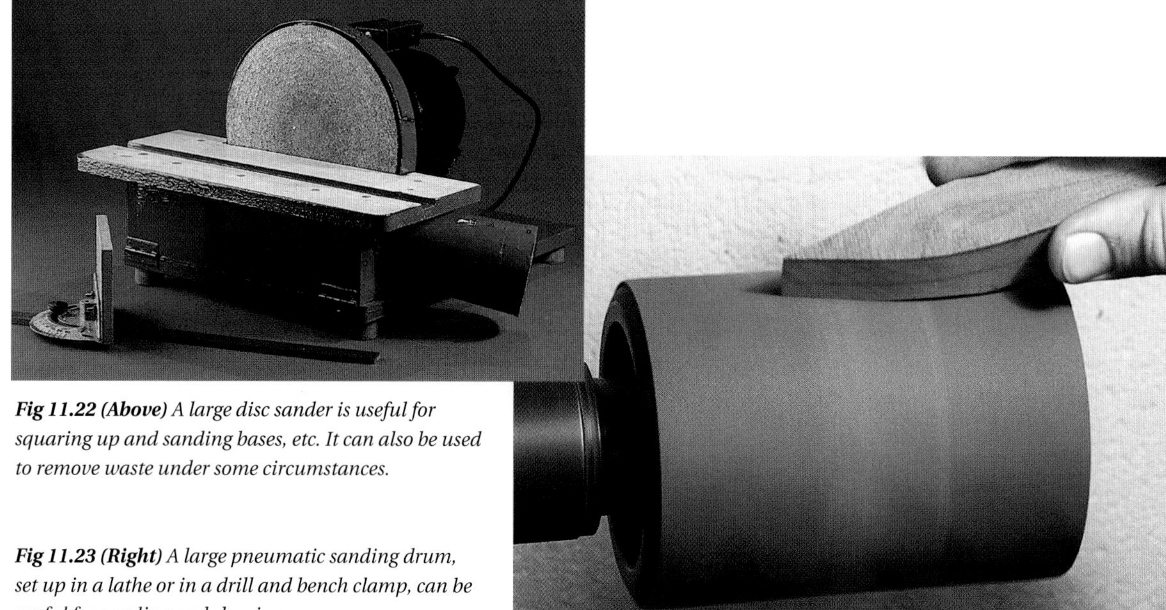

Fig 11.22 (Above) *A large disc sander is useful for squaring up and sanding bases, etc. It can also be used to remove waste under some circumstances.*

Fig 11.23 (Right) *A large pneumatic sanding drum, set up in a lathe or in a drill and bench clamp, can be useful for sanding and shaping.*

SUPPLIERS INCLUDE:

Axminster Power Tools
Picador
Sand-Rite
Woodcraft
Delta
Roto/Carve (Multi-Carver contact roll sander)

Disc and belt sander

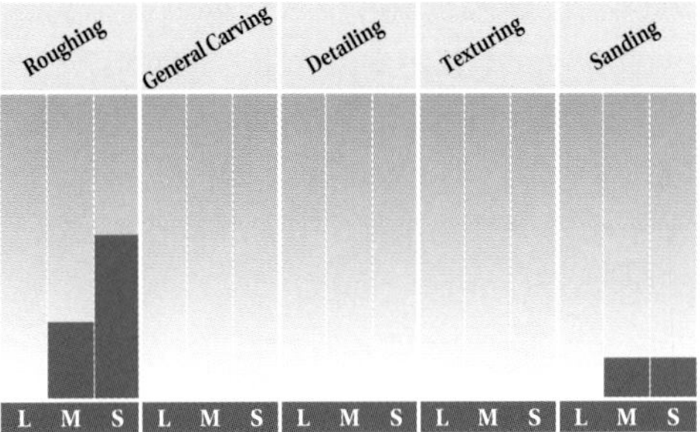

little ingenuity, and possibly some parts from Picador, you can fix the larger Sandboss pneumatic sanding drum on a totally enclosed ¼ or ⅓hp motor to make a similar machine. The American company Woodcraft Supplies have a 3in diameter by 8in long (75 x 200mm) pneumatic drum in their catalogue, which is intended to be fitted horizontally in a lathe or, with a special adapter, vertically in a drill press. Very large pneumatic-drum sanding machines are available from another US company, Sand-Rite. They manufacture a range of drums with diameters from 2 to 8in (50–200mm).

Safety

Sanders require dust extraction, *and* you should always wear respiratory protection too. Although they are relatively safe to use, make sure you hold the work firmly so that the sander cannot snatch workpieces from your grip and hurl them across the workshop. With disc sanders, only use the half of the disc that is travelling *down* toward the table. When using large sanding discs, make sure the machine cannot slam the work on to the table with your fingers trapped underneath.

Copy-carving and sign-making machines

There are several machines on the market which can be used in the small workshop to reproduce a master carving. Most use a router motor directly linked to a stylus, which traces over the surface of the master pattern. The stylus and router are supported on some form of pantograph arrangement which allows movement of the cutter head, and the stylus is manually guided over the master pattern (Fig 11.24). Roughing cuts are taken first, and then smaller cutters and matching styli are used to create a near-finished carving.

Some copying machines, such as the Marlin, Kimball, and Micom Re-Peter Mk 5, are really intended as two-dimensional copy-routing and sign-carving machines. However, they could be used for low-relief carving, though it might require a little ingenuity. These sign-carvers are very similar to engraving machines in operation, with the motor and a stylus follower mounted on an arm, either on

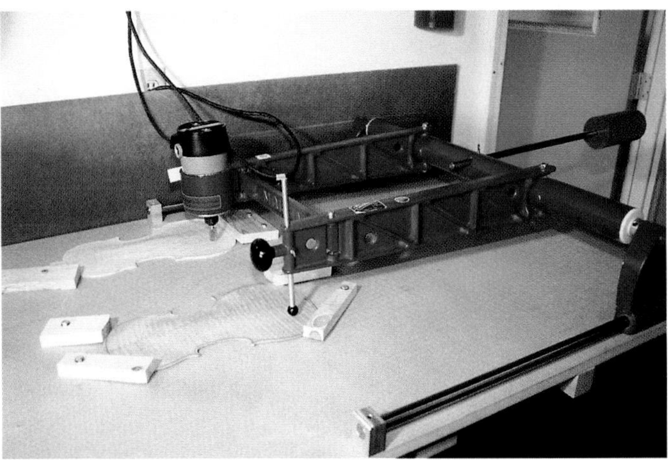

Fig 11.24 *Sign-carving machine being used to contour a musical instrument back. (Photo by courtesy of Terrco)*

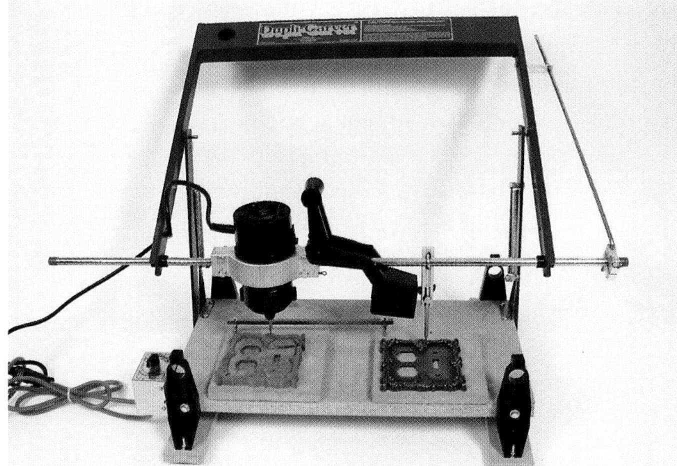

Fig 11.25 Dupli-Carver copying a shallow relief. (Photo by courtesy of Terrco)

Fig 11.26 Dupli-Carver copying a small bust. (Photo by courtesy of Terrco)

a pantograph like an engraving machine, or on *x*- and *y*-axis runners. Trend sell a well-built sign-carver attachment which will accept a portable router.

Other machines, like the well known Dupli-Carver, the Micom Re-Peter Mk 3, and the Wivamac, are capable of more complex three-dimensional carvings. The design of the Dupli-Carver (Figs 11.25 and 11.26) enables intricate undercutting operations to be performed, as the cutting head and stylus are capable of rotation as well as *x*-, *y*-, and *z*-axis movement, making it the most capable copying machine that I know of – even if it is not the most substantially constructed. For the UK market Rod Naylor modifies these machines and supplies them with a powerful and yet relatively quiet, UK-voltage, professional die grinder, making them suitable for the hardest-working professional workshops (Fig 11.27).

Another style of copy-carving machine uses a circular-saw-type blade to remove the waste. These have a long history, and have been in use since the nineteenth century for such jobs as gunstock blanks, clog soles, and decoys. They tend to work faster, but are not capable of producing the same level of detail as the router-head carvers. An American company produces a model which will fit to an existing 10in (255mm) circular saw bench, called the Roto/Carve. It looks interesting, with an

Fig 11.27 A Dupli-Carver being used with an angle grinder and carving disc to rough out a carving from a master pattern. (Photo by courtesy of Rod Naylor)

SUPPLIERS INCLUDE:

Rod Naylor
Micom
Roto/Carve
Terrco
Hamlin Holdings Ltd
Willy Vanhoutte

action more like that of a copy-turning lathe than other copy-carvers. Because of the way it works it is very suitable for producing long, slender carvings, and is able to create work up to 54in (1370mm) long; however, I have never seen one in the flesh. The company also produces a specially profiled cutting blade for the sawbench; this almost eliminates the stepped finish which usually results from using a saw blade, leaving much less final sanding and cleaning up to do. This type of machine would be useful for the repetitive manufacture of relatively simple shapes like decoy ducks, and especially elongated items such as gunstocks, spindles, etc., which have little in the way of projections.

Copy-carving machines are all relatively expensive and take up a fair amount of workshop space, so they are only really a worthwhile purchase for those who want to produce multiple copies of carvings to sell commercially, or who have to reproduce existing work very accurately.

All the machines mentioned above produce only one copy of the master at a time, but if you want large-scale production or reproduction, larger machines which can produce more than one copy at a time are available. Terrco, who make the Dupli-Carver, also build the K-Star, and Willy Vanhoutte make a larger model; both of these can carve two items at once, while still not being too big for the average workshop (Fig 11.28). For real mass production, Terrco also manufacture the Northstar and Master Carver machines, which are custom-built and have from 2 to 24 cutting spindles – well beyond the scope of the home workshop.

Copy-carving machine

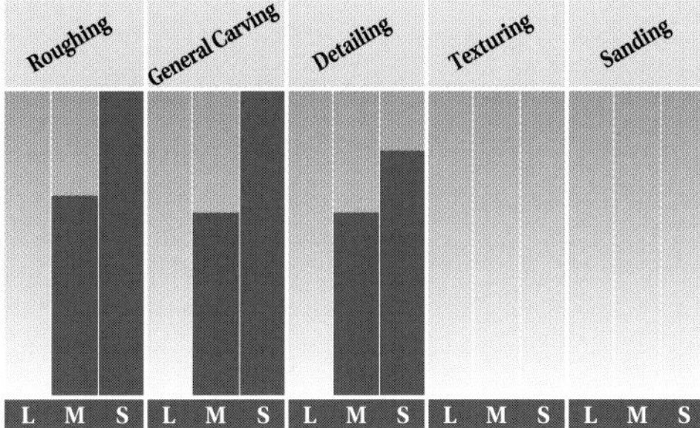

Fig 11.28 A twin-head copy-carving machine for higher production rates. (Photo by courtesy of Terrco)

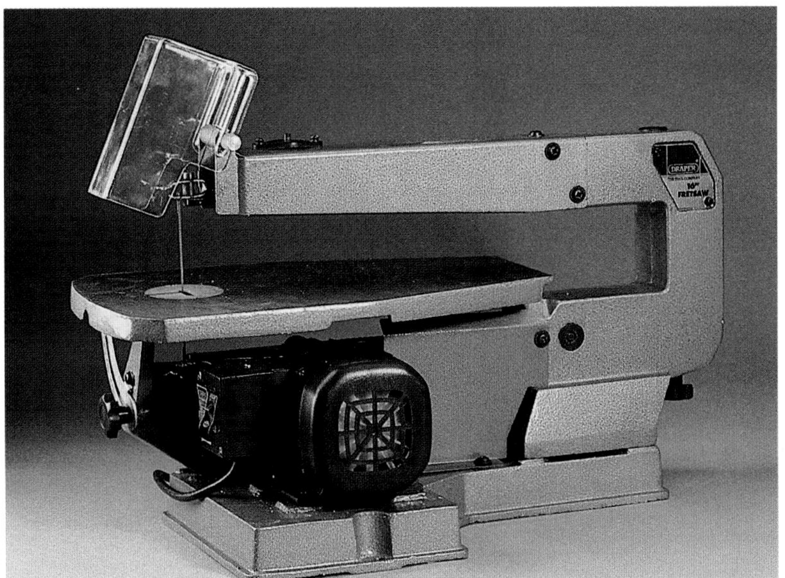

Fig 11.29 A fretsaw is useful for preparing pierced work for mirror frames, intaglio pieces, and shaped blanks for relief carvings.

Fretsaws

Motorized fretsaws, or scrollsaws (Fig 11.29), are widely available, but their use in carving is mainly restricted to cutting relatively thin, shaped panels for relief carvings. They are especially suited to cutting out blanks for pierced decorative relief carvings, such as for mirrors, frames, and friezes.

One with a powerful motor will cut timber at least 1½in (38mm) thick; the one I use will cut timber up to 2in (51mm) thick. I have had a Hegner machine for nearly 20 years; they are used extensively in schools, and are particularly well built. Other machines are available with a wide variety of prices and specifications, and Kity have added a well-built machine to their range, looking very similar to the Hegner.

A variable speed control is advantageous, as is a foot switch, which will leave both your hands free to manipulate the work. A wide range of blades is available for fretsaws, and accurate cutting depends on the selection of suitable blades for the material you are cutting. Hegner supply a range of good-quality blades, but I particularly like the American Olsen blades, which are available in the UK from Shesto. These cut very cleanly, leaving very little burr or tear-out on the underside of work.

● **Take care that work cannot be snatched from you when working with powerful workshop machines like sawbenches, drills, etc. Clamp the work securely and make sure the guards are fitted and properly adjusted. If you are not confident about the procedure you are about to attempt, don't carry on.**

SUPPLIERS INCLUDE:

Kity
Axminster Power Tools
Rexon
Draper
Hegner
Shesto
Delta

CHAPTER TWELVE

Pyrographs

THE pyrograph (Fig 12.1) is not usually considered to be a carving tool, but merely a means of decoration; however, its use in the field of realistic bird and animal carving has enabled carvers to reach new heights in the realism of fur and feathers. It can enable you to apply surface decoration and textures which are much finer than those achievable by any other tool. The units used for this are a far cry from the simple electric-soldering-iron-type of pyrograph found in craft shops, though. They employ special alloy wires which are forged and sharpened into various scalpel-like pens or shaped knives. Heating is accomplished by passing a very heavy low-voltage current through the wire forming the knife. Precise adjustment of the power supply enables fine control over the temperature of the tips and hence over the line widths and spacings that can be achieved. On very low heat settings it is possible to impress lines into the surface of the timber without burning or discoloration. On the other hand, the colour of the burnt lines can be used as decoration, and by burning at different heat settings various shades of brown-black can be achieved. The heated pens can be used to selectively burnish and colour small areas of a carving, such as the eye, instead of trying to dye it or insert a different type of timber. Although they have precise

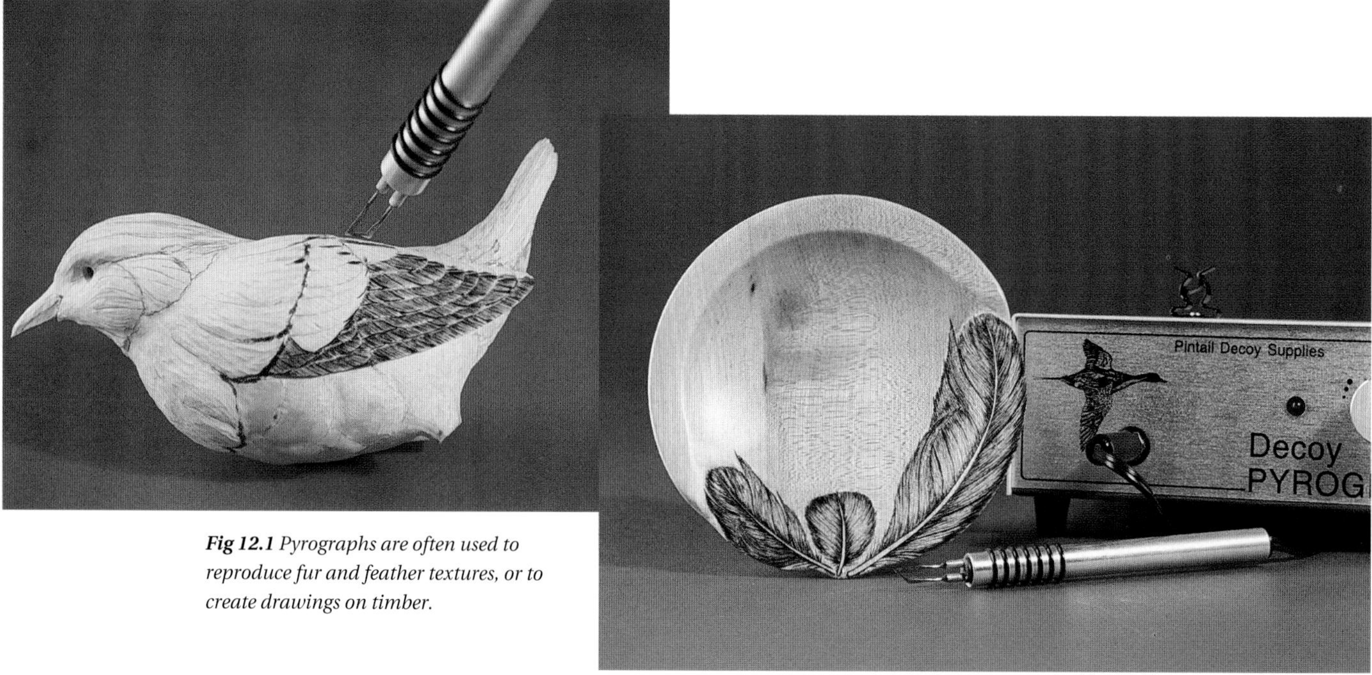

Fig 12.1 Pyrographs are often used to reproduce fur and feather textures, or to create drawings on timber.

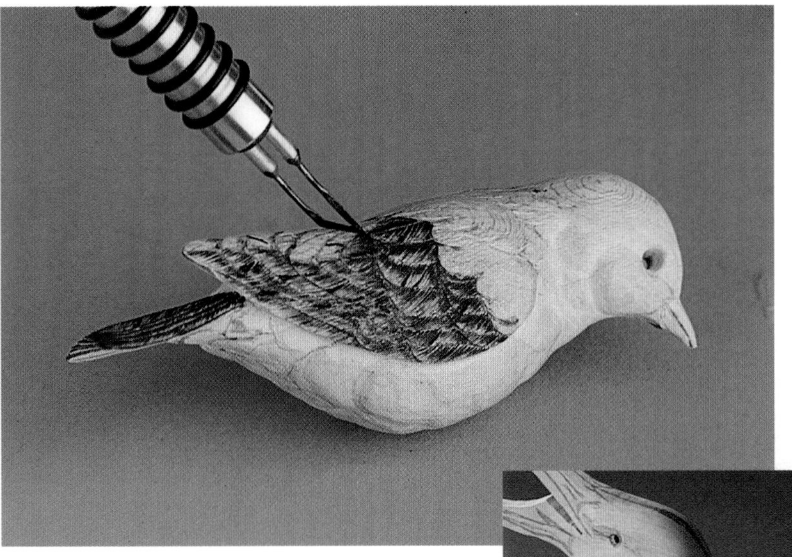

***Fig 12.2** The heated pen can also be used to 'carve', forming undercuts and cleaning up areas left rough by conventional edge tools.*

***Fig 12.3** The pen is usually held so as to burn lines perpendicular to the surface; this avoids undercutting fine texturing, which may be weak and break away.*

tip-temperature control, you cannot just set the pen and use it: different areas of the timber react inconsistently due to varying density and grain direction, so you have to make minor adjustments. Pens have a fairly low thermal mass, gaining and losing temperature quickly, which can affect the way they work. A large-output transformer limits this effect: mine has a 50VA transformer, the largest available in UK-built units.

Most bird carvers use the burnt lines merely as surface decoration, as they will later paint their carvings; but darkly burnt areas can also be used as shading under semi-transparent layers of colour, or you can even burn in many different shades by using different heat settings.

Pyrographs can also be used to form undercuts or clean up inaccessible areas in a carving (Fig 12.2); but it is inadvisable to undercut fine texturing, which may become too fragile (Fig 12.3).

A wide variety of shapes and styles of burning pens is available, including specially forged handpieces for writing, and to create fish scales on carvings. Handpieces plug into the power supply and are easily changed. Some also have interchangeable tips, but you have to wait for them to cool before you can safely change them, and their proximity to the heat can make the connections unreliable due to oxidization. There are several manufacturers of pyrograph power supplies, mainly in the USA. I have been

SUPPLIERS INCLUDE:

Pintail
Leisure Time Products
Colwood
Nibsburner
Shesto

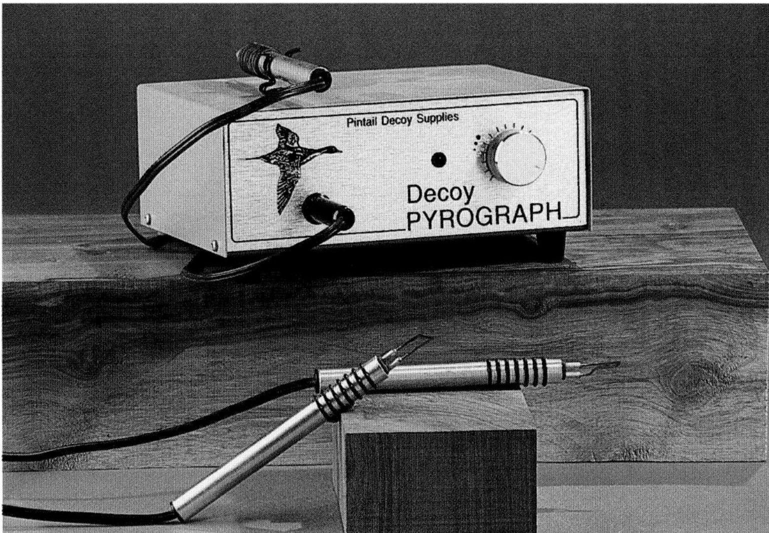

Fig 12.4 *The Pintail Decoy Pyrograph is a reliable British-made unit that has been on the market for many years.*

using the British-made Pintail Decoy Supplies unit (Fig 12.4) for the last ten years, and it has proved very reliable. There isn't a UK manufacturer for the handpieces, however, but two makes, both from the USA, are available to fit it: the ones made by Colwood, which have cool plastic handles and cork grips, and the alloy Detail Master handpieces from Leisure Time Products. The latter can get a bit warm with continuous use, but with rubber gripper rings fitted, they work well. I have quite a few handpieces from both manufacturers, but for most jobs you can

Pyrograph

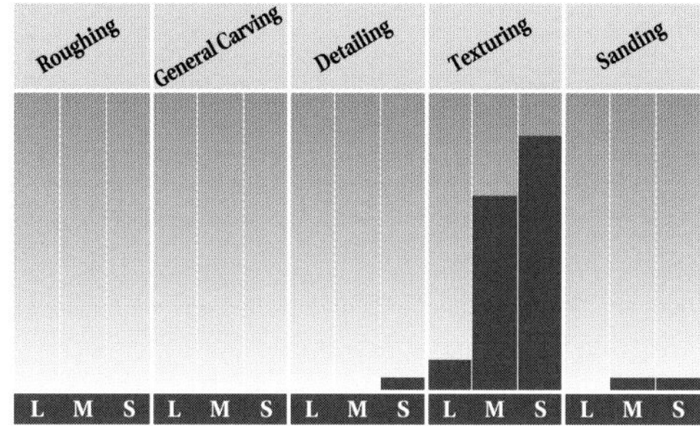

get away with two shapes: one with a rounded, sharpened tip for use in confined spaces or on concave surfaces, and for general-purpose use one with an oblique knife-edge like a craft knife (Fig 12.5).

Safety

Some smoke is obviously generated by the burning process, which should not be breathed in, as you never know what chemicals it contains – especially if you burn through other chemical substances

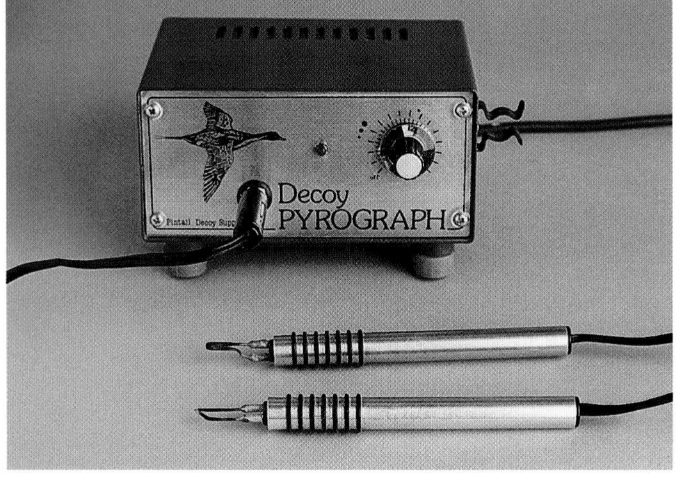

Fig 12.5 *A wide range of different sizes and shapes of heated burning pens are available for use with a pyrograph; these two meet most of my needs.*

such as glue or fillers. Extraction can be used, or, if it is only a very small amount of wood smoke, dilution would probably be adequate. This can be achieved by using a small fan to draw the air past the work and disperse it into the atmosphere. You could also wear a suitable mask or respirator.

Keep your workbench clear and put the handpiece down safely if it is still switched on, preferably held in a tool clip. When turned to a high setting it will easily ignite wood dust and shavings.

Keep the burning tip clear of all cables, both low-voltage and mains, as when hot it will slice straight through them, and it is sharp enough to cut the insulation even when cold.

- **Difficult to classify, pyrographs are nonetheless useful at times, so they had to find a place in this book. They are particularly good for creating fur and feather texture effects, cleaning chopped and messy corners, or burnishing areas to achieve colour.**
- **Soldering-iron-style pryographs are not particularly good; the heated scalpel style is more versatile, with a wide variety of pens available.**
- **Keep burning pens well sharpened and do not force them – allow the heat to do the work.**
- **Don't use the extreme point of the pen, especially when burning long lines: using a greater length of the pen tip allows it to run in the line it is burning, rather like an ice skate.**

Suppliers

I have tried to make this list as comprehensive as possible for UK suppliers, but that is an extremely difficult exercise, and I apologize in advance for any errors and omissions. The US addresses included are those gleaned from my own dealings with various US companies over the years, and from the regular advertisers in the American magazines I read. I'm afraid this part of the listing is far from comprehensive. If you live outside the UK I suggest you refer to your local specialist magazines, or contact addresses below to ask for local suppliers. Seeking contact with other carvers and woodworking societies may also supply more local information. While every effort was made to ensure accuracy at the time of writing, please bear in mind that company names, addresses, and telephone numbers change, and some also cease trading.

Airstream Dust Helmets
PO Box 975, Elbow Lake, MN 56531, USA
Tel. 800 328 1792
Safety equipment

Al-Ko Britain Ltd
Number One Industrial Estate, Medomsley Road, Consett, County Durham, DH8 6SZ
Tel. 01207 590 295
Workshop machinery and chainsaws

Allen Power Equipment
The Broadway, Didcot, Oxfordshire, OX11 8ES
Tel. 01235 813 936
Echo chainsaws

Andreas Stihl Ltd
Stihl House, Stanhope Road, Camberley, Surrey, GU15 3YT
Tel. 01276 20202
Chainsaws and associated safety equipment

Arco Ltd
PO Box 21, Waverley Street, Hull, HU1 2SJ
Tel. 01482 327 678
Safety equipment

Atlas Copco Tools Ltd
PO Box 79, Swallowdale Lane, Hemel Hempstead, Hertfordshire, HP2 7HA
Tel. 01442 61201
Portable power tools

Avery Knight & Bowlers Engineering Ltd
James Street West, Bath, Avon, BA1 2BT
Tel. 01225 425 894
Power chisels

Axminster Power Tool Centre
Chard Street, Axminster, Devon, EX13 5DZ
Tel. 01297 33656
Portable and workshop machinery including bandsaws, dust extraction, and safety equipment

Bailey's
1520 South Highland Avenue, PO Box 9088, Jackson, TN 38314, USA
Tel. 901 422 1300
Specialist chainsaw carving equipment including extra-small chainbars and chain

BJR International Ltd
266 Harrogate Road, Bradford, BD2 3RH
Tel. 01274 626 805
Router tooling

Black & Decker
210 Bath Road, Slough, Berkshire, SL1 3YD
Tel. 01753 511 234
Portable power tools

Robert Bosch Ltd
Box 98, Broadwater Park, Denham, Uxbridge, Middlesex, UB9 5HJ
Tel. 01895 838 383
Portable power tools and air-powered tools, Dremel flexi-shafts and tooling

Bowman Innovations
King Street Buildings, Suite 33, King Street, Enderby, Leicestershire, LE9 5NT
Tel. 0116 286 1611
Power-Gouge carving disc

BriMarc Associates
8 Ladbroke Park, Millers Road, Warwick, Warwickshire, CV34 5AE
Tel. 01926 493 389
Arbortech carving discs and equipment

Calder Polishing Company
Unit 10, Calder Trading Estate, Bradford Road, Brighouse, West Yorkshire, HD6 4DJ
Tel. 01484 401 699
Small electric and air-powered grinding and polishing equipment

Canland UK Ltd
8 Little Park, Princes Risborough, Buckinghamshire, HP27 0HS
Tel. 01844 344 825
Sandboss pneumatic sanding drums

Carroll Tools Ltd
16–18 Factory Lane, Croydon, Surrey, CR0 3RL
Tel. 0181-781 1268
Foam-cushioned sanding drums and drill clamps

Clarke Power Tools
Lower Clapton Road, London E5 0RN
Tel. 0181-986 8231
Workshop and portable power tools, compressors and air-powered tools

Clico (Sheffield) Ltd
Unit 7, Fell Road Industrial Estate, Sheffield S9 2AL
Tel. 0114 243 3007
Saw-toothed machine bits

CMT Tools (UK)
8 Wainwright Road, Bexhill, East Sussex, TN39 3UR
Tel. 01424 216 897
Router cutters and accessories

Colwood Electronics
15 Meridian Road, Eatontown, NJ 07724, USA
Tel. 908 544 1119
Pyrographs and burning pens

Craft Supplies Ltd
The Mill, Millers Dale, Buxton, Derbyshire, SK17 8SN
Tel. 01298 871 636
King Arthur's carving discs, power chisels

Craftwoods
PO Box 527, Timonium,
MD 21094-0527, USA
Tel. 800 468 7070
Flexible-shaft carving tools and cutters, power chisels

CSM Trade Supplies
6 Peacock Lane, Brighton, East Sussex, BN1 6WA
Tel. 01273 600 434
Specialist abrasives, Flex Porter Cable and Belt It abrasive file sanders

Dalloz Safety Ltd
Fountain House, High Street, Odiham, nr Hook, Hampshire, RG29 1LP
Tel. 01256 703 581
Pulsafe powered respirators and other safety equipment

DCE (Dust Control Equipment)
Humberstone Lane, Thurmaston, Leicester, LE4 8HP
Tel. 0116 269 6161
Dust extraction equipment

Delta UK
Westwings House, Station Road, Guiseley, West Yorkshire, LS20 8BX
Tel. 01943 873 535
Workshop machine tools

Desoutter Ltd
319 Edgware Road, Colindale, London NW9 6ND
Tel. 0181-205 7050
Air-powered tools

DeWalt
210 Bath Road, Slough, Berkshire, SL1 3YD
Tel. 01753 567 055
Portable power tools

Done to a Turn
Brynhaul, Maenclochog, Clunderwen, Pembrokeshire, SA66 7JX
Tel. 01437 532 476
Kirjes pneumatic sanding drums

Dremel
PO Box 1468, Racine, WI 53401-1468, USA
Tel. 800 437 3635
Flexible-shaft carving machines and tooling

Draper Tools Ltd
Hursley Road, Chandler's Ford, Eastleigh, Hampshire, SO5 5YF
Tel. 01703 266 355
Portable power tools

Elektra Beckum Machinery Ltd
6 The Quadrangle, Abbey Park Industrial Estate, Romsey, Hampshire, SO51 9AQ
Tel. 0181-938 3642
Bandsaws and circular saws

Elu Power Tools
210 Bath Road, Slough, Berkshire, SL1 3YD
Tel. 01753 572 112
Workshop machinery including bandsaws

English Abrasives Ltd
PO Box 85, Marsh Lane, London N17 0XA
Tel. 0181-808 4545
Abrasives

Falls Run Woodcarving
9395 Falls Road, Girard, PA 16417, USA
Tel. 800 524 9077
Flexcut chisels for power chisels

Faron Enterprises Ltd
76 Langford Cottages, Midhurst Road, Lavant, Chichester, West Sussex, PO18 0JR
Tel. 01705 502 999
Ambient-air dust extraction equipment

FASTCo
231 Corstorphine Road, Edinburgh
EH12 7AT
Tel. 0131-314 6247
Chainsaw training advisors

Fein Power Tools (UK) Ltd
Group House, Mackadown Lane, Kitts Green, Birmingham, B33 0LQ
Tel. 0121-789 7844
Portable power tools

Fercell Engineering Ltd
Unit 60, Swaislands Drive, Crayford, Kent, DA1 4HU
Tel. 01322 563 131
Dust extraction equipment

Festo Ltd
Automation House, Harvest Crescent, Ancells Business Park, Fleet, Hampshire
Tel. 01252 775 000
Portable power tools

The Foredom Electric Company
16 Stoney Hill Road, Bethel, CT 06801, USA
Tel. 203 792 8622
Flexible-shaft and other rotary carving equipment and tooling, including Typhoon burrs

Freud Tooling (UK) Ltd
Unit 2, Treefield Industrial Estate, Gildersome, Leeds, LS27 7JU
Tel. 0113 245 3737
Portable power tools

Garryson–Insley Ltd
Spring Road, Ibstock, Leicestershire, LE67 6LR
Tel. 01530 261 145
Tungsten carbide burrs

Gesswein (Woodworking Products Div.)
255 Hancock Avenue, Bridgeport, CT 06605, USA
Tel. 800 544 2043
High-speed carving equipment and tooling

Hamilton Power Products
PO Box 2355, Colchester, Essex, CO3 5FY
Tel. 01206 762 470
Flex Porter Cable abrasive-belt files

Hamlin Holdings Ltd
132 Widney Lane, Solihull, West Midlands, B91 3LH
Tel. 0121-705 0407
Sign-carving machines

Hegner UK
Unit 8, North Crescent, Diplocks Way, Hailsham, East Sussex, BN27 3JF
Tel. 01323 442 440
Moviluty flexible-shaft carving tools and tooling

Helmet Integrated Systems Ltd
Commerce Road, Stranraer, DG9 7DX
Tel. 01776 704 421
Powered respirators

Hermes Abrasives Ltd
Severalls Industrial Park, Wyncolls Road, Colchester, Essex
Tel. 01206 844 623
Abrasives, sanding accessories

Hitachi Power Tools (UK) Ltd
Precedent Drive, Rooksley, Milton Keynes, MK13 8PJ
Tel. 01908 660 663
Portable power tools

Husqvarna Forest & Garden UK
Oldends Lane, Stonehouse,
Gloucestershire, GL10 3SY
Tel. 01453 822 382
Chainsaws and associated safety equipment

In-Lap Dust Collection Systems
3122 Washington Avenue, Box 081576,
Racine, WI 53408, USA
Tel. 414 633 8899
Dust extraction equipment

Jack Sealey Ltd
Easlea Road, Moreton Hall Industrial Estate, Bury St Edmunds, Suffolk,
IP32 7BY
Tel. 01284 757 500
Portable power tools and workshop equipment, including compressors and air-powered tools

Kango Ltd
Shrewsbury Avenue, Woodston Industrial Estate, Peterborough, Cambridgeshire,
PE2 7BX
Tel. 01733 371 707
Portable power tools

King Arthur's Tools
2818-D Industrial Plaza Drive,
Tallahassee, FL 32301, USA
Tel. 904 877 7650
Carving discs for angle and die grinders

Kity
Unit 9, Guildford Industrial Estate,
Deaconfield, Guildford, Surrey, GU2 5YT
Tel. 01483 453 502
Workshop machinery including bandsaws

Klingspor Abrasives Ltd
Dukeries Chase, Chaylands Avenue,
Worksop, Nottinghamshire, S81 7DN
Tel. 01909 500 250
Abrasives

Leisure Time Products
2650 Davisson Street, River Grove,
IL 60171, USA
Tel. 617 639 1000
Pyrographs and burning pens

Liberon
New Romney, Kent, TN28 8XU
Tel. 01797 367 555
Polishing and finishing materials and equipment

Macford Products Ltd
1 & 2 Enterprise City, Meadowfield Avenue, Spennymoor, County Durham,
DL16 6JF
Tel. 01388 420 535
Maxicraft flexible-shaft carving machines

Machine Mart Ltd
211 Lower Parliament Street, Nottingham,
NG1 1GN
Tel. 0115 956 5555
Portable and workshop tools, including compressors and air-powered tools

Makita (UK) Ltd
Michigan Drive, Tongwell, Milton Keynes,
MK15 8JD
Tel. 01908 211 678
Portable power tools

Metabo
Hursley Road, Chandler's Ford, Eastleigh,
Hampshire, SO53 1YF
Tel. 01703 266 355
Portable power tools

Micom Ltd
Industrial Estate, The Street, Maldon,
Essex, CM9 7XP
Tel. 01621 856 324
Sign- and copy-carving machines

Minden Industrial Ltd
16 Greyfriars Road, Moreton Hall, Bury St Edmunds, Suffolk, IP32 7DX
Tel. 01284 760 791
Portable power tools

MJK Engineering
Unit 5, Moorlands Business Estate, Balme Road, Cleckheaton, West Yorkshire, BD19 4EZ
Tel. 01274 851 129
Electric and air-powered die grinders and accessories

Navesink
820 Nut Swamp Road, Red Bank, NJ 07701, USA
Tel. 908 747 5023
Pyrographs and micromotors

Nibsburner
3255 Blue Mountain Way, Colorado Springs, CO 80906, USA
Tel. 719 576 8686
Pyrographs

Nilfisk Ltd
Newmarket Road, Bury St Edmunds, Suffolk, IP33 3SR
Tel. 01284 763 163
Dust extraction equipment

NMA (Agencies)
34 Elmfield Road, Birkby, Huddersfield, West Yorkshire, HD2 2HX
Tel. 01484 531 446
Workshop equipment incl. bandsaws

Norgren Martonair Ltd
PO Box 22, Eastern Avenue, Lichfield, Staffordshire, WS13 6SB
Tel. 01543 414 333
Air-powered tools

Norton Abrasives
Bridge Road East, Welwyn Garden City, Hertfordshire, AL7 1HZ
Tel. 01707 323 484
Abrasives, sanding accessories

NSK America Corp.
700-B Cooper Court, Schaumburg, IL 60173, USA
Tel. 708 843 7664
Small electric die grinders

Numatic International Ltd
Chard, Somerset, TA20 2BB
Tel. 01460 68600
Dust extraction equipment

Nu-Tool
Carcroft Industrial Estate, Wellskye Road, Adwick-le-Street, Doncaster, South Yorkshire, DN6 7DU
Tel. 01302 721 791
Workshop machinery incl. bandsaws

L. R. Oliver & Co. Inc.
9974 Dixie Highway, Fair Haven, MI 48023, USA
Tel. 810 725 4440
Karbide Kutzall carving discs and burrs

P & J Dust Extraction Ltd
Unit 1, Lordswood Industrial Estate, Revenge Road, Chatham, Kent, ME5 8PF
Tel. 01634 684 526
Dust extraction equipment

Partner Jonserad Power Products UK
Oldends Lane, Stonehouse, Gloucestershire, GL10 3SY
Tel. 01453 820 305
Chainsaws and associated safety equipment

Perma-Grit Tools
The White House, Pointon, Sleaford, Lincolnshire, NG34 0LX
Tel. 01529 240 668
Tungsten carbide abrasive burrs and tooling

Peugeot Power Tools Ltd
Unit 9, Guildford Industrial Estate, Deaconfield, Guildford, Surrey, GU2 5YT
Tel. 01483 453 502
Portable power tools

Pfingst & Co Inc.
105 Snyder Road, PO Box 377, South Plainfield, NJ 07080, USA
Tel. 908 561 6400
Flexible-shaft carving machines

Picador Engineering Ltd
Foxhills Industrial Estate, Scunthorpe, Lincolnshire, DN15 8QJ
Tel. 01724 281 305
Workshop sanders

Pintail Decoy Supplies
20 Sheppenhall Grove, Aston, Nantwich, Cheshire, CW5 8DF
Tel. 01270 780 056
Karbide Kutzall carving discs and burrs, Pfingst spares, flexible-shaft carving machines and tooling, pyrographs

Pro Machine Tools Ltd
17 Station Road, Barnack, Stamford, Lincolnshire, PE9 3DW
Tel. 01780 740 956
Workshop machinery incl. bandsaws

Protective Specialties Development Group
PO Box 39060-CC, Philadelphia, PA 19136, USA
Dust extraction equipment

Racal Health & Safety Ltd
12–16 Greenford Road, Greenford, Middlesex, UB6 8XT
Tel. 0990 168 118
Respirators and safety products

RAM Products
5 Elkins Road, East Brunswick, NJ 08816, USA
Tel. 908 651 5500
Small electric die grinders

Razertip Industries
Box 1258, Martensville, SK, Canada, S0K 2T0
Tel. 306 931 0889
Pyrographs

Record Power Ltd
Parkway Works, Sheffield, South Yorkshire, S9 3BL
Tel. 0114 244 9066
Workshop machinery including bandsaws and powered respirators

The Rex Oliver Co
9665 Kretz, Algonac, MI 48001, USA
Tungsten carbide tooling

Rexon Ltd
Summit 1, Mangham Road, Barbot Hall Industrial Estate, Rotherham, S61 4RJ
Tel. 01709 361 158
Pillar drills

Rod Naylor
Turnpike House, 208 Devizes Road, Hilperton, Trowbridge, Wiltshire, BA14 7OP
Tel. 01225 754 497
Copy-carving machines and tooling, including Tornado cutters

Roto/Carve/Sand
2754 Garden Avenue, Janesville, IA 50647, USA
Tel. 319 987 2511
Copy-carving machines, sanding equipment

Ryobi Power Equipment (UK) Ltd
Pavilion 1, Olympus Park Business Centre, Quedgeley, Gloucestershire, GL2 6NF
Tel. 01452 724 777
Portable power tools and chainsaws

Sand-Rite Manufacturing Co
321 N Justine Street, Chicago, IL 60607, USA
Tel. 800 521 2318
Pneumatic sanding equipment

Sedgwick & Co Ltd
Swinnow Lane, Leeds, LS13 4QG
Tel. 0113 257 0637
Workshop machinery

SCM Enterprises
W168 N11318 Western Avenue, Germantown, WI 53022, USA
Pyrographs and mini-die grinders

SECO Engineering Co Ltd
32 Reading Road South, Fleet, Hampshire, GU13 9QL
Tel. 01252 622 333
Belt It abrasive-belt grinding machines

Shesto Ltd
Unit 2, Sapcote Trading Centre, 374 High Road, Willesden, London NW10 2DH
Tel. 0181-451 6188
Foredom carving equipment and tooling including Typhoon burrs

Skil UK
PO Box 98, Broadwater Park, Denham, Uxbridge, Middlesex, UB9 5HJ
Tel. 01895 838 743
Portable power tools

Skilbond Direct Ltd
Dudley House, The Valley Centre, Gordon Road, High Wycombe, Buckinghamshire, HP13 6EL
Tel. 01494 448 474
Electric mini-die grinders

Stayer Power Tools Ltd
Unit 9, Guildford Industrial Estate, Deaconfield, Guildford, Surrey, GU2 5YT
Tel. 01483 453 502
Portable power tools

Startrite
(For address see Record Power)
Bandsaws

Stretton of Coventry
870 Foleshill Road, Coventry, CV6 6GS
Tel. 01203 688 144
Flexcut chisels for power chisels

Sugino Corporation
1700 N Penny Lane, Schaumburg, IL 60173, USA
Tel. 847 397 9401
Auto Mach power chisels

TCL Supplies
213 Portland Road, Hove, East Sussex, BN3 5LA
Tel. 01273 736 896
3D wood-boring bits

Terrco Inc.
222 1st Avenue NW, Waretown, SD 57201, USA
Tel. 605 882 3888
Copy-carving machines

Thorite Ltd
Laisterdyke, Bradford, West Yorkshire, BD4 8BZ
Tel. 01274 663 471
Compressors, air-powered tools, and accessories

Timbercrafts
Rt 214, Lanesville, NY 1245, USA
Tel. 914 688 7877
Chainsaw carving supplies

Titman Tip Tools Ltd
Kennedy Way, Valley Road, Clacton-on-Sea, Essex, CO15 4AB
Tel. 01255 220 123
Tungsten carbide tooling

Trend Machinery & Cutting Tools Ltd
Penfold Works, Imperial Way, Watford, Hertfordshire, WD2 4YF
Tel. 01923 249 911
Sign-carving machines and tungsten carbide tooling

Ultra Speed Products Inc.
18500 East Aschoff Road, Zig Zag, OR 97049-9707, USA
Tel. 503 622 4387
Air-turbine carving units

Wealden Tool Company
31 Bainbridges Industrial Estate, East Peckham, Kent, TN12 5HF
Tel. 07000 565 000
Router cutters and accessories

Willy Vanhoutte
Industriepark 11, B-8370 Beernem, Belgium
Tel. (+32) 50 78 17 94
Copy-carving machines

Woodcraft Supply Corp.
210 Wood County Industrial Park, Parkersburg, WV 26102-1686, USA
Tel. 800 225 1153
Pneumatic sanding drums

Metric Conversion Table

inches to millimetres and centimetres
mm = millimetres cm = centimetres

inches	mm	cm	inches	cm	inches	cm
⅛	3	0.3	9	22.9	30	76.2
¼	6	0.6	10	25.4	31	78.7
⅜	10	1.0	11	27.9	32	81.3
½	13	1.3	12	30.5	33	83.8
⅝	16	1.6	13	33.0	34	86.4
¾	19	1.9	14	35.6	35	88.9
⅞	22	2.2	15	38.1	36	91.4
1	25	2.5	16	40.6	37	94.0
1¼	32	3.2	17	43.2	38	96.5
1½	38	3.8	18	45.7	39	99.1
1¾	44	4.4	19	48.3	40	101.6
2	51	5.1	20	50.8	41	104.1
2½	64	6.4	21	53.3	42	106.7
3	76	7.6	22	55.9	43	109.2
3½	89	8.9	23	58.4	44	111.8
4	102	10.2	24	61.0	45	114.3
4½	114	11.4	25	63.5	46	116.8
5	127	12.7	26	66.0	47	119.4
6	152	15.2	27	68.6	48	121.9
7	178	17.8	28	71.1	49	124.5
8	203	20.3	29	73.7	50	127.0

About the Author

David Tippey's interests in woodworking and metalwork were natural developments from his interest in model-making, which began when he was a teenager. On finishing school he went on to study photography at Kitson College in Leeds, before joining industry. He became the technical director of a Harrogate electronics company, manufacturing printed circuits, until in 1984 he changed career to become landlord of a pub in the Yorkshire Dales.

His spare-time interests have always been practical, spanning a wide range of projects, from model boats, aeroplanes, and amateur radio as a teenager, to antique restoration, model engineering, and silverwork, but these all took a back seat after a magazine article on American decoys prompted the purchase of a book on decoy carving, and his first carvings emerged. Since the opportunity to carve full-time arose in 1988, the scope and style of his carving has increased, moving away from just the decoy duck to a much wider avian theme.

For a complete change from the highly detailed style covered in his first book, *Carving Realistic Birds* (GMC Publications, 1996), David also carves stylized, simply painted birds which draw their inspiration from the flowing, graceful shapes of their subjects, and occasionally an engagingly simple, tactile, natural-finish wooden bird, revealing the beauty of the wood from which it is fashioned.

Photo: Nick Hough

His work has found its way into collections in Britain, Europe, and North America, and has been featured in various magazines and on television. He regularly writes articles and reviews for woodworking magazines, and is also active in teaching woodcarving, running courses at local colleges, and individual birdcarving courses at his own studio.

David is the founder of the North-Western Group of the British Decoy Wildfowl Carvers Association, so almost all of his time is dedicated to carving in some form or other. The great spotted woodpecker has become his logo.

Index

GMC Publications

Books

Woodworking

Bird Boxes and Feeders for the Garden — Dave Mackenzie
Complete Woodfinishing — Ian Hosker
David Charlesworth's Furniture-Making Techniques — David Charlesworth
Furniture & Cabinetmaking Projects — GMC Publications
Furniture Projects — Rod Wales
Furniture Restoration (Practical Crafts) — Kevin Jan Bonner
Furniture Restoration and Repair for Beginners — Kevin Jan Bonner
Furniture Restoration Workshop — Kevin Jan Bonner
Green Woodwork — Mike Abbott
Making & Modifying Woodworking Tools — Jim Kingshott
Making Chairs and Tables — GMC Publications
Making Fine Furniture — Tom Darby
Making Little Boxes from Wood — John Bennett
Making Shaker Furniture — Barry Jackson
Making Woodwork Aids and Devices — Robert Wearing
Minidrill: Fifteen Projects — John Everett
Pine Furniture Projects for the Home — Dave Mackenzie
Router Magic: Jigs, Fixtures and Tricks to Unleash your Router's Full Potential — Bill Hylton
Routing for Beginners — Anthony Bailey
The Scrollsaw: Twenty Projects — John Everett
Sharpening Pocket Reference Book — Jim Kingshott
Sharpening: The Complete Guide — Jim Kingshott
Space-Saving Furniture Projects — Dave Mackenzie
Stickmaking: A Complete Course — Andrew Jones & Clive George
Stickmaking Handbook — Andrew Jones & Clive George
Test Reports: The Router and Furniture & Cabinetmaking — GMC Publications
Veneering: A Complete Course — Ian Hosker
Woodfinishing Handbook (Practical Crafts) — Ian Hosker
Woodworking with the Router: Professional Router Techniques any Woodworker can Use — Bill Hylton & Fred Matlack
The Workshop — Jim Kingshott

Woodcarving

The Art of the Woodcarver — GMC Publications
Carving Birds & Beasts — GMC Publications
Carving on Turning — Chris Pye
Carving Realistic Birds — David Tippey
Decorative Woodcarving — Jeremy Williams
Essential Tips for Woodcarvers — GMC Publications
Essential Woodcarving Techniques — Dick Onians
Further Useful Tips for Woodcarvers — GMC Publications
Lettercarving in Wood: A Practical Course — Chris Pye
Power Tools for Woodcarving — David Tippey
Practical Tips for Turners & Carvers — GMC Publications
Relief Carving in Wood: A Practical Introduction — Chris Pye
Understanding Woodcarving — GMC Publications
Understanding Woodcarving in the Round — GMC Publications
Useful Techniques for Woodcarvers — GMC Publications
Wildfowl Carving – Volume 1 — Jim Pearce
Wildfowl Carving – Volume 2 — Jim Pearce
The Woodcarvers — GMC Publications
Woodcarving: A Complete Course — Ron Butterfield
Woodcarving: A Foundation Course — Zoë Gertner
Woodcarving for Beginners — GMC Publications
Woodcarving Tools & Equipment Test Reports — GMC Publications
Woodcarving Tools, Materials & Equipment — Chris Pye

Woodturning

Adventures in Woodturning — David Springett
Bert Marsh: Woodturner — Bert Marsh
Bill Jones' Notes from the Turning Shop — Bill Jones
Bill Jones' Further Notes from the Turning Shop — Bill Jones
Bowl Turning Techniques Masterclass — Tony Boase
Colouring Techniques for Woodturners — Jan Sanders
The Craftsman Woodturner — Peter Child
Decorative Techniques for Woodturners — Hilary Bowen
Faceplate Turning — GMC Publications
Fun at the Lathe — R.C. Bell
Further Useful Tips for Woodturners — GMC Publications
Illustrated Woodturning Techniques — John Hunnex
Intermediate Woodturning Projects — GMC Publications
Keith Rowley's Woodturning Projects — Keith Rowley
Multi-Centre Woodturning — Ray Hopper
Practical Tips for Turners & Carvers — GMC Publications
Spindle Turning — GMC Publications
Turning Green Wood — Michael O'Donnell
Turning Miniatures in Wood — John Sainsbury
Turning Pens and Pencils — Kip Christensen & Rex Burningham
Turning Wooden Toys — Terry Lawrence
Understanding Woodturning — Ann & Bob Phillips
Useful Techniques for Woodturners — GMC Publications
Useful Woodturning Projects — GMC Publications
Woodturning: Bowls, Platters, Hollow Forms, Vases, Vessels, Bottles, Flasks, Tankards, Plates — GMC Publications
Woodturning: A Foundation Course (New Edition) — Keith Rowley
Woodturning: A Fresh Approach — Robert Chapman
Woodturning: A Source Book of Shapes — John Hunnex
Woodturning Jewellery — Hilary Bowen
Woodturning Masterclass — Tony Boase
Woodturning Techniques — GMC Publications
Woodturning Tools & Equipment Test Reports — GMC Publications
Woodturning Wizardry — David Springett

Upholstery

Seat Weaving (Practical Crafts) — Ricky Holdstock
The Upholsterer's Pocket Reference Book — David James
Upholstery: A Complete Course (Revised Edition) — David James
Upholstery Restoration — David James
Upholstery Techniques & Projects — David James

Toymaking

Designing & Making Wooden Toys — Terry Kelly
Fun to Make Wooden Toys & Games — Jeff & Jennie Loader
Making Wooden Toys & Games — Jeff & Jennie Loader
Restoring Rocking Horses — Clive Green & Anthony Dew
Scrollsaw Toy Projects — Ivor Carlyle
Scrollsaw Toys for All Ages — Ivor Carlyle
Wooden Toy Projects — GMC Publications

Dolls' Houses and Miniatures

Architecture for Dolls' Houses — Joyce Percival
Beginners' Guide to the Dolls' House Hobby — Jean Nisbett
The Complete Dolls' House Book — Jean Nisbett
The Dolls' House 1/24 Scale: A Complete Introduction — Jean Nisbett
Dolls' House Accessories, Fixtures and Fittings — Andrea Barham
Dolls' House Bathrooms: Lots of Little Loos — Patricia King
Dolls' House Fireplaces and Stoves — Patricia King
Easy to Make Dolls' House Accessories — Andrea Barham
Heraldic Miniature Knights — Peter Greenhill
Make Your Own Dolls' House Furniture — Maurice Harper
Making Dolls' House Furniture — Patricia King
Making Georgian Dolls' Houses — Derek Rowbottom
Making Miniature Gardens — Freida Gray
Making Miniature Oriental Rugs & Carpets — Meik & Ian McNaughton
Making Period Dolls' House Accessories — Andrea Barham
Making Tudor Dolls' Houses — Derek Rowbottom
Making Victorian Dolls' House Furniture — Patricia King
Miniature Bobbin Lace — Roz Snowden
Miniature Embroidery for the Victorian Dolls' House — Pamela Warner
Miniature Embroidery for the Georgian Dolls' House — Pamela Warner
Miniature Needlepoint Carpets — Janet Granger
The Secrets of the Dolls' House Makers — Jean Nisbett

Crafts

American Patchwork Designs in Needlepoint — Melanie Tacon
A Beginners' Guide to Rubber Stamping — Brenda Hunt
Celtic Cross Stitch Designs — Carol Phillipson
Celtic Knotwork Designs — Sheila Sturrock
Celtic Knotwork Handbook — Sheila Sturrock
Collage from Seeds, Leaves and Flowers — Joan Carver
Complete Pyrography — Stephen Poole
Contemporary Smocking — Dorothea Hall
Creating Knitwear Designs — Pat Ashforth & Steve Plummer
Creative Doughcraft — Patricia Hughes
Creative Embroidery Techniques Using Colour Through Gold — Daphne J. Ashby & Jackie Woolsey
The Creative Quilter: Techniques and Projects — Pauline Brown
Cross Stitch Kitchen Projects — Janet Granger
Cross Stitch on Colour — Sheena Rogers
Decorative Beaded Purses — Enid Taylor
Designing and Making Cards — Glennis Gilruth
Embroidery Tips & Hints — Harold Hayes
Glass Painting — Emma Sedman
An Introduction to Crewel Embroidery — Mave Glenny
Making and Using Working Drawings for Realistic Model Animals — Basil F. Fordham
Making Character Bears — Valerie Tyler
Making Greetings Cards for Beginners — Pat Sutherland
Making Hand-Sewn Boxes: Techniques and Projects — Jackie Woolsey
Making Knitwear Fit — Pat Ashforth & Steve Plummer
Natural Ideas for Christmas: Fantastic Decorations to Make — Josie Cameron-Ashcroft & Carol Cox
Needlepoint: A Foundation Course — Sandra Hardy
Pyrography Designs — Norma Gregory
Pyrography Handbook (Practical Crafts) — Stephen Poole
Ribbons and Roses — Lee Lockheed
Rubber Stamping with Other Crafts — Lynne Garner
Sponge Painting — Ann Rooney
Tassel Making for Beginners — Enid Taylor
Tatting Collage — Lindsay Rogers
Temari: A Traditional Japanese Embroidery Technique — Margaret Ludlow
Theatre Models in Paper and Card — Robert Burgess
Wool Embroidery and Design — Lee Lockheed

The Garden

Bird Boxes and Feeders for the Garden — Dave Mackenzie
The Birdwatcher's Garden — Hazel & Pamela Johnson
The Living Tropical Greenhouse: Creating a Haven for Butterflies — John & Maureen Tampion

Videos

Drop-in and Pinstuffed Seats — David James
Stuffover Upholstery — David James
Elliptical Turning — David Springett
Woodturning Wizardry — David Springett
Turning Between Centres: The Basics — Dennis White
Turning Bowls — Dennis White
Boxes, Goblets and Screw Threads — Dennis White
Novelties and Projects — Dennis White
Classic Profiles — Dennis White
Twists and Advanced Turning — Dennis White
Sharpening the Professional Way — Jim Kingshott
Sharpening Turning & Carving Tools — Jim Kingshott
Bowl Turning — John Jordan
Hollow Turning — John Jordan
Woodturning: A Foundation Course — Keith Rowley
Carving a Figure: The Female Form — Ray Gonzalez
The Router: A Beginner's Guide — Alan Goodsell
The Scroll Saw: A Beginner's Guide — John Burke

Magazines

Woodturning • Woodcarving • Furniture & Cabinetmaking • The Router
The Dolls' House Magazine • The ScrollSaw • BusinessMatters • Water Gardening

The above represents a full list of all titles currently published or scheduled to be published.
All are available direct from the Publishers or through bookshops, newsagents and specialist retailers.
To place an order, or to obtain a complete catalogue, contact:

GMC Publications
Castle Place, 166 High Street, Lewes, East Sussex BN7 1XU, United Kingdom Tel: 01273 488005 Fax: 01273 478606
Orders by credit card are accepted